HOODOO
FOR EVERYONE

HOODOO
FOR EVERYONE

MODERN APPROACHES TO MAGIC, CONJURE, ROOTWORK, AND LIBERATION

SHERRY SHONE
AKA THAT HOODOO LADY

North Atlantic Books
Huichin, unceded Ohlone land
aka Berkeley, California

Published by
North Atlantic Books
Huichin, unceded Ohlone land
aka Berkeley, California

Cover art © Vodoleyka via Shutterstock
Cover design by Jess Morphew
Book design by Happenstance Type-O-Rama

Printed in the United States of America

Hoodoo for Everyone: Modern Approaches to Magic, Conjure, Rootwork, and Liberation is sponsored and published by North Atlantic Books, an educational nonprofit based in the unceded Ohlone land Huichin (*aka* Berkeley, CA), that collaborates with partners to develop cross-cultural perspectives, nurture holistic views of art, science, the humanities, and healing, and seed personal and global transformation by publishing work on the relationship of body, spirit, and nature.

North Atlantic Books' publications are distributed to the US trade and internationally by Penguin Random House Publisher Services. For further information, visit our website at www.northatlanticbooks.com.

Library of Congress Cataloging-in-Publication Data

Names: Shone, Sherry, 1971– author.
Title: Hoodoo for everyone : modern approaches to magic, conjure, rootwork, and liberation / Sherry Shone aka That Hoodoo Lady.
Description: Huichin, unceded Ohlone land aka Berkeley, California : North Atlantic Books, [2022] | Includes bibliographical references and index.
| Summary: "A beginner's guide to an inclusive Hoodoo practice—history, spellwork, folklore, and herbs"—Provided by publisher.
Identifiers: LCCN 2021054432 (print) | LCCN 2021054433 (ebook) | ISBN 9781623177089 (paperback) | ISBN 9781623177096 (epub)
Subjects: LCSH: Hoodoo (Cult) | Magic.
Classification: LCC BL2490 .S56 2022 (print) | LCC BL2490 (ebook) | DDC 133.4—dc23/eng20220228
LC record available at https://lccn.loc.gov/2021054432
LC ebook record available at https://lccn.loc.gov/2021054433

1 2 3 4 5 6 7 8 9 KPC 27 26 25 24 23 22

This book includes recycled material and material from well-managed forests. North Atlantic Books is committed to the protection of our environment. We print on recycled paper whenever possible and partner with printers who strive to use environmentally responsible practices.

CONTENTS

Foreword   vii

1 Hoodoo Origins   1

2 Fundamentals of Hoodoo Practices   55

3 Ethical Hoodoo   117

4 Worthy Hoodoo Fighters   147

5 Putting It All Together   179

6 Cleansing   217

Appendix   249

Bibliography   283

Suggested Reading   287

Biography   289

FOREWORD

This book is an eloquent approach to hoodoo. Sherry makes this craft, this art form, tangible for all seekers. Within the first few paragraphs, the reader is immediately engaged and practicing. I have known Sherry for years now, and she is a ball of sunshine who speaks the truth in such a grounded way that you just want to sit back and soak it all in.

With her background and awareness, Sherry is able to bridge a gap between one of the most widely recognized religions in the USA, Christianity, with the ideal of the ancestors who knew other ways prior to being indoctrinated into the Christian faith. This is a gap that is not always gracefully addressed. Sherry does not turn her back on the Bible, even as a practitioner of the craft. In fact, she embraces it more and helps us to shift our thinking with regard to a doctrine we were taught as children from a pastor in church. If you are looking for a book that "will go there with you" ... this is your book. This book is truly liberating!

From the beginning, she addresses ethics and responsibilities! Whenever we engage in any type of working, ethics will guide us safely to our goals for everyone involved. A step-by-step guide to discovering self-respect and respect for the other (be it another individual, an ancestor, a guide, a divine relationship).

More than a book on hoodoo, Sherry helps the reader take a minute and take a look inside: "Who are you?" I love this ... as self-knowledge is the key to a healthy individual. We read about what hoodoo is, the experiences that it can provide, and the magic that it can accomplish.

This book is the second one out of a series. Her first book, *The Hoodoo Guide to the Bible*, starts us off. If you are picking this one up first, that works just fine; however, I would encourage the reader who enjoys this book to find the other one as well. The book in your hands will introduce us to historical places, people, and events that hoodoo practitioners can discover—as well as how to practice hoodoo.

But wait; there is more. Prepare yourself for a wonderful storyteller. Getting wrapped up in the stories with Sherry can make you, the reader, feel as though you are there with her. Experience a beautiful perspective of the phenomena—the world around you.

So wash your hands, make a cup of tea, and walk with Sherry through the pages of this book. It is an honest, exciting journey. I truly love my encounters with her, and I expect that you will too.

Granddaughter Crow

HOODOO ORIGINS

A REFLECTION OF HOODOO

Welcome to *Hoodoo for Everyone*, where I will do my best to introduce you to this beautiful folklore magic of hoodoo! Hoodoo is the African American folklore tradition created right in the Southern United States by enslaved Africans. In that tradition enslaved Africans needed, and I mean really needed, freedom, liberation, and in my words, deliverance. Before there were honey jars, red brick dust, goopher dust, and many other things you may have read are hoodoo, there was the need to be free. A serious freedom that meant life or death.

Hoodoo workers originated from healers that resided on the plantations. Some of them were folk doctors, rootworkers (called so because of the roots they dug up from the ground to use in their practice), medicine women, and midwives (those that cared for the pregnant or lactating enslaved Africans and their infants) who could work in the house and came from Africa with an understanding of these traditions. They would make salves out of animal fats, teas out of plants and tree bark, and pain remedies from animal parts (like horse hooves). They used boneset to ensure broken bones were healing and onions and garlic to cure colds and flu, among other things—anything to get enslaved Africans back to work in the fields.

Hoodoo workers were sought after, revered, and feared. An interviewee from the book *African American Slave Medicine* by Herbert Covey tells us that "hoodoo and conjure workers were the most feared and held power of the slaves in those days. They would hold a secret meeting place where you could get charms to harm your enemies. The conjure worker would be working when it was dark by the light of the moon and wave their arms and hands and speak to the moon. In a kettle they would put snakes and things (no one ever knew everything) and they would all join dancing around the fire and beating the drums faster and faster. They would chant and pray until they fell into a heap."

Doesn't sound like "light and love" to me. Does it to you? This is my belief of hoodoo. It is for those that require swift urgency when you can go to no one else. When your mortgage is late, when an illness isn't going away, when your spouse or partner is leaving, when you are being evicted, when your community is being shot at, when your lives are at stake. This is what hoodoo is for—it's not pretty. It isn't meant to be. So you will not read what you normally hear about hoodoo in this book. I will give you my own experience in hoodoo through my story and the stories of the updated hoodoo people, places, and objects. This is not the hoodoo you may have read about or have seen on social media. This is hoodoo that I have created for those of us who have been hurt, abandoned, misunderstood, or cast aside because we are not traditional or conforming. These are updated hoodoo foundations.

One thing that hoodoo workers, plantation owners, and overseers could agree upon is keeping the body clean. In the enslaved African's quarters there was soap, and there were quarantine areas where the newly enslaved could be isolated from the existing ones to ensure disease prevention. They would use castor oil, vinegar, whiskey, rum, and animal fat to ward off infections, diseases, and illnesses. This, of course, wasn't because they truly cared about their "workers" but because they needed to protect their human investments. In ritual work this is mirrored in the cleansing of objects, tools, altars, and most importantly, us as spiritual containers. Before we begin any hoodoo or conjure practice, we are asked—and really required—to be clean. If you didn't have soap, then you could wash with salt or lye or vinegar. If you didn't have that, then you would go to a running creek (never stagnant water) and bathe (never where the animals drank or relieved themselves if it could be avoided). I cannot imagine the cold of having to bathe in a creek in the Southern winters—the thought of it makes my bones ache. Our shared ancestors endured this just to be clean.

That said, let's get your hands washed. Start with your favorite soap, salt, vinegar, lemon, essential oils—whatever you want to use. Use the warmest water you can (I won't ask you to recreate the pain of bathing in cold water like our ancestors did). Then come back and begin reading again. Remember that this is the ritual. Before you use a sacred text or practice hoodoo work or start any spell, start with a clean body. This means washing your hands before you read any sacred texts and cleaning the space that you will work on before you start. This means cleaning your thoughts of any impurities (except for the energy that you need to either attract or banish) as much as you can and have focus on what you want and need to be delivered from.

I'll wait.

Okay, now that we're back, let's start with an introduction to how this book was birthed.

This book happened after I was celebrating my first one, *The Hoodoo Guide to the Bible*, with my wife. We were discussing my childhood. My family roots go back to Mississippi, Texas, and Kansas. From the South to the Midwest, we began as enslaved people and became freed people and then sharecroppers, lawyers, educators, ministers, authors, artists, and social media influencers. My greatest memories have been expressing and experiencing the faith that I learned to cultivate in our church home in Kansas. It was a very well-known evangelical church. I was baptized and saved there. Being saved is a ritual process where you proclaim that you will be a witness to God and that you will serve and be obedient to God's laws for the rest of your life. It was something that my family expected us all to do, and if we didn't, we would expect to be shunned and talked about until we succumbed. I did as I was trained. So did my mother. My mother's mother. Her mother's mother. And so on. Our lineage in that church went back almost seventy years. Even today, when I go back to my hometown in Kansas, I will, out of respect, visit the church. I am acknowledged by the current pastor. I am honored that the organist is playing the keys of the organ that has a brass inscription on it that reads "In Memory of Essie Mae Brown." Essie Mae Brown was my great-aunt (daughter of Gran Gran). To this day, I pay tithes there from time to time to ensure our ancestors keep our family safe. Tithing is a ritual that is taken from the Bible: "You must without fail give a tenth of everything your seed produces in the field year by year" (Deuteronomy 14:22). This translated into anything that you produced monetarily. Anything that you were gifted (like your physical and spiritual talents) was included in this. For example, in hoodoo, when I receive funds electronically, I still move 10 percent of it to a savings area that I use for some type of service to others. It is not my money but Spirit's money to donate, to share with others, to use to uplift someone other than me.

Do I believe in everything I was taught in the Bible and at church? No. I am and was conflicted by the hurtful things that the teachings included, like scripture that did not always shine the best light on my understanding of a caring deity. Our pastors taught us from the Old and New Testament. These stories of slavery, murder, and tragedy were intertwined with stories directly adjacent to stories of forgiveness, love, and tolerance. I couldn't grasp how this religion could embrace this self-hatred and sacrifice and call it love. As I grew up and went to school, I learned more about the history of our country and how enslaved people built this country but were shunned and executed. My inner conflict grew larger still when I began to develop feelings for both girls and boys. During cheerleading practice I enjoyed the scent of my best friend's bubble gum and her hair. When we finished winning a football game, I wanted to date the biggest quarterback on the team. In choir I was attracted to the androgynous tenor dressed in a suit and tie that sang "Against All Odds (Take a Look at Me Now)" by Phil Collins.

On Sundays and Wednesdays after school, I went to the Young People Willing Workers training courses that were taught by Black Pentecostal pastors, deacons, and their wives. I was instructed that to love a deity meant obedience. Obedience didn't just stop with the deity. It also meant obeying the church's covenants, our parents, our government, and our teachers at school. I studied and obeyed. I watched my sense of self change slightly. I wanted to be more like the women that I saw in movies like *Heathers* and *Pretty in Pink*. These women looked nothing like me, but I still saw more in them than I saw in the mirror.

When it came to my magical expression, any visions and dreams that I had that came true were to be used exclusively for the church and our church members. My grandmother's gifts of sight and spirituality were passed down to me from my mother, and my conjure and ability to call ancestors to do things on my behalf was from my father's side of the family. My father's side of the family was known as "backwoods," meaning they did work for evil. They would go into the swamps and dig out roots that they would boil and serve as medicine. They didn't take prescriptions like most of my family; they used teas and oily salves that they would spread over themselves when they needed to have something fixed. I think that is why it is so easy for me to be different now—I grew up with this being my normal.

I could see the future, I spoke in tongues, and I read the Bible. I read it for a different reason than others in my flock. I read it because I wanted to use some of the powerful words that appeared in the stories to make my own words sound better. Something about the words gave the stories more power. In our training we were told that we were required to study the Bible because God demanded it and one day he would test us on it, kind of like the SATs. I did not want to fail, so I read. I read so much that I found stories where there were strong women that led and won wars. I read the stories about love, sex, diversity, freedom from enslavers, and drama and wondered if I was reading a different Bible than the congregation. Perhaps. It was probably because I was told a long time ago by my great-grandmother on my dad's side that I could always tell a different Bible tale if I didn't like the one read to me. That's what I would do with the Bible and how I started changing words around in the Bible without any fear. I would read between the lines of the story or make up my own that met my needs. I guess I was doing exactly what my ancestors did generations before me—making do with what I've been given to get what I want.

When I was with my dad's family, I was brought up practicing "the work" or "workin' the roots" or "laying a trick." We never called it hoodoo; it was just something we did. We cleaned the carpets and bathroom floors with eucalyptus water each time we mopped to keep the house positive. When we burned ourselves on the stove, our granny would put margarine or butter on the burn and pray over it, telling us it was healed and sending us outside to play like nothing happened. We ate black-eyed peas each New Year's Day to give us good luck. When my grandfather argued with us, my grandma would give him coffee with sugar, and there would be little messages underneath the sugar bowl to remind him to stay sweet. When I gave birth to my daughter, my great-grandma put one thimble of Lysol in my bathtub to encourage my stitches to heal. Before I married my first husband, my gran gran had a vision that he wasn't the one for me and tried to warn me. I married him anyway.

My practice of hoodoo reflects who and what I believe in now, but that doesn't mean I do everything the way I was taught back when I was a child. For example, some hoodoo work requires a small offering of urine or blood (human or animal) to ensure the spell is bound to you and will work faster and stronger. I know that the bacteria and other pathogens in such items that are applied to the body or consumed could result in infections and disease, so I don't include them. Sacrificing red ants, which is traditional in conjure spells to increase the anger of a situation (like making someone uncomfortable enough to move or quit their job) is common, but killing red ants for a spell seems wrong to me ethically; instead I choose to use hot peppers and sulfur. Instead of wiping urine into my baby's mouth to eliminate thrush, I may take the infant to the doctor for a quick checkup, or I may use plain yogurt to wipe that baby's mouth, because now we know a bit more about the benefits of yeast.

In hoodoo eggs and animals are sacrificed (like in other cultures and religions). This is fine as well, but as a practicing hoodoo worker I do not use this. Instead I use herbs, roots, intention, faith, and direction to obtain the same results. I use photographs that I take with my phone to bring in the power of the herbs instead of foraging those that I know are facing extinction (High John the Conqueror root comes to mind, and there are others).

I use the Bible to perform rituals and incantations, and I customize the text, rewriting it to match my needs (changing pronouns and phrases without diluting the message) and eliminating parts of the Bible I no longer want to see or pass along in my own rituals.

If I know anything about working with ancestors and guides, I know that being yourself, your true self, in your work gives you the best results. In my truth, this means that changing up and upgrading hoodoo techniques from the old-ways hoodoo (which some may call black-belt hoodoo) to a newer understanding is natural and would be what our ancestors would want. My book walks you through my journey and gives you a myriad of ways to upgrade your hoodoo techniques to a more modern approach. Now that you know the background of my book, I can't wait to tell you even more.

WHO AM I? I'M THAT HOODOO LADY

Did you first see me on Instagram? What about reading my first book, *The Hoodoo Guide to the Bible*? Maybe you listened to a podcast where I was a guest. If so, thank you! Let me tell you even more about me. I'm a hoodoo practitioner that goes by the name Sherry Shone. This is my persona (I discuss personas later in the book and my reasons why I practice as such). I also am called That Hoodoo Lady. Some may say I'm a blanca or negro bruja (white or dark witch); some would say I'm a healer and others may just say I'm good at what I do for others. Whatever they say I am, I respond to That Hoodoo Lady as a badge of honor. I speak, like many of you, to my ancestors and spirit guides for answers to questions for myself and others.

I use old-ways magic called hoodoo, which is a North American folklore magic created by enslaved Africans. You can skip ahead to definitions where I tell you more but know that it is a beloved tradition of

the Black (African American) people. It is one of several folklore traditions, but I think it is the best and most pure of all oral tradition folklore. It is practiced by hundreds of thousands, if not millions, of people.

As a hoodoo practitioner my job is to make sure that I pass along
knowledge of this previously oral tradition of hoodoo. To do this, I need
to tell the history of its people, the Black people of North America who
were transported into enslavement by way of the diaspora. Our history
is interwoven with other melanated cultures. America is founded on the
ideals of freedom and built by the hard work of immigrants and those
impacted by the diaspora.

The diaspora is the involuntary dispersion of a group of individuals
from one geographic location to another, such as from the birthplace
of all humankind (Africa) to Europe or North or South America. Our
ancestors from many cultures have been impacted by the diaspora. This
is universal. Therefore, our shared pain is universal. Our shared experience of being displaced and abandoned is universal. Our need for connection and community in a world that is not ours is universal. This may
be why many of us feel we do not belong anywhere, because our roots
were shifted from us without our permission. Hoodoo is so precious to
me because hoodoo was made by a people that needed deliverance, and
deliverance is a universal need. At some point our families and communities felt unheard. We have, as a humankind, felt disenfranchised.
As a people, we have felt disrespected or abused. These feelings bring
about the need for change, an uprising and demand to obtain freedoms
that were given to others with privilege. This need drives us to want
deliverance, and, in my truth, hoodoo fulfills that need with its way of
giving those that practice it a "life manual" that is like the Bible through
its verses and supplemented by herbs, roots, incantations, folklore, and
song. But first, hoodoo demands that its practitioners know and respect
and provide offering to their ancestors of the tradition. The offerings
are given at places like crossroads, in running waters, at cemeteries,
on holy or sacred ground, at energy vortexes, libraries, justice centers,
prisons, hospitals—the list goes on and on.

It cannot be said enough that appreciation of Black culture is encouraged and necessary to be a good hoodoo worker. I would never want to

go to a chef that doesn't taste their own food. I use hoodoo and practice it with how I grow my herbs, how I pray, how I live my life, and how I get what I want from this life. But I do this only by living in my own truth and by studying African American stories, myths, and folklore. I continue to practice and consume the world and history as it pertains to African Americans and respect and converse with its ancestors. In updated hoodoo respect of the past includes moving forward with the purpose of getting what is needed, without practicing hoodoo in a manner that no longer serves me (or my guides).

When people tell me they want to learn hoodoo, they come from many backgrounds, but hoodoo calls them, and that is fine by me. Before I teach them how to make a petition paper or spiritual bath or even a healing gris-gris bag (a small fabric bag, instead of an animal skin bag, filled with spell magic), I ask them to study Black history, Latin history, Indigenous history, Asian history, feminine history, and civil rights from around the world. These are the backbones of a good rootworker. We will do the same type of journey so that you are climbing each rung of the ladder. It is impossible to be a good, and even great, rootworker without going up this ladder (and not intentionally down the ladder). Knowing your own history and connecting to ancestors, legends, and guides is so crucial.

I have spent several years in my physical body—this shell of flesh and blood and emotions and confusion and chaos. I don't expect perfection in myself, and my readings are never, ever perfect to me. They are perfect for the situation, and the guides, ancestors, and deities deliver perfect messages, but I many times fall short, and that's okay. Knowing myself and being present in the reading and giving every client the deliverance that they need is the true goal, not my own glory.

I've had clients that have triggered just about every personal issue that I have wrestled with. Obesity, neglect, abuse, trauma, chronic conditions, failed relationships, poverty, job loss, promotions, wealth, happiness, love, parenthood, loss of parents—see, the entire gamut is who I am. All of me connects to each and every client guide, ancestor, and deity, and together we build the roots that make a beautiful experience for the client to give them deliverance, which is the only goal. Not to make a cool social media post. Not to get more likes on Instagram or TikTok. It is more important to heal in good faith, intention, and direction than to have a popular podcast where you speak about it. Please understand this is part of hoodoo foundations. Our ancestors, yours and mine, had serious issues that required a serious hoodoo deliverance solution. Their very existence was built around the spiritual medicine worker giving them information that would *save their lives*—many times figuratively but other times literally. Allow that to marinate into your being.

My next advice is to take a moment to reflect on who you are. What draws you to hoodoo? What is it helping? What could be some triggers that you may want to work on before working with a client? Another story: In my first year as a reader, I had some serious concerns about a particular trauma that I hadn't dealt with in therapy, with a licensed professional. But clients would come to me, and I would see this trauma in them, in their messages from Spirit. I would tell them what their guides, ancestors, and deities would want them to know and, like I said, we hear what we need for hear for ourselves, and there it would be. This huge sign in front of me—"Get help, Hoodoo Lady. Take your own advice, Hoodoo Lady. We—your loving guides, ancestors, and deities— want this to be healed for you." The more I read, the more it came up (sometimes I can be fairly stubborn) until I started talking about the issue with my therapist. Sessions later and with techniques that helped me to overcome and live with the trauma without pain, I noticed I no longer had clients coming to me with my triggering trauma. Of course, I certainly had other experiences where new things would pop up, but expect this in your own #updatedhoodoo work. You will be challenged. You will hear what you need to hear from your guides, ancestors, and deities—believe me, it will happen, and it's okay. It's what we do as healers. We heal ourselves first.

My Religious Experience

I was raised in an evangelical church in Kansas. I have such vivid and happy memories of getting dressed up and going to church, where I could sing and watch the exciting service. Have you ever seen an evangelical church service? If you haven't, then I will try to explain. Imagine a fashion show, concert, and rally for your favorite public speaker, all in the same building and performing in that order. The congregants are in their finest outfits with hats, gloves, and elaborate hairdos. They are escorted into the church by gloved ushers. You take your seat as close to the pulpit as possible (so that you don't have to sit in the back with the latecomers). Everyone nods in approval at your being present, and after a few moments the service begins. There are opening announcements, songs, prayers, and then my favorite, the testimony service.

Testimony service is an opportunity for the congregation to tell the church (yes, the entire church) their sorrows and fears, and then they praise and worship by calling out or crying or running up and down the church aisles as they are filled with spirit.

This is the part of the service that I enjoyed the most because I am a believer in immersion in conjure. Immersion, meaning that the guide or spirit is completely overtaking you (or the practitioner). Conjure, meaning you have asked something, or some would say demanded something, to carry out a wish, desire, or direction. I believe that in practicing hoodoo you can ask a spirit or energy to join you with another guide (for example, an ancestor of the client) when they are asked, and that exchange will influence every part of the host (how they dance, speak, or even sing). Once the energy has blessed the person with deliverance, then the body is returned to its rightful owner.

Hoodoo is so important in this regard. When you practice hoodoo (and if you are protected and ask), the guides or spirit can come into your body and work with you to help you get what you need. It is the reason that I am a practitioner (because it is so like my church upbringing).

After the testimony service and the immersion was awakened, it wasn't the end of the experience. I did not always relish the next part: after offering, where we give our dollars and change to a brass or gold-plated bowl, the message would be delivered. Sometimes the message was inspiring, and we could leave feeling like we were flying. Other times, it was not uncommon to leave feeling shamed, hurt, resentful, or angry because of the verse that was chosen.

Here are examples of Bible verses that I found particularly harmful and the messages that followed:

Wives, submit yourselves unto your own husbands, as unto the Lord. (Ephesians 5:22–24)

This would be followed by a forty-five-minute lecture on why women needed to do everything their husbands dictated because it was following God's law. I could see all of my friends that were my age practically rolling their eyes. Shockingly, though, I saw some of them nodding and then later praying for a partner that they could be obedient to.

By law a married woman is bound to her husband if he is alive, but if her husband dies, she is released from the law that binds her to him. So then, if she has sexual relations with another man while her husband is still alive, she is called an adulteress. But if her husband dies, she is released from that law and is not an adulteress if she marries another man. (Romans 7:2–3)

My great-grandmother followed this to a T. She was divorced and never remarried until her ex-husband (my great-grandfather) died. Then she remarried at the age of eighty-five, because the Bible told her so.

When a man strikes his slave, male, or female, with a rod and the slave dies under his hand, he shall be avenged. But if the slave survives a day or two, he is not to be avenged, for the slave is his money. (Exodus 21:20–21)

This verse is particularly troublesome because I can imagine the context in which it was used during slavery. How many enslaved Africans were given their worth as a product or resource to be avenged by currency only so that another enslaved African could take their place? How many were told that they had to serve a deity that cared so little for them that they would need to serve here on earth with the reward of ascending into a heaven to serve another white man that was now their heavenly master?

How can these words be used for anything other than subjugation or enslavement or damage? How can you have encouraged or uplifted or supported by saying and preaching these words? Those are horrifying, but to a true Bibliophile this is the good and bad of it.

The love of hoodoo is very much like these verses. They are raw and outdated and cannot be apologized away. It is our past and it needs a true change in language to be something that I feel comfortable using. It needs to be restructured to fit this new world. We are no longer enslaved as a people. We are still going through strife and drama, but we have other ways to bless, protect, and banish that do not require the exact ways of old. They require our respect of the old and offerings to our ancestors, but they do not require that we blindly go back to an era that no longer serves us.

Some may say this is disrespectful or sacrilegious, and I'm okay with that because I know that my magic works with or without the approval of any other hoodoo practitioner.

MY SPIRIT EXPERIENCE

My great-grandmother (Gran Gran) loved to tell us stories of her upbringing in the Midwest. Being on buses and trains and having to sit in the back or in coach while everyone else was free to roam where they wanted. Her stories would transport us back to that time of segregation, but in her words, it wasn't always truly bad. She asked us to look back so that we could respect and enjoy our current lives that much more. We would ask hundreds of questions, and she would answer all of them. One story was of her pretending to be my mom's nanny so that my mom could sit at the front of the bus while Gran Gran stayed in the back. She attributed her faith to being the reason she could endure this without fighting back. Her prayers kept her strong, joyful, and witty.

Gran Gran lived in the time of segregation, but she never spoke about segregation as a necessarily bad thing. It was just a part of her life. It was her experience, and she had no other way of understanding other than that. Her life was built within walls of segregation and separation, and this became her comfort and her own protection. She didn't want to go into the white person's world. She feared it. She saw those that dared open their mouths be killed and maimed. She would speak out but only if she could do so quietly. She mended, ironed, and cleaned for wealthy families for a living. She raised my grandmother and great-auntie alone. Her husband was what some would call a tramp or a train tramp. He made his living working on trains and never stayed in any place for too long. He would send a few dollars now and then to help her out, but really, she was alone—Gran Gran didn't complain.

Gran Gran would say, "When I was working for the whites, rearing their children, cooking their meals, mending their clothes, I treated their families like my own, but I never got too familiar. I knew that they were mostly good Christian people and put food on their children's table, but I also knew that there was something else about them. Something that was deep inside that would switch like a light to dark. There would be a flicker as that energy would take over, and then they would let you go from your job or try and touch you where they had no business touching you, and you just need to pray and give it to God that he would see you through." Her employers (like many of us in today's times) were her new enslavers. They were to be feared because of their ability to take away your financial security, and they were also someone that you were tethered to. Their life was directly tied to yours and vice versa. Your success was their success. If they failed, then you too, as their worker, would fail. Gran Gran's story started in 1899, and her journey ended in 1998 (ninety-nine years later). She was mugged, abused, abandoned, and traumatized in those ninety-nine years. But she was also deeply loved, admired, respected, prayed for, wanted, needed.

Marriage and love relationships were sacred to Gran Gran. They were sacred because of the teachings she received in church. She longed and hoped for a deeper love from my great-grandfather (her husband), but this was not to be. He left shortly after my grandmother was born—never to return. Too many of our stories begin this way. We start as a family of maybe two or three or more, and then members of that family slowly depart, and new ones enter. This shift can be counted upon the same way as the shift of the earth's tectonic plates. Our lives are meant to shift. Let's sit with that for a moment. From the time we are born we are meant to not stay still. We are not stagnant. Change cannot occur without another force moving against us to cause the need to adjust. Animals, plants, and the building blocks of DNA are constantly moving and adjusting every day if not every second. In hoodoo there is also a change happening that requires us to attune to new thinking and new values.

The stories that were once gladly told no longer have the same effect, so now we have new ones. The old meanings of words are irrelevant from their definitions twenty or thirty years ago. When I first researched and had a need to name what my spiritual gift of hoodoo was, I first knew it in the church as the "spirit." This spirit lived inside of me and could be contacted whenever I needed help or guidance. The spirit also provided me with a new roadmap when I needed one. It encouraged me to keep going. It spoke to me and told me where I should walk, what words to speak, whom to speak to, and whom to avoid. This spirit was something passed down from parent to child just like eye color or personality.

When I was younger this spirit sounded like my mom and grandma. This spirit was feminine and warm like milk that would be served with toast. Comforting and honey sweet, the voice would gently remind me to do chores, to pick out the most fun outfits. The spirit I had I could see in other creatures like ants, birds, and puppies. I would hold them in my hands and notice their differences from me. The ants with segmented red or black bodies or sometimes a mixture of colors that amazed me. So fragile and tiny with a goal to build and bring food back home to the queen. The ants would track over my hand and arm and tickle me. I would follow them all the way to the raised hills or holes in the cracks of my bedroom. I never really knew where they were going, but I still, in my child's mind, knew it was somewhere spectacular. It just had to be to have to live every day in the ground. I thought of what it would be like to be able to climb as high as your body could take you but be so small that you knew nothing of how much larger the world was around you.

In puberty, my spirit voice was altered ever so quietly. It was now deeper in tone and richer in quality. It was heavier and slightly condescending, with undertones of anger that I didn't understand. It was the least favorite of my spirit voices. It would warn me when to finish homework and when I could let assignments slip. The spirit introduced me to the notion of guilt in faith. What I mean by this is that there was a vengeful, spiteful deity that punished and hurt me if they were angered. The new spirit voice gave me doubt. Doubt about my looks, my physical body, of course, but also my insecurities about my intellect, my status in my family (where my brother would tell me I was adopted and should be ashamed), and my ability to be loved as who I was. This spirit could be brutally honest, telling me that my clothes, hair, and identity were false and reminding me to do better, always better. To run or jump or climb or ascend to my end, even though as a teenager I had no idea what that was.

One day I was in the middle of a conversation with a friend at lunch. The subject of race came up when we looked at the tables. Black people were pepper and white people were salt. Then, after giggles, came the comparisons from each of us on which we were (salt or pepper). I (even now it is a cringe-worthy moment for me) told my white friends that I was a mixture. They objected—I had to make up my mind. I had to decide what I was. I shook pepper and salt onto the table and gladly pronounced that I was both but (cringe part) at least I had some white in me. The spirit taught me shame of self. It seemed that the more I tried to pray or ask others to help build me up, the louder the spirit got. If only I could tell my twelve-year-old self that this spirit would go away after puberty and to not believe it—it was a false entity. But that wasn't my destiny. This voice encouraged me to reject my faith because I could never trust or please it. It taught me I didn't have a direction—that my direction correlated with what my parents and grandparents wanted. I certainly didn't have intentions. I had needs and desires. I desired cool clothes and to be in a Huey Lewis and the News music video on MTV. But I didn't see anyone that looked like me on TV, so it only gave the spirit more evidence that I was an anomaly. I knew in my heart I didn't want to be different, so I asked the spirit to remake me into something that would blend in and not stand out. The spirit wasn't always bad—it kept me out of danger.

When I was a child waiting at a bus stop in the Colorado winter, I didn't question it when it told me that it was not okay to go into a warm car provided by a stranger. When the stranger approached me, all smiles and well wishing, the spirit showed me fear. I saw images of what the stranger saw. It was like I could see past their eyes and into their mind. The images I saw were twisted and dark, where they wanted nothing more but to expose me to another life—a life of sex work, drug addiction, and damage by adults. I saw all of this as the stranger held open the car door. The spirit showed me a small, filthy apartment that smelled like mold. The spirit showed me a door that had a lock on the outside for which the stranger possessed the only set of keys. I could hear whimpering and muffled cries from the door. I could hear myself behind the door. I jerked my hand away from the stranger's car door and told them that my mom would call the police if I didn't meet her at the next bus stop.

The spirit gave me these images all the time. Before I went places, I would see in my mind ahead of time what was to come. Fear was some of those images, and the spirit could give visions of nightmares. Nightmares that only my gran gran could calm down. I would see buildings crumbling to the ground, plane crashes, the Charles Manson murders, the rape and assault of women in hotel rooms we stayed in on family vacations. The mental picture movies were just as real as anything I saw when I looked out a window. The spirit was training me in spiritual things while I was in my junior and senior year of high school. While others were learning algebra, I was learning to pray away the visions or use them to prepare for what was coming and avoid what was there to harm me.

In hoodoo you will come across many spirits claiming to be here for you. If they are here for you then they will not mind you challenging them or asking them a question from time to time. I learned in adulthood that it was okay to question my spirits, ancestors, and guides. My spirits are now so much a part of me that I would not know myself without them. I made peace with them once I connected with ancestors and learned about other ancestors that had experiences like mine. For example, Mother Harriet Tubman would have visions and dreams because of a head trauma. These visions helped her to see the way forward in her ranks as a leader in the Underground Railroad and in the military. Learning to trust my spirits gave me an internal self that is closer than any family or friend or lover, all in the same body. But there are drawbacks.

With having these spirits inside of you as a hoodoo worker, you have constant conversations—all the conversations and all the decisions and misunderstandings that come when you have two or more ideals and personalities—unless you learn to stop them. In hoodoo you will take inventory of everyone in the room of your mind and, as you recognize members, you will need to learn their voice. Is their voice truthful or full of judgment and fear? Is the voice yours, or does it belong to your client? Is the voice ancient or a new soul? Do they come in peace and love, or are they there to teach about evil, fear, or vengeance? The spirits that you encounter are just there because they want to be part of the conversation (or because you called them). I'll show you more about working with the spirits later, but take a moment to scan your body and take note of what spirits are inside of you. Have they always been there? Do they support your decision to learn about hoodoo, or are they trying to tell you that you should run away? Keep those words they are saying to yourself for now. Later, we will ask them more and come to an understanding.

The spirits guide us and can help us move in the direction we are going. Direction is the last tenet because of this. Without direction we would be a ball thrown by a pitcher that never finds a bat or glove. We would just be energy without a goal.

WHAT IS A HOODOO WORKER?

A hoodoo worker is someone that believes, lives, and practices hoodoo—the hoodoo work of old where there were enslaved Africans that needed deliverance from their enslavers. They would use herbs and roots and their background from African rituals to heal and protect themselves and those that asked for their guidance.

A hoodoo worker has respect for their ancestors that are descendants of enslaved Africans. Their turmoil and struggle are in their blood, and understanding this is so key to being a good hoodoo worker. Understanding that through deliverance and the need for real solutions in a time of need is the true reason for hoodoo. It's not for getting or taking someone's partner. It's about deliverance from causes and issues that resonate with those that ran in the middle of the night, hungry and scared, from sure death if they were caught. It is larger than picking out a pretty crystal or a special type of incense. It is a deep feeling in your soul that you need to be freed from whatever condition ails you and having the courage to seek it, receive it, and be grateful for it.

A hoodoo worker is also a rootworker. Someone that works with natural herbs, roots, and plants to bring about healing and change. They were called rootworkers because of the physical plants that were used and how the roots of these plants were processed to bring forth the energy and healing power from them. For example, herbalists use valerian root to calm and combat insomnia symptoms. The plant grows tall—up to two or three feet (in my backyard anyway)—and it has little pink or white flowers that bloom from the tall stalk. It is a favorite treat for butterfly larvae, and my bees and hummingbirds hang out with it. In some states and countries, it is classified as a weed because it is so easy to grow, and it can take over your yard if you aren't careful—and your neighbors' too. The most potent part of the plant is its roots. They are the source of the valerian oil—the liquid gold if you will—that provides insomnia and pain relief. A true rootworker would know this and would dry the root and use it in tonics, teas, and in powdered forms to give their patients relief.

True rootworkers understand the living things all around them and how to grow and cultivate them—very much like our ancestors did before. Start simple with updated hoodoo. Consider your ancestry and begin by researching just one plant that would have meant something to your lineage. Maybe it's peppermint, ginger, thyme, lemon balm, chive, or pepper that speaks to you. If so, then go to a plant nursery or search for photos of your plant choice and do research on the healing properties of the plant.

Next, use the healing properties of the plant and correlate those to hoodoo work. A peppermint plant is used for its leaves, stem, and oil that is extracted. It has been used in the Eastern and Western medicinal traditions. It is aromatic (smells great), can reduce or eliminate spasms, pain, sore throats, indigestion, cold, toothaches, and nausea. Historically it was used in Egypt, Greece, and Rome. It is synonymous with other mints in the mint family, and there is a myth that it was once a nymph that was being seduced by Hades. Persephone (Hades's bride) was so upset at this betrayal that she transformed the nymph into mint and made it cower on the ground (it is a ground cover) so that people would overlook it and step on it. Not to be outdone, Hades gifted mint with its sweet smell so that if you did step on it, the sweet smell would overtake you and you couldn't resist it. In hoodoo this far-from-low plant is used to calm down angry communications. It is used in teas to entice your lovers into wanting to have sex with you. It gives you fresh breath if chewed so that you are more appealing. You can place crushed mint in a sock or pantyhose and add your prayer and blessing. You then carry this bag like an amulet for pain relief, to get over a heartbreak, or to give you sweet dreams.

If you were a native African woman, maybe you would start with the peanut. In Africa peanuts are a necessary legume (seed) that have protein and fats and contribute to combating malnutrition. Peanuts (or groundnuts as they are also called) are one of the raw materials that boosted the continent's economic stability well into the 1970s. In later years, with the misinformation (or information for some) that peanuts were causing allergies in children and health concerns about using peanut oils, the revenue for this legume dried up. This affected mostly women as this was one crop they could grow without interference. The market has shifted to Eastern Europe as traders are more apt to believe that the quality standards and farming practices are safer and farming equipment is superior. This adds to the poverty and decline of women-owned enterprises. As a hoodoo worker, if I were making a spell for a client that wanted to cause the decline of another's business, I would use peanuts as a way to increase that client's finances. I would add a peanut to a doll that I made for someone to encourage nutrition and to make sure the recipient of the doll was well fed.

As someone with a rich Irish lineage, you might do a search on the internet that will help you find that Irish trees include the oak, alder, birch, and pine. Flowers and plants that are part of this heritage are daffodils, woody plants, sea campion, bog asphodel, and sundew plants. I would pick one of these plants and do my research to understand it to really get to the root (pun intended) of its being and then take that plant (virtually or physically) to my altar. Observing it for the life that it has. Touching each leaf and stem or digging into the soil and appreciating the roots that are fed from the nutrients in the soil. Covering the root system up, then taking care of the plant by learning how to best support it in its setting. Let the plant remain on your altar for as long as it takes you to form a relationship with it. To understand its needs for water, sunshine, and interactions. All plants have a need for interaction. The breath you give it when you speak to it. The wind that caresses its body. The interaction with other plants in your home or in its plot of land.

In the book *The Hidden Life of Trees*, forester and author Peter Wohlleben walks the reader through his scientific discovery that the forest is a hidden network of a living organism with each tree in the forest participating and communicating with each other—even if it means giving up one life for the greater good of the forest. Personally, I think of this when I think of our human condition in hoodoo. Each hoodoo or rootworker is responsible for keeping the human nature or construct healthy, even when it means the personal sacrifice of giving of yourself through prayer, fasting (if you choose to do this), and healing of the world through rootwork, herbology, and plant-based medicine. As rootworkers and hoodoo workers, we are responsible for continuing life by understanding the life-based systems around us *and* by being respectful of living things—even if it means our own discomfort.

WHAT IS A CONJURE WORKER?

Did you ever watch the series *True Blood* on HBO? I remember that series mostly because of the show's opening sequence and scenes (well, there were also some really good sex scenes). There were scenes of worshippers falling in rivers and lakes, being baptized by water. People speaking in tongues, dancing, and praising. Bible thumping. All mixed in with other parts of our society. Alcohol, drugs, sexual freedom, sex workers, and the like. Quite a juxtaposition, but really, to me it showed that we are all parts of one body. We are a full frame of our past, present, and future led by possession and conjuration.

Another kind of conjuration occurs in hoodoo rituals when we specifically call out a deity, guide, or ancestor to do something on our behalf as a pledge. When I say, "Thy will be done" or "In the name of," I am speaking to my intended deity out of respect and humility and making things happen through my will and theirs.

If I can persuade you to love or fear or suspect or enjoy something, then I truly have the gift of conjure. I can also use conjure when I use incantations (chanting or speaking) in a spell to help bring about change or increase or health. It is very relative as energies are movements of space and shifts of emotions. As a conjurer, I take this role seriously and understand the consequences of doing conjure. I recognize that using my toolbox of "making shit happen" is all about my own ethics and morals. In conjure, there is no judgment. No rule of three, which is common in Wicca. If I do something that brings about darker or more dubious solutions, then I know the impact, and I welcome it.

ANCESTORS, DEITIES, AND GUIDES

Later in the book, I will tell you about my tenets for hoodoo (intention, faith, and direction). Before I get you started with that, I think it's a perfect time to tell you about the other three foundations of hoodoo. These are knowing about ancestors, deities, and guides. All of us have them. Some of ours are shared across bloodlines or cultural identifiers or even gender identity. Some are chosen by us through cultural appreciation and education. My understanding and explanation may differ from yours, but it is truly how I think of these foundational references when I do any hoodoo work. I never undertake a work, conjure, or hoodoo ritual or spell without taking an ancestor, deity, or guide along for the ride.

Ancestors

Think back to last week or last month or even ten years ago. Who is a central figure that has influenced an important event, whether it was joyous or tragic? I can think of many, because unfortunately the list is populated by guides at the blink of an eye. Ancestors that were tortured and killed at the hands of bigots. People that were killed by lovers and then legislation was passed in their names. Humans, our precious trans beings, who have been slaughtered because they dared to show their true faces at a workplace or at a restaurant, and the hatred of some other soul snuffed them out. Beings that stood firm in the face of adversity with the same fear as enslaved ancestors, knowing that if they attended a protest or voted a certain way or spoke at a podium that it might be their last day on earth. These are the ancestors, guides, and deities of whom I speak and are worthy of our hoodoo conjure and offering.

You may also think of a movie you like about the classic parent and child relationship. When you think of that relationship there is a bond. Many times blood, but surely a relationship of trust and love (in most cases). In some cases, there can be other bonds and ties in that parent and child relationship that are not the happiest, but the relationship is still there. That relationship is due to heritage. The lineage is passed down from generation to generation—from parent to child and that child as a parent to their child and so on. Ancestors are characteristically part of a root system from a family tree that expands over time.

I have a big tree called a monkey puzzle tree or monkey tree in the front yard of my home in Oregon. The monkey tree, also known as the *Araucaria araucana*, has been on the planet for hundreds if not millions of years. Its ancestry is a conifer, and it gets its name from people that said "it would puzzle a monkey to climb that." The monkey tree is from Chile and Western Argentina. It is very tall, with spiky foliage and a very rough exterior for bark. Each limb of the tree reminds me of monkey tails with twists and turns. But the danger of the monkey tree is the sharpness of each triangle-shaped "leaf" that comes out of it. The tree leaves are rough and wide at the base and spiky at the tip, making them very sharp—like knife tips. It's impossible to prune, even with your best pruning shears, because of the roughness and terribly sharp exterior. The leaf tips can dig into your sturdiest gloves, and even worse, your flesh. The folklore behind the monkey puzzle tree is that the tree deserves your respect, and if you pass it and are not quiet, then it will turn your tail into a monkey tail. I do not know about that, but I do know that many that pass by the tree wonder about the legend.

The tree speaks to me of ancestry because of the years that it has lived on this earth. There is mystery behind the tree. The pinions the females produce carry the seed of new trees worldwide. The tree itself becomes its own beauty and its own danger. If you approach the tree to prune it, you better be ready to understand its nature. You have to protect yourself with gloves and clothing that covers you or else the leaves will dig into your flesh and prick you. I can imagine that any monkey that tried to climb this tree would think twice when approaching it. But the tree itself is gorgeous and regal. Standing tall with taillike limbs that stretch out and encourage you to witness it in all its glory. Only when you get close do you see what it's really made from and have to decide to get to know it better.

That's an ancestor to me. An ancestor may be someone you know from your biological or chosen family of origin. They may be someone you revere. Someone that is elevated when you tell stories of childhood or experience. They may be someone that gave you a name at birth. Maybe they were someone that made you your favorite dish or gave you your first toy. Either way, ancestors leave their marks. They are a root system that you are built from that continues moving up. They are complex, and can be sharp and biting and kind and welcoming, but they require blood. The blood that comes only from someone who is close enough to learn from the root system. Ancestors require preparation—like the preparation that I have to undertake before I prune the monkey tree in my front yard.

Ancestors, deities, and guides can be so many things. They can be lovely to look at and may cause others to admire them, but only those that are close know what they really are. Ancestors are teachers of the family system. Ancestors give you the traits that make you who you are. Ancestors provide the life lessons that give you a sense of self—even if that education means that to save yourself you never go near that family system again. Ancestors are blood or lineage or family of origin (whether by birth or by choice). They can resemble your own faith, intention, or direction, or they can begin your understanding of faith, intention, and direction. Ancestors are life beings that were here in our physical world. They experienced common life problems that we have and understand what it is like to begin and end in this world. Because of this, we reach out to ancestors when we have issues with life and want practical guidance from someone who has been there before. Ancestors, because they are descendants or offspring from your root system, will have a history for you that you cannot get from a guide or a deity.

When you have a client in front of you for whom you are doing a deliverance work spell or conjuring an ancestor, then you will be introduced to someone you do not know. You will have no previous understanding of the ancestor without introducing yourself. Just like my explanation of how I approach my monkey tree, stay mindful when reaching out to your client's ancestors. Your client's ancestors will (because they are in the same lineage as your client) have the same complex issues and concerns that follow them (unless there has been healing or severing of those issues). Because of this they are excellent resources for information about your client and their history, *but* ancestors were once human. They can lie and will lie. They can hurt and will hurt. They can interfere, and they *will* interfere. They are not all happy and rainbows, because life on earth is not so. Many of your client's ancestors had experiences, trauma, and emotions that they may still carry with them into the next world. Because of this, I recommend new hoodoo workers work with only their ancestors to reach other ancestors so that the ancestors can work together without entangling you in their stories. Otherwise, it would be like having someone else's tree in your front yard that you've never pruned or watered or even know how to take care of.

Your Plant-Based Roots

When you learn about plant life and how to care for plants, it will inspire you to understand why the culture embraces this plant. When you are attracted to hoodoo, it may be because certain plants are calling you to work with them. Many times, it is because the plant just happens to thrive in the environment that sustains it. The plants you find in Ireland may be similar to those that naturally grow in the Pacific Northwest, where the soil is wet and boggy nine months out of the year. Where the moss grows like carpet across rocks, bridges, and walkways. Its presence indicates a rainforest in the making—even if it's on a suburban landscape of people just trying to get to work and to their favorite coffee spot. Deeply consider how this same plant has outlasted even our eldest ancestors and that the network of the plant system will continue—even as we, the humans that claim to own the earth, do nothing but try to destroy it when it encroaches into our firepits or sidewalks, rooftops, or siding.

Deities

When I think of deities, I think of the gods and goddesses. Whether you are basing this understanding on religion or an archaeological stance or an understanding that our history was made from something systematically larger is your choice.

When I think of a deity, I think of the many different things out there that, to me, are beyond comprehension. Clouds, for instance. Clouds are made of condensed water—floating water droplets suspended in the atmosphere, just hanging there. Water droplets that have a purpose—its purpose is to express cooled water from above or even from below. The clouds' purpose is also to give us rain and snow. Even more than that, clouds are found on many planets other than earth because the chemicals that make up water are also prevalent in our universe. They are required for the solar system to be what we need to *be*. Why is that? Out of all of the universes out there something makes ours so unique to support not just the solar system but our little pebble just far enough from the sun to not be scorched and not too far to not be able to sustain life.

I think of deities as being as vast and wide as the billions of universes that exist when we think of an atmosphere that sustains life here on earth. The deity is in the atmosphere that is supported by the clouds, supported by the rain and snow it produces that provides the water we need to keep our trees and plants and animals living. The deity cares about and loves everything we meet (if this is your belief). If not, then maybe your deities are the laws of physics, gravity, transmutation, combustion, and integration. These are other examples of deities that can or cannot be seen but are powerful and enrich our experiences here on earth. For millions of years, before we had a reflection of nature in the oceans and in the skies, something created all of the galaxies and universes upon universes in existence. I would be ignorant if I thought it was something I was meant to fully understand, but it does require my offerings, because in hoodoo it sustained and kept my ancestors (our shared ancestors) safe in uncertain times.

There were humans that worshipped several gods at once or one god or no gods. This isn't a religion. The human beings that we have been shaped from began by observing things they couldn't understand and applying categories and words onto them to make them safer and approachable for us. Those names then became as large as the original ones. Our human forms in magic are expressed in our hoodoo, and it is bigger than a group of people in a building giving tithes. Our connection with a deity (spiritual or factual) completes us in a way that love, faith, and intention do not.

The religion that some of us follow now meets our needs of connection and order. Some of us need this to respect our traditional ethics and morals, and others do not—they follow different laws and express them in their own way. None of us follow the same path, even if we are part of a group. Each of us has our own understanding through a unique experience of this ball of self. This body of flesh, tendons, bones, heart, and mind that starts with our first breath and ends with our last. True deities are full of faults and errors because they are shaped from our human mind, and our minds are never faultless. It is okay to question your deity. Ask for clarification. Write your grievances and, in prayer, send them to your deity for answers. If you seek other answers, then read and grow and study in that new context. Deities don't always answer the way you may think they need to. I have had deities answer my questions in tarot readings, at the grocery store in advertisements I see for products, at stop signs, in words of comfort from friends, when I hear a song that speaks to my heart and opens my soul and allows me to work in a more concentrated fashion. The deity gives our spells a focal point, like if we are looking at the destination address on a map app. Our deity is helping us get there, and once we do, we give them a good or negative review in the form of an offering we place at their feet (virtually or physically) like a review on Yelp. There are places to leave offerings for deities. The best way to know what to leave them is to ask them what they want and where they want it.

My deity (like my guides) likes things to be left in places they find consecrated and holy for them. I bow my head and kneel out of respect to my deity when I ask them for help. If my plane is going down and I call out a deity's name and the plane corrects itself and I walk away safely, then I will give an offering at a church or religious institution. But I could easily also send a thank-you note to the airline or spread the love and gratitude by making my friends a meal, calling someone that I love, doing social justice hoodoo work, volunteering my time, helping someone in need, communicating my love for animals by respecting them and not harming them, or caring for nature and not destroying it.

Guides

What is a guide? Any elevated being that identifies as someone that leads you. They rarely demand the same of you; there are some that can, and you can decide for yourself if you want to follow them. Guides can be ancestors or deities. In addition, according to Merriam-Webster, they can also be

- a mythological or legendary figure, often of divine descent, endowed with great strength or ability,
- an illustrious warrior,
- a person admired for achievements and noble qualities,
- one who shows great courage,
- the principal character in a literary or dramatic work.

Considering what I said before about how women have been treated, apply the same to men. Gay men that told others that they loved another man and then were killed on their way home. Men that were abolitionists and hung from the same tree as Black people because they dared to speak out for what they knew in their hearts was right. Indigenous men that wanted nothing more than to protect their families from those that infiltrated their homes and ways of life. Their protection was misconstrued as "savage," and they were taken from their families and their lives were taken by gunfire.

Guides have this in common. They are never perfect. They are willing, strong, weak, damaged, addicted, and persistent regardless of gender, nationality, or religion. Some were fathers and mothers and breadwinners and career minded, or they were homemakers. They built governments (and destroyed them). They supported every gender and race, even if they didn't understand them.

Who are my guides? In this book I will tell you about a variety of heroes that are worthy of our offering and can offer hoodoo deliverance. My guides are everyday people (like my great-grandfather, my mother, my father, and so on).

I love my guides. I am guilty of even putting them on a pedestal that is only high enough for my own imagination. Even as a hoodoo practitioner, I must remind myself that my treasured ancestors are not just to be put up on a shelf in my office or den in a golden or bronze frame for others to admire. They are here to continue doing work for all of us to carry out their goals—even in death. I remind myself that they need honor and offering. I bring them flowers or wine or play their favorite music. That is a time-honored way to express devotion and adoration in a public and straightforward way. Unashamed and free and open. In any practice of spirituality, our ability to be the ancestor's physical manifestation of their works, and express their works in our own.

In this book I focus on everyday guides that you may or may not know. I tell their stories—sometimes their real story, sometimes their imagined life from what I have researched. I follow up with a Bible verse that I have hand-picked for them; their intention, faith, and direction; and a spell to use when conjuring them.

My hope is that you go through each of these verses in your own practice and study. That they encourage you and keep you steadfast whenever you do anything heroic.

A hero is by definition "a mythological or legendary human often of divine descent having great strength or ability." Many of us may not have those relations, whether blood or known; choose from the ones I have below. Review the verses and notice how you read and understand them before and after the heroic tale, then work through my recommended spells and add to them or subtract from them as necessary to meet your needs for deliverance in hoodoo.

CULTURAL APPRECIATION, APPROPRIATION, EDUCATION, AND ERADICATION

One event that I held was on cultural appropriation. I discussed my views on how cultural appropriation manifests itself in metaphysical ceremonies, magic, herbalism, and hoodoo. Hoodoo was birthed out of abuse, being caged, and wanting to escape. Our ancestors have fought for the ability to be free and to enjoy our free will. Hoodoo can be practiced by anyone of different races *if and only if* they are respectful and honor those that lived the truth that demanded the hoodoo tradition (to provide deliverance where there is adversity).

On the other side of hoodoo, it can be easy for me to succumb to the negativity. I think we are all susceptible. In this body—the only body I can use in this lifetime—I have chosen this family and this body in this race. There are many times in this body that I am reminded of my physicality. When I attempt to run up a hill and I struggle to catch my breath. When I go outside and soak in all the sunlight without any fear of damage, because my skin craves the warmth. When I awake and head to the mirror and run my fingers through coils and curls and have to decide whether I want to wet it so that I can comb through it or leave it be, dry and crown-like in its formation. When I go to a shopping mall, masked and armed with the knowledge that I may be followed, I may be mistaken as a shoplifter, I may be questioned about my purchases and if they are mine. The frustration I feel when someone attempts to comment on my curves, my hair, my skin color, my lips, my intellect, my anger—everything that makes me who my deity knows I am. My tendency to sleep after eating carbs or turkey. My speech patterns. My love of chicken and watermelon and my struggle to *not* like it just to prove others wrong. My need for faith. My desire for deliverance. My work in conjure and possession and possessing and willingness to consume this faith fire that is in my belly. Beat into my race by generations of being told that this person—this Jesus—died for everyone, including me but, in the year of 2021, knowing that the very same people that take our words and style also want to crush our ability to procreate by murdering our children and males.

This flattery and fear of my culture that I chose is heartbreaking and killing more of us by, as Malcom X famously said, any means necessary. I feel it when I go into downtown Portland and see the thousands of victims of houselessness. Tarps draped across chain-link fences and stretched onto tree limbs, trash cans, or even inoperable vehicles to provide protection from the elements. Mental health issues are ignored, but my culture's dances and singing are copied and then sold through a more palatable suburban, indoor-cycling influencer. It can be easy to fall into the negativity. You go to a church for years and years, donating your hard-earned coins because you have been taught that this is the way to obtain deliverance and experience the heartache of finding out that all of those dollars go into the leader's bank account so that they can drive a better car than yours, live in a neighborhood that you would never be allowed in, and live a life that you prayed for.

Why does that happen? Why do we culturally appropriate? Appropriate meaning taking someone else's social, cultural, and artistic aspects for your own. Am I guilty? Yes. When we were growing up, I wanted to have long, flowing hair that ran down my back, because that was a status symbol. Long, straight hair was good. My hair was bad. That's what I knew, so I strived for that. It showed in other ways too. When I went for jobs, I made sure I spoke in a manner that was acceptable. I hid anything that would celebrate my culture. I did not wear cornrows. I didn't wear long, painted fingernails. I didn't pop gum. I didn't speak to "them" the way I would have spoken to friends and family. I went to operas and musicals that celebrated another culture and then, in return, I learned that their ways were the best ways. I learned culinary arts and how to cook with their herbs. I began to hate my own culture's ways. I didn't want greens anymore—that wasn't what they ate, so I wanted spinach and pea shoots. I still get caught in the trap of wanting what I am not.

Maybe you are in the same trap. Feeling that your own culture or background isn't enough. Wanting to be something, anything, but you.

It is understandable. We want what we see and admire. We imitate and become infatuated with what excites us and feeds our curiosity. For me in my truth, in this body, taking hoodoo into my blood helped me and freed me from wanting to be someone I was not. I learned that my being is deeper than a pair of sneakers or how I walk or dance. My being is all about how I treat others. How I love others. How they love me. How I respect others that are not like me in the everyday world. How I begin to research and learn about my people's ways and take those into my own day-to-day, and to embrace and love them is to embrace and love myself.

In the song "Letter to My Trap" by Yo Gotti and Mike WiLL Made It, Gotti and WiLL rap that the draw and attraction of running a drug business, the thrill that it brings, the money that it afforded them, was the first love of the protagonist. The song continues to tell the tale that the singer wants and deserves the respect from the very thing that almost took everything from him. When my clients come to me, when I read for myself, when I hear of readers helping to give their clients what they need, I find that many times they want absolution or an apology or some kind of closure from the thing that has kept them bound. Even if they started the relationship or addiction with full knowledge of the possible outcome, the thing harming them is still there. They want to move forward. Using spells of self-love is key in those situations. It may be difficult or even impossible for the client to get closure without help from a therapist or other mental health care, but that and the work of spiritual cleansings, prayers, blessings, and hoodoo spells and rituals give them back their voice and their freedom; it is part of the process.

Self-love is the cure for appropriation. Appropriation is dangerous because it feeds the fear of "other." It gives to the energy of "you—exactly as you identify as—are not enough and you need to take on another culture to feel comfort and love and satisfaction."

Appropriation. Adoption. Seizure. Annexation. These are words that describe what it is to appropriate something. To take some aspect or thing as your own. We do this in positive ways all the time, like when we foster and then adopt a pet. We appropriate it in that manner. We adopt it, we benefit from it, and hopefully they benefit from us including them in our lives. It's an exchange of energies that requires some type of trust and contract of intention of responsibility.

Appropriation can also mean something darker, like during slavery. The enslavers appropriated and seized human beings as their own. The enslavers purchased them; used their skills, talents, unique ideas, and culture for themselves; and benefited from them with no regard to the harm they were causing. Imagine this scenario: I go to your home as a welcomed guest. Using a family recipe, you make me a meal that I enjoy. I then ask you for the recipe because I thought it was so wonderful. You share it with me because, after all, we are friends, right? Then one year later you learn that I have taken that same recipe and branded it in my name as "That Hoodoo Lady's Meal." I go on social media and TV and make commercials telling the story of the recipe. I embrace the recipe and present it as my own. I'm living a lie, yes, but everyone sees my brand on the recipe, so now they think it really did start with me. And you, as the original creator of the recipe, get no credit for it. No one even knows of your existence in the recipe's story, because I have not credited you for any of the work.

Take another example: hairstyles. I wear my natural hair as an afro sometimes and other times as locs. There's a specific loc pattern called Sisterlocks. It is a patented locking system for coiled hair by Dr. JoAnne Cornwell. She spent years perfecting the locking technique that allows coiled hair to stay locked without the use of waxes or oils. The hair grows quickly and in thin but beautifully strong intertwined strands. With this process, it takes at least six months to a year for natural Afrocentric hair to turn into fully locked tresses. There are certified Sisterlocks consultants that take hundreds of hours of training classes to do their clients' hair in the same manner. It's a pattern passed from teacher to student, systematically and ritualistically to ensure the quality of the Sisterlocks brand is maintained. There are others that want to use this system but do not want to invest in the Sisterlocks training classes to pay for Dr. Cornwell's intellectual property, so they simply buy a wig in the same style or use waxes or oils to mimic the style. When asked, they proudly smile and tell their tale that they, too, have Sisterlocks, knowing that they have not done one minute of the work required to use that name.

When you culturally appropriate, you seize, assume, adopt, and have the arrogance to assume that you can use a recipe, a hairstyle, an experience as your own without going through the same experience as that individual. When you say you are a hoodoo worker and do not honor, train, acknowledge, or follow hoodoo patterns that are passed down from teacher to student, you weaken the system, you are basing your experience on lies, and you shame the name. This is why hoodoo is so protected and protective of its training. There are hoodoo workers that have spent decades learning and mastering their craft, only to show one person outside of their inner circle, culture, or familiar experience and have their hard work touted on that person's Instagram or TikTok as their own—shameful!

Because of cultural appropriation some hoodoo workers hide and tell half spells to keep their work close to their hearts. Some workers will tell you the whole spell from beginning to end only if you are from their community or their racial background. Others may share but tell you only about ingredients that are impossible to find to make sure you can't duplicate the spell if you are unknown to them (or if they don't feel you are advanced enough in your practice). I have found this in other traditions as well. I remember going to a Santeria priest for deliverance with a work issue. He asked me to bring an egg. I, not knowing any better, brought a plain white egg from the grocery store. Once I got there he asked me questions about the egg: Where was it from? What color was the chicken? Did I remove any of the feathers from the egg? All those things would help him with giving me deliverance. And when I didn't answer in the way he needed, he canceled my session, and I had to go get another egg that he could work with.

As you read other hoodoo books, remember this: you will need to have your own connection to Spirit and the deity of your choosing. It is a personal journey, and while I can provide guidance, I am not always correct about what you need to do in your hoodoo journey. I wrote this book to help you with an inclusive hoodoo. When you are reading other practitioners' work or even asking them for help, depending on where they were raised and taught you may get half of the picture if you are the wrong color, gender, or even from the wrong state or city.

We hoodoo practitioners do not have a membership or society that we all belong to. There are hoodoo practitioners that do say they are authorized to teach and certify you, but when you are considering this, remember that our ancestors never had an online class to share their teachings and they never held a correspondence course. Hoodoo work was passed from parent to child, from aunt to niece or nephew, and so on. I love to remind my clients and students in my classes of this verse in the Bible: "Study to show thyself approved unto Spirit, a worker that needeth not to be ashamed, rightly dividing the word of truth" (2 Timothy 2:15). As a worker of deliverance (hoodoo worker), it is up to each of you to search and find your own truth. I hope to inspire you in my writings, but in the end, search your own spirit to receive if my teachings (or anyone's teachings) are true.

If you recognize this, then you have passed the first step. The second step is to understand the seriousness of choosing this path. Being a hoodoo worker is a life choice—it must be in your truth and walk. It is how I work, how I practice magic, how I eat, and how I pick what I put into my body when it needs healing. The work is quite simple, but it is also very individual.

I never do the same work twice that I'm aware of. That's what I love about hoodoo. It's all mine, and when you practice, it will be all yours. But you must be aware of the full slavery experience, the full experience of being impacted by the diaspora with all of your culture, ways, and history stolen.

Now unto them that can keep you from falling, and to present you faultless before the presence of glory with exceeding joy, to the only wise Highest One, be glory and majesty, dominion, and power, both now and ever. Amen. (Jude 1:24–25)

OUR BLACK CHURCH: A STUDY IN GUILT

As I mentioned before, I have been raised in a very religious background. My wife jokes that in our family all of us are ministers, whether we want to be or not. The Black church merely represents the religious institution of Protestant communities that arose post-slavery with predominately Black members. It is known for Pentecostal attributes like chanting, singing, fasting, praying, tithing, long services, speaking in tongues, and anointing. I have come to also associate it with the civil rights movements, voter movements, protest movements, and drugstore counter sit-ins, with the Black church and its congregation leading the charge.

The Black church began with the enslavement of Africans that were involuntarily relocated by way of the diaspora. The traditions of the African religions were stripped from them as were other cultural references. Black nationalism and Black theology are at the roots of this. Pride in self based on the tragedy of our roots. Who but a proud and chosen people would be persecuted as much as Black people, and isn't the deity, or deities, of our African roots strengthening us by making us suffer?

White enslavers allowed enslaved Black people to teach other enslaved people through the Bible each Sunday to indoctrinate them into believing that it was this new god's will for them to serve and be led by their white enslavers. After slavery, the Black church was at a crossroads—do they continue with the teachings of their enslavers, or do they build their own religion that supports and uplifts their people? In the Black church there is a mixture of these ideas. Whatever you believe as a hoodoo practitioner, know that the church and its roots are highly sensitive topics for workers. There are some that think of their church roots and beliefs as their saving grace and follow them obediently to support the strength of their hoodoo's efficacy.

Then there are workers like me who struggle with the pain of being led by a church that seems to encourage shackling of our freedoms in the name of religion. Encouraging continued abuse of power by telling us each week to hold on and be strong in the face of mass infractions of our liberties with the hope that one day a deity will save us. We hoodoo workers who do not believe this are nontraditional. We subscribe to beliefs that there are several ancestors, guides, and deities of new and old that tell us to stand up and be proud. To fight back by any means necessary and in peace. That we can be from all walks of life, any religion, any gender, any orientation or none at all, and still be practicing and very effective workers of intention, faith, and direction.

The Ritual Anointing

Every New Year we would go to service with a bottle of olive oil so it could be blessed. We would all line up and wait for the bottle to be prayed over, and after the service we would take the bottle home to use all year long. When I got a cough, my grandma would dab me with blessed olive oil and—bam!—the cough would be gone. When I had a paper or quiz or something important to prepare for school, I would anoint it before turning it in and I would anoint myself before studying and—bam!—I would get a great grade for it. Daubing myself with this oil was so ingrained in me that even to this day I have asked my home church to bless oil and ship it to me, because I believe in its utility.

The Ring Shout

In the church that I attended we held testimony service. This is the part of service where each member would get an opportunity to tell the congregation their deepest secrets and how they have been changed, delivered, and overcome. As a kid, it was the best! I got to hear the juiciest gossip for free. I especially liked that part of the service where we would either form a circle or dance around the church in circular formation, singing and stomping and hollering, allowing our true selves to be unashamed and loud. No worries or stress, just unadulterated praise! Tremendous.

I was reading for a group months ago and my ancestors asked me to ask a participant to do this ritual for their own deliverance. Maybe you can try this too. Find a spot outdoors where you are the most comfortable and can be loud. Draw a circle on the ground, even if it's an imaginary circle. Now, stomping your feet as best as you can, call up the dirt and dust and allow the wind to carry you to the next place. Circle and chant and scream and laugh and cry and shout! Let your words turn into another form of language. Do not hold yourself back. Light a fire if you'd like. Circle and kick up the storm clouds in front of your car's headlights until the lights go down. This practice should bring you back into that native part of yourself that you may have hidden before. This is organic magic at its best. Once you have completed your ritual dance, gather a small amount of the dirt that you stomped on and take it back with you. Mix this dirt with herbs such as rosemary, myrrh, or rose. Keep it on your altar to remember the wild person you are allowing yourself to be. Tell your testimony with pride. Note: It's important to say that if your guides or ancestors ask you to use other herbs, do that! Trust your own ancestors and guides over what I (or any other hoodoo worker) may tell you. As you read further, I will help you with ways to build stronger connections to Spirit, guides, ancestors, and deities.

OUR FASHION, HAIR, AND LIFESTYLE

I have been happily nappy now for years. My coils and tight curls are my crown of glory, but they haven't always been. The Africans that traveled over the ocean were rumored to have inserted seeds and grains of rice into their braids and cornrows to spread the grain wherever they landed and ensure they would have a crop that would be a subsidy. The afro has been a sign of strength and freedom. The pick worn in the back of the afro says that the person is standing tall and demands respect. It is also used as a weapon. To see these hairstyles, our fashion, and our way of life duplicated with disregard to cultural appreciation is a shame—the disregard of the history of the dressing up suits, the box braids, the covered hair with a rag or do-rag, the food, the style, the lifestyle. Research must be done if you are a hoodoo worker to understand the Black culture and respect it before building any spells.

For this section, I'm focusing on hair. In hoodoo it is important to use hair in your rituals and spells because hair is so personal. In barbershops back in the day, the clients wouldn't let the barber sweep up the hair; they would carry it back home with them for fear that it would be used in a spell. Using hair is good for conjuring up the energies of the person that it was attached to. If I am making a doll of a lover or friend, I would ask them to donate their hair to adorn the doll, which gives it even more life. In updated hoodoo I want you to think outside of what someone may tell you to do in a book.

Hair has been connected to the person and is part of that person's DNA and their spirit. Hair contains our DNA and is one of the few pieces of our body that can be used for forensic evidence. Only hair that has the follicle has true DNA in it, so consider this with your spell work. If you cut the client's hair or the client cuts their hair and gives it to you, then the magic could be perceived as lost. However, cut hair is just fine for dolls and hoodoo bags. Even adding your pet's hair when making pillows or amulets adds a personal touch that cannot be achieved with anything synthetic.

OUR BODIES

There are a few ways that I think of the Black body. The Black body takes many forms and has several stereotypes. Let me give you examples.

The Athlete

Athleticism is stressed in the Black community. If you want to get out of a bad situation, like poverty or abuse, then you will need to be an athlete. Sports will get you through, as many parents, grandparents, and others recommend. Become a football player, a basketball player, and even, as of late, a golfer or a hockey player—anything but focus on education in school. This comes with its own burdens. In my youth, my great-grandmother would tell us that our bodies were built this way because we were born from the ancestry of enslaved Africans that were the survivors of all the others. Our DNA was made to make us run faster because we had to run away from the enslaver's whip. We were stronger because we had to pull cotton and bear children and withstand the brutality. Our coordination and agility were from generations of playing similar sports in Africa and it was the one thing that wasn't taken from us.

Athleticism was another resource, another way to make money on the backs of our race. If you could gamble on it, then it was an acceptable skill for an enslaved person, and later your neighbor, to have. Imagine growing up without athleticism as a Black child, only wanting to learn more about science or math or the arts, and being asked, "Wouldn't you rather go shoot some hoops instead?" As you observe our world around us, acknowledge this stereotype for what it is—a myth. Do not participate in your hoodoo while engaging in this myth. Cleanse yourself in water, salt, and vinegar, followed by placing a small amount of sugar on your tongue. Acknowledge to yourself that you have perpetuated this myth. You bathe in these ingredients to ensure your body really understands that it needs to tighten up, and the vinegar draws out negative or false beliefs. Once you have done this, then move forward, not looking back. As you become more aware through working with your deities, guides, and ancestors, you will see that athleticism is in the DNA of any human being and not assigned to a certain race. Speak out when you notice that young Black children are being pushed into sports just because of their race. Encourage, in your hoodoo, the promotion of Black excellence in other, nontraditional roles and activities. Like all children, Black children have great capabilities and beautiful minds; they only need to have it opened to other possibilities. So many of our Black children and adults were lost when they did not choose athleticism despite being told it was their only choice. This then led to them choosing other goals, maybe some not as positive. Maybe joining gangs for a sense of community. Maybe being drawn in by the attractiveness of substance abuse when they really needed mental health care. As a hoodoo practitioner, you are expected not to become Black but to understand the Black experience if Spirit is asking you to do this work. From there, the hope is that understanding this experience will make you even more powerful and grateful for your own experience, which is equally as profound.

The Big Momma

The Big Momma, always cooking, cleaning, and caring, knew how to heal everything with roots and herbs and soulful comfort food. She was always jovial and laughing, with a large belly and hips and a wide grin. The stereotype of the Big Momma never included a Big Partner that would love her. It was always her giving of herself, giving of her time, giving of her energy for all her children and everyone else's children. An ever-flowing river of wisdom. Her lessons that she taught were priceless but shaped how other cultures see our Black women. The obese bodies were unattractive because they were shapely or fuller than most. We were damned to be single. No person would find us sexually attractive. We were there, just as our ancestors were, to care for other children. It was our destiny.

The issues with this stereotype are so vast it's hard to express, but to tell a singular race that their women were put on this earth only to be nannies for others—even to the point of insisting we use our breasts and breast milk not just for our own children but also for others—and that it is a service we should do with joy is horribly cold. If you practice hoodoo, then the women who are hoodoo workers—who birthed this tradition from their own spirits and minds when they were being tortured and ridiculed for something as random as the size of their butts and thighs—deserve your respect. Do not dress like them in hoodoo and perpetuate this stereotype. Do not bind your hair or pretend that your body is fuller than it is by using padding or plumping or additives when you practice hoodoo or conjure. Do not attempt to mimic language patterns or gestures to be more unlike yourself. It disgraces your own culture, and it disgraces our ancestors.

The Promiscuous Girl or Round the Way Girl

Sir Mix-a-Lot's hit "Baby Got Back" was a very popular rap song that has been certified double-platinum, earning gold for digital downloads in 2005. It is actually the artist's response to how the media characterizes full-figured female bodies. It was written by Sir Mix-a Lot and Amylia Dorsey after they saw a 1980s Budweiser commercial and noted that thin bodies were always highlighted and rarely was there a celebration of a curvy body. The song, to them, broadened the definition of the female body. Take that as you wish, but the Black female stigma is that she is always willing to have sex and wants and needs to be taken by anyone or everyone, at the discretion of the pursuer. She does not object or have any other needs, but sexual gratification and her free-spirited dress, clothing, and hair only add to the fictionalized and fetishized notion. The National Organization of Women (NOW) reported that 18 percent of women (in particular Black women and other women of color) will be sexually assaulted in their lifetime.[1] This didn't start in the 1980s for Black women. Not by a longshot. History has told us that the hypersexualization of Black women has been reported since the 1400s and includes forced reproduction, enslavement, rape, and sexual coercion.

As a Black woman, I cannot express how many times my body is ogled by others and how, as an adolescent, I was told by adult men how "good" I looked and that I looked like I "wanted it." Even when I didn't know what "it" was. I did observe that other white women could express themselves in the same fashion as I did, and it was seen as "fun" and "creative." From cornrows to latex pants, they, it seemed, could wear anything and they wouldn't endure the negative consequences that I did. I was called "loose" or "too free." I was told by Destiny's Child that I was "Nasty" and to go and put some clothes on, even when the group themselves would later stomp proud and empowered on stage with a one-piece suit on. There were so many confusing statements of how our bodies, Black bodies, were not ours but only tools for others to view and obsess over and then to control. If I wear locs then I am unprofessional and cannot and should not be in corporate America. If you choose to embrace this experience of Black bodies and modify your style to appropriate it as your own, then be honest about whether you are embracing a culture or putting on a costume that you can take off one day. The Black being can never be taken off; they will always be held under the scrutiny of a world that holds them under a different lens.

Because Black women are more liberated and empowered by their bodies, this empowerment is reflected in their dress, hair, and fashion. Clothing is tighter, shorter, looser, more stylish, and showed every curve and natural flow. It is an expression of who we choose to be. While the struggle is far from over, celebrities like Lizzo show that all body types can be viewed and admired from afar but are no longer the sources of ridicule or enslavement.

As a hoodoo worker, it is our role to respect and bring humanity to our clients. To not shame or ridicule those that choose to celebrate their bodies in their fashion, hair, and lifestyle. We are to be lights of deliverance and not part of the culture that disrespects women and expresses false notions of immorality if women choose to dress or undress as they choose.

The Black Penis

I am as guilty as the next person of falling for this stereotype when I dated within and outside of my race. I did not start having sex until much later, but in junior high and high school, in the snickerings and gossip of us preteens, there was the myth of the unusually large Black penis. It was just known that if there was a Black man, their penis was either the stuff of legends or you should run and hide rather than have sex with them. Even my grandma told me that sex was nothing I should deal with when it came to race. She begged me to choose a suitor that wasn't Black, actually. Of course, scientifically and physiologically this is nonsense. The average penis when erect, according to a *Journal of Sexual Medicine* study in 2013, is 14.15 cm (just shy of six inches) with a circumference of 12.23 cm (around four inches, give or take).[2]

As a cis female and hoodoo worker, I cannot speak to what negatives or positives the male endures with this stereotype, but I do know that as a hoodoo practitioner you may have clients that ask you to conjure or apply rootwork to encourage sexual prowess, endurance, or virility. To understand this experience, I (as I usually do) recommend doing research to understand how this stereotype impacts Black males: the expectation by many of their sexual partners that they will be able to perform sex (with limited or no experience) to the satisfaction of any partner, wielding an above-average penis that is the envy of their counterparts. The pressure they felt when they thought they were only average, not knowing that average is actually what a partner may be hoping and dreaming for. The Black penis myth says that the sexual organ is the most important part of the Black male and that any other body part (such as their mind) is trivial at best. That to have a Black man means that you have won some prize of a lover, because surely the goal of any sexual encounter is to be stretched beyond human capabilities and to be made painfully sore. This myth, in the wild, is powerful because it is still very much present now, even though science contradicts it.

As a hoodoo worker, break down walls of sexual stereotypes and false desires. Conjure up for your clients consensual, glorious, agreeable sex that isn't relegated to our sexual organ size or performance. Many of us know that the most sexual part of our body is our brain.

As hoodoo workers, it is our responsibility to share in #updatedhoodoo that freedom includes freedom from stereotypes, especially those that bind us in our sexual practices.

In updated hoodoo we respect each other's cultures, freedoms, and lifestyle choices. We do not shame or curse those who have abilities or solutions that are unlike ours. We celebrate each other's diversity without appropriating it. We learn and research what we are curious about, including our very understanding of hoodoo and conjure. We listen and study and become tools of deliverance, as this is the way of the practitioner and the healer. It is the way of intention, faith, and direction. We intend to practice hoodoo that is true to our roots. We have faith that we are doing everything in conjure with integrity, even if we have to use liberation as a weapon, and we seek direction that helps us attain that goal.

OUR AFRICA, OUR FUTURE

Liberation is not a new term to most of us, and it certainly isn't to our home, Mother Africa. Africa, with rich and fertile soils, plant life, and resources, has been the mecca of colonizers since 500 BC. Alexander the Great occupied Egypt to establish trading routes, military headquarters, and a communications center. Carthage, which means "new city," was founded around 814 BC on the North African coast. It had wars with the Romans until 150 BC, when Rome overtook them. The Romans were then overtaken by the Arabs in the medieval period, where the languages and religion shifted from African traditional religions to Islam.

When European ships arrived on the African coast to exchange goods and services in the 1600s, the Europeans learned from the African suppliers, farmers, and crafts people. This practice continued when Europeans landed on Indigenous lands in North America. This is cultural colonialism and cultural imperialism at its core: nations such as those in Europe that go into another country and control that country's values, language, education, and religion so that they can expand their own economic opportunities. Some may argue that the imposing of European, Christian values onto Africa caused the continent's decline, and others may say that it benefited Africa by providing exposure and revenue opportunities for those that were powerful enough to trade with them. What we should remember is that the need to overtake Africa was not just spiritual but political. At this time (1700s–1800s), European countries including France, Germany, Italy, and Spain were in conflict with each other for more control of Africa, as they needed its larger land area—Africa was a jewel to conquer because of the land mass and opportunity for industrialization. In areas where the colonies had not succumbed, the residents would be swooped up by the slave trade or colonized by stripping away their sense of self through reeducation.

Between 1881 and 1914 this control dominated the Africa that once was a proud place of origin. There were survivors of this in Ethiopia, Liberia, and the Dervish State, but Africa as a whole was formalized as colonies by Portugal, France, and Britain. This was done to continue the Industrial Revolution and the booming technological advances that could ravish Africa's raw material. Once the revenue and economic values were integrated, then religious and racial cleansing continued. Europeans telling Africans that their way of life was unclear and hedonistic and their traditions evil (traditions such as polytheism, animism, the love and worship of multiple gods, plant-based healing, and spiritual guidance over what was then nontraditional). The results were wars, poverty, and eradication of materials, animals, water, and ways of life that were once thriving.

There was intercontinental trade of its products: grains, legumes, millet, sorghum, sugar, tea, barley, dates, bananas, peppers, and wheat. When millions of Africans were uprooted, the need for these exports did not stop. However, the harsh climates and labor reduction due to slavery, famine, disease, and government distress left many once-flourishing societies in Africa at the point they are now: needing to benefit from the advances of science and agricultural technology but having limited finances to do so. Africa needs regional economic development—this is a deliverance need that is rarely discussed. As hoodoo workers, we have a chance to satisfy a very urgent need of our ancestors—saving our homelands from destruction.

Fast-forward to today and Africa is still impacted by the destruction of these takeovers. There are food shortages (famine), guerrilla warfare, political, social, and societal consequences. The centralized and postwar European powers that were put in place to establish systems with their authoritarian policies (many imposed by force) added to the conflicts and distress. The laws, taxes, forced labor, excavation, and agricultural production are maintained (or not maintained) by British rule—even indirectly.

In hoodoo we honor what was done in Africa by the products we choose for our work. I use peanuts, grains, syrup, and other objects from Africa (ethically sourced) if possible. If I cannot find these, then I honor them by incorporating the closest referential object (like a sweet potato instead of a yam or local honey instead of sorghum). Using African products also means that when I practice hoodoo, I look to African religions for referential guidance. I call upon orishas from the Yoruba religion the same as I do saints from the Bible. Conjure is fluid to me, and I know that my future as a hoodoo worker means embracing all that has made me who I am and bringing that knowledge to educate others.

FOLKLORE AND MYTH

African culture revolves around myth (like several others—Chinese, Indigenous, Grecian, Romans, Jewish). The tales consist of a template. They start as an introduction of the character and a setup of the situation. The character is immortal, mortal, human, or creature of fantasy. They have powers (that emulate human personality traits that we deal with each day). There is a battle between a positive and negative force and then a winning outcome. The moral of the story gives the reader a reminder of a life lesson so that they don't make the same mistakes as the protagonist of the myth.

In the book *Mythology and the Bible*, Corinne Heline gives us a different view of the Genesis version of the beginning of humanity. I have provided several examples that show how the story tells the same information but for diverse cultures. We all use similar myths, which is incredible to me considering the span of us as beings in geography.

In the beginning, before the creation of earth matter, was a formless state personified in the deity Chaos. The daughter of Chaos was Night, the darkness inhabiting primordial space, the living space of esotericism.

She was the mother of every divinity whose origin was shrouded in the darkness of uncertainty. She was the mother of Light and Day. Their offspring was Eros, or Cupid, who aided them in the creation of Gaea (Mother Earth). Eros pierced the breast of Gaea with the arrow of life, which he filled with love, his power. After the infusion of love, the earth was awakened and all plant and animal life flourished.

How much more welcoming is what we may have been told or shared before? Another folklore story that I love is the story of Olorun, the creator of life:

> *"In the beginning, all that existed were the water, land and sky, which was ruled by Olorun. Another god named Obatala went to Olorun to ask if he could create land for living things to exist. When he was granted permission, Olorun visited Orunmila, Olorun's first son, to consult with him about his wish. In response, Orunmila told him that he must obtain a gold chain, a snail's shell filled with sand, palm nuts, corn, and a special egg that encompassed the essence of both the male and female orishas. Obatala hung the long gold chain from the sky and climbed down to earth, only to find that he could only go so far due to the chain's length. When he reached back to pour the sand from the snail's shell to form dry land, he dropped the special egg and released Sankofa. When he reached the earth, Obatala spread the sand and planted the pine nuts. He even founded a hill and called it Ife. After a while, he decided to fashion human beings to keep him company because his task was quite lonely. He founded the city of Ife, and the gods and goddesses visited him and his creations on earth frequently."*[3]

Another is the story of life through Bumba.[4] A creator named Bumba made the sun, sky, and moon. According to legend, Bumba existed before any human being was even thought of, but with cosmogony of African folklore, this means that we were all created by each other and no one being is higher than or more important than another. Bumba bore three children that continued the creation process. Through this communal creation story, the children are those that make up everything needed for the continued lifespan of beings, nature, and animal life. All is for the sake of the community, and all are beings and products of the earth. In hoodoo we use animism, the belief that we are all connected beings and all animals, plants, and objects have a spirit and a purpose. This is important when you are building your rituals and learning whom your guides, ancestors, and spirts are. They can be anything—from a human being to a spirit animal to your grandfather's favorite tree. This is also why in many hoodoo oral traditions you will see workers use spiders, snakes, herbs, roots, and altar objects as a focal point.

Folklore is so important in a hoodoo or conjure worker's journey. The folklore is the sharing of oral tradition. My story, your story, and our story are mixed in with myth. There are tales of Ponce de Leon and the Fountain of Youth, Anansi the mischievous spider, and the Indigenous Coyote; these are all folklore characters. There are also places and objects—the spinning wheel, the enchanted forest, the looking glass, the Holy Grail.

Folklore is our customs and beliefs told verbally. Sometimes they are known as false stories, but I feel they are usually the best stories of all because many times there is a ring of truth to them or I have found they come from a place of fact from long ago. Take the Fountain of Youth. A mysterious myth, but aren't some of us still enchanted with the idea of never growing old and using our magical gifts to try to hold on to our youth, our freedoms, and our abilities for one more day or year?

The first time I was exposed to an actual written text that supported my upbringing was when I read *Folk-Lore from Adams County, Illinois* by Harry Middleton Hyatt.[5] This is a complete accounting of Hyatt's experience interviewing hoodoo practitioners from different ethnic backgrounds in and around Quincy, Illinois, in the Adams County community. Hyatt, an Anglican reverend, spent his life documenting the folklore and hoodoo spells, conjure, and ways in one of the most prolific accountings of hoodoo that I am aware of from that time. There are other books that I recommend highly from the last thirty years, but this book is my go-to when I want to look at historical ancestors and guides. It is the closest I think I will get to a written accounting of the hoodoo oral tradition.

In the book, Hyatt attempts to stay absolutely true to the recorded interviews. Terms that may offend many now were documented to ensure that the real experiences and stories remained true to the source. Dialect and vocabulary in the interviews were recorded without omissions. This is exactly how my gran gran and her family would tell me how to do things and how I learned. They did not clean up their language; I either got it or I was scratching my head for an idea and had to pray that my guides would give me direction.

For example, as noted in the book, for weather warnings the practitioners would say, "St. Matthias breaks the ice. If no ice, he makes ice." This means that if the ground has thawed out before St. Matthias Day (before February 24) and if there isn't any ice, it will only get colder.

When we see folklore sayings, they are used in hoodoo as life lessons or reminders of what our ancestors felt and believed a long time ago. They are also indicators of what we can and should beware of—warnings, messages, morals, tales from neighbor to neighbor and family member to family member. Some would call them fake news, but to me they are the lifeblood of true hoodoo. Here are a few folklore sayings you may have heard:

- Put your foot upon a chair that you are sitting in.
- Spit pomegranate seeds at a building to purify it before entering.
- To cure sore eyes, sleep with rotten apple slices covering them.
- A russet potato can draw out the color of bruises and black eyes.
- Wear a necklace of black beads until it breaks to make a wart disappear.
- If your apron slips off you while you are preparing supper, then your lover is thinking about you.
- If you burn biscuits, then your partner is sore at you.
- The first person you dream of when you sleep under a new quilt will be your future partner.
- The first guest before breakfast will bring three more before night.
- If someone hoodoos you (puts work on you or a spell) you must go to a hoodoo worker of the opposite gender to cure you.
- To prevent yourself from being hoodooed after your wedding, always jump over a broom before entering your new house for the first time.
- If a bird (usually a robin) pecks on the window of someone that is sick and its beak turns bloody, it is a sign that person will die.
- April showers bring May flowers.

- A young girl that whistles and a bleating sheep always come to the top of the heap.

- What goes up must come down either on the head or on the ground.

- Sleep in the moonlight to make your skin clear.

- After giving birth, the mother must walk around the house nine times with a thimble of blessed water to ensure the child has a happy beginning.

Maybe some of these sound familiar. If so, you may have a background in some hoodoo folklore sayings. My great-grandma, grandma, and other elders spoke to us this way frequently. You couldn't bring out brooms or step on anything without hearing their superstitions. You caught up on them or you were left out. I still practice some of them to this day. I swear by wrapping my feet in onion, ginger, and cloves, in noncling wrap when I get a cold. I eat black-eyed peas every New Year. I place a knife below my mattress to make sure my marriage bed is never in pain. I don't let visitors come into my home through the back door when they first visit (ever), and I always ask people to take off their shoes before walking around in my home so that any residual dirt from their past is not brought into my house.

This folklore then made up the spells that are the cornerstone of rootwork. For example, there is folklore that says that if a cat walks in front of you, then that means a death will happen, but if you cross your fingers when you see it, the death will pass you by. I see cats and I cross my fingers. Is it preventing death? Who knows. But I won't test my luck.

The Creation of Death Mythology

There is a story in mythology that the gods meant for humans to be immortal and that death was introduced when either animals or people made some mistake and as a result incurred the wrath of the gods. Some of us are very afraid of death. In the tarot the Death card doesn't represent a natural (or unnatural) death but actually a change that might be coming to you. When you are doing possession or conjure work, you will be working with the tight rope that links you to the next realm.

The people of Luyia relate that a chameleon placed the curse of death on the people when a man refused to give it food.[6] Another tale about the chameleon is that it was to deliver the news of eternal life to the people. But a lizard arrived first and told the people of death instead. In hoodoo and conjure I would conjure a lizard tail, a snake's rattle, or a chameleon, take from them their essence and spirit (their true nature), and make them work for my ritual. If I need to hide myself from someone that wants to harm me, I will conjure and bring forth the energy of a chameleon, a lizard, or a snake because they are known to transform themselves and mutate to blend into their backgrounds. I would not use a peacock or a crow; they call attention to themselves. Let the true animal's spirit come through and try not to alter them. Allow them to alter you in how you view your conjure spells.

Folktales give us parables and stories that remind us of our human attributes and are transferred to the world of creatures and animals to give us life lessons. To me they are very similar to what we see in Bible stories and other sacred texts. When you read my stories about the Tall Man and the Blue Lady and then dream or write a tale of what they mean to you or what they are teaching you, then this would be a myth that you could bring into your own Book of Shadows.

When you are creating a Book of Shadows, a journal, a spell book, or your own MS Excel spreadsheet of spells as hoodoo practitioners, remember that this is a sacred object. As I have said with my very own book, before touching, handling or sharing this book with anyone, wash your hands, come with a clean heart and mindset and never ever let someone take your hoodoo book of knowledge from you.

◇◇◇◇◇◇ CHAPTER 1 EXERCISES ◇◇◇◇◇◇

Researching Your Ancestor

Take a moment to think of trees that you pass every day—all of us pass at least one during our journeys. Research the history of this tree and learn about its ancestry. What species does it come from? Does it have any folklore? If so, what is it? How does it ensure its heritage continues?

What secrets does it hold? How is it like or unlike your own family heritage? Once you know about the tree, then go by the tree and ask it what it wants from you. Does it need water? Does it want to hold your secrets? Does it need nourishment? If so, what kind?

Now think of a family or chosen family member. It can be blood or one of our shared ancestors. Do your research on this ancestor the same way you did the research on the tree.

Fill in the blanks about the ancestor:

Ancestor's name:

Ancestor's lineage:

Ancestor's common or familiar name (aka nickname):

Ancestor's likes and dislikes:

Ancestor's objects, foods, pets, favorite people, places, etc.:

Ancestor's secrets:

Ancestor's energy (is it a lighter energy, more protective, harmful, loving, kind, awkward, angry, spiteful?):

How did the ancestor leave this earth?

Why would you use this ancestor?

Why would you not use this ancestor?

The importance of doing this exercise is to understand how to research an ancestor. As a hoodoo worker you will do this many times in your practice. You will be speaking spiritually with ancestors of your own and of your clients. Research any ancestor first and respect them before proceeding to ask them for any help.

Cultural Appropriation, Eradication, Education, and Appreciation Exercise

Think of a cultural practice you are aware of.

Describe this cultural practice in detail. Include how you first learned about it, who taught it to you, how observing the practice made you feel, what objects or spirits were called. Really go into detail.

Now name an example or way that you have observed or even personally

1. appropriated this practice,

2. eradicated this practice,

3. appreciated this practice,

4. educated yourself about this practice.

When you come upon another cultural practice, take this into consideration. Ask yourself what your intentions are before taking the practice into your own hoodoo or conjure work. Represent the truth and honor the culture that the practice has come from, and perform this practice only *if* you have permission to do so and you respect this practice. If permission is not given to you, then appreciate it and let it be.

NOTES

1   Black Women and Sexual Violence," National Organization for Women, https://now.org/wp-content/uploads/2018/02/Black-Women-and-Sexual-Violence-6.pdf.

2   Debby Herbenick, PhD, et al., "Erect Penile Length and Circumference Dimensions of 1,661 Sexually Active Men in the United States." *The Journal of Sexual Medicine* vol. 11,1 (2014): 93–101, doi:10.1111/jsm.12244.

3   "8 Interesting African Creation Myths the World Should Know About," *Atlantic Black Star*, January 19, 2016.

4   "Creation Myths in Africa," Biblioteca Pleyades, www.bibliotecapleyades.net/mitos_creacion/esp_mitoscreacion_0.htm.

5   Harry Middleton Hyatt, *Folk-Lore from Adams County, Illinois* (London: Forgotten Books, 2015).

6   "African Mythology Gods and Goddesses list—Creation Myths, Examples, Stories and Creatures," The Mystica, https://www.themystica.com/african-mythology.

FUNDAMENTALS OF
HOODOO PRACTICES

In chapter 1 we covered a ton of information about what hoodoo is. Now let me share some of my own personal experiences with hoodoo. Hopefully this book is becoming familiar to you, and you are learning some helpful ways to increase your knowledge as a hoodoo worker.

Let's review the basics from chapter 1.

- ♦ Know what conjure workers and hoodoo workers are. Do not confuse hoodoo workers with other workers (those practicing Vodou, Santeria, or Lucumi, for instance, are not hoodoo workers). Many of us conjure (or call upon Spirit to do work with us or on our behalf) and can be called conjurer workers but not hoodoo workers. As a conjure worker you are making something do something outside of its will. A hoodoo worker practices the oral tradition of hoodoo as instructed and led by their enslaved African ancestors from North America. Hoodoo workers use natural ingredients (plants, water, salt, lemon, personal concerns) and they also can use modern items like a digital image instead of a picture. Hoodoo workers are respectful of their surroundings and try to not bring attention to themselves unnecessarily.

◆ Pick out your own ancestor, deity, and guide that speaks to you. Start with your own lineage or bloodline if possible. Introduce yourself gently and do not force them to come to you. Whenever I find a new guide, I first do research on them and determine what they are going to give me and what they will ask of me. If the price is too great, I walk away.

◆ Know the difference between cultural appreciation, appropriation, education, and eradication:

    ◆ I appreciate something when I leave it with the culture that it comes from.

    ◆ I appropriate when I take something from a culture without respecting or acknowledging the culture it comes from.

    ◆ I educate when I share my culture with another culture, and in return I may learn from that culture. I can leave it alone or I can take the education (with permission) and integrate it into something that I want to enhance, always acknowledging the source.

    ◆ I eradicate when I disregard the origin of something from another culture and I totally take it on as mine and purposefully do my best to ensure that culture is destroyed.

◆ Research and learn some folklore and myths from your ancestry. You can start with some text from Harry Middleton Hyatt. Slavic folklore, Indigenous folklore, Appalachian folklore, and Jewish folklore are some topics to search to get you started. Myth is the beginning of how hoodoo was formed. There's always some truth there. Find the truth, add your own spice to it (with herbs, chants, waters, oils, and prayers), and you will be fine. Other resources include *Living Folklore: An Introduction to the Study of People and Their Traditions*, *The Social Science Encyclopedia*, third edition, and the International Society for Ethnology and Folklore. Many folklores and oral traditions may be triggering or contain inflammatory notions and language. Adjust these stories and take from them the lessons that you can apply to your hoodoo work (the same as you would with Bible verses).

TRIGGER WORDS

A word about trigger words in this book: a trigger word is any word that inspires someone to act. Consequently, it's usually a verb. They're called trigger words because of the common phrase "pull the trigger," which is used as a euphemism for making a decision. There is an opposite side to triggers where the words are impactful and may cause distress. This is not always desired, but in the form of this work I want to help the reader understand that my use of scenarios and stories in the chapters is to trigger an action response and not to cause emotional distress.

The action is to transform or to change or to kick-start your own journey in becoming a hoodoo worker to others. Just as Bible verses can be claimed and made to serve a higher purpose in your spell work and your hoodoo, I hope that you take power back from the very institution and religious chains that may still bind you by hearing these tales of true heroism in all their meanings.

I do hope you understand above all things that hoodoo can be and is inclusive. It is inclusive because it includes any of those that seek its wisdom. Your culture or racial background does not matter. Your determination and thirst for the knowledge does.

Your religion or desire to not participate in a religious structure is not a prerequisite to being a practicing hoodoo worker. Cultural appreciation is required. What is cultural appreciation? Cultural appreciation is when you have asked and have received permission to participate in a cultural tradition or event. If your culture is not represented natively by African Americans, then your participation as a hoodoo worker could be classified as possibly a mutual exchange of norms and understanding as a way to bring about a deeper relationship that benefits all of us as a society. I am exchanging ideals with you about my culture, and you are learning. You are also sharing your ideals and culture as you introduce your ancestors, guides, and deities into your hoodoo experience. Everyone benefits from each other and grows together. Without knowledge of our past, we will repeat it. Without cross-sharing and understanding and appreciating our diversity, we will remain separated.

This carries itself to other aspects of our ability to share information and learn about each other. As a lesbian hoodoo worker, I bring to my experience, my sexual orientation as one aspect of myself when I introduce my identity to you in this book. Perhaps you will share characteristics about yourself that will add to our knowledge. This may include physical characteristics, intellectual standards, ethics, spiritual wants or needs, boundaries, and gender identity. As a hoodoo worker, I will have a vast background of identities that make me who I am and so will you. To truly work together in community and in conjure, a respect and cross-pollination of ideals is important to build a rich mixture of ways that we use to be better hoodoo workers. As the Bible says, "*Study to show thyself approved unto the Spirit of Old, a workman that needeth not to be ashamed, rightly dividing the word of truth*" (2 Timothy 2:15).

To me, this is what we are tasked with every day in our lives. We are challenged to study, that is, be unashamed in speaking and living in our own truth. What is your truth? Is your truth your gender? Your marital status? Your housing or lack of housing? Your medical or mental identification? Your job or lack of employment? Your body size? Your hair texture? Your religion? Your background or country of origin? Then walk unashamed in that truth. Is it as a Black lesbian? Then be the unashamed and approved Black lesbian that you are called to be by your ancestors. Is it a nonbinary youth leading an art festival on a day that you have been raised to believe was a day of rest? Then work at that art festival, rightly dividing what is just and unjust, in freedom and bravery without lowering your eyes or feeling embarrassed because of the body or identification your deity has chosen to give or what identity you have chosen to take.

Our lives are to share and to bless and to reach out to each other's hearts. Hoodoo is more than candles, graveyard dirt, and dolls. It is about community, history, and knowing ourselves inside and out and then finding deliverance through deities and guides that help us along the way.

EXPERIENCE A THAT HOODOO LADY READING

Welcome to a That Hoodoo Lady reading. Have a seat and make yourself comfortable. To get us started I will spray my own personally made blessing water into the air to assure our ancestors that this is a sacred space. In old-ways hoodoo I may have asked you to add in a drop of your blood or urine, and then I would have sprayed the doorstep with it to ward off evil spirits. But I know differently now, and my blessing water is blessed in a Bible verse, and I add ginger, peppers, and locally sourced flowers to make the water personal yet powerful.

We'll receive messages from the ancestors, guides, historical places, and events that are personally wanting to help you with your issue. You don't need to worry if the ancestor or guide looks like you or comes from your background. These guides are part of our fabric. The human fabric. You do not need to look like me (a Black lesbian) to work with me as a hoodoo client, and if you are led to, you can even further your journey and become a hoodoo practitioner yourself. The hoodoo tradition arose from the needs of enslaved Africans in the American South who wanted deliverance from the strife and pain they endured. They were beaten and made to submit. They were forced to learn a new language and a new religion. They know how it feels to be cornered and made to suffer. The guides I show you will work with you. They will speak with you, and they will show up only for you when you call in your hours of need for deliverance—deliverance as a place of strength and not weakness. These guides I work with are powerful and some are very human. Others are plant life. Some are historically important places where there was a triumph or even tragedy. There are so many options.

Is your phone turned off? Are you here? Are you present? During slavery we wouldn't have this space all alone. We would be in the fields or near a tree. So let's take ourselves to that starting place. We will say an opening prayer that works for me, our guides, and you.

It can be religious or secular—I am flexible. It may be a chant or words that we find helpful from a line of poetry. Either way, its purpose is to protect us from anything that is not like the Highest Upon High and keep it from entering. I will ask that anything that is not relevant to your reading today stay outside of this place, and reassure it that if *you* want, you will pick it up on your way out.

Then I start to drum on my djembe. The beat of the drum may sound foreign, or it may soothe you. I will drum until I find the right vibration for your ancestor. I know you have questions, but I am so grateful you can wait as we make a strong connection.

If I cannot find it through the drum, then I will pick up my thumb piano. The thumb piano is something that helps me with African American guides specifically. It is a rectangular wooden block with small metallic keys that emit tones. I will pluck one bar after the next until I find the sound that speaks to your soul. I use that chord to find your soul key, and I add that to my information about you.

Then we talk, just like you were talking to a dear friend. I ask you about what is going on and why you came to see me. We laugh and joke, or we cry together, or I hold space for you while you go into the deepest parts of yourself and come back with answers. Hoodoo is serious business, and I am so grateful you are trusting me. Let's go deeper. I open my Bible and flip through the pages. I ask you to tell me when to stop flipping and you choose a verse. This is called bibliomancy, an ancient divination technique used by several practitioners of all and no faiths. I read the Bible verse, and it tells me what we need to do next. It tells me what herbs, roots, or incantations I need to use when creating your spell. It tells me your secret intentions for deliverance. The direction that the deliverance must go and your intentions. It keeps us honest, and it is precise. It cuts through all the bullshit and lands us precisely where we need to be.

We then travel there together. I will start by tapping on my steel drum to call out the magical key that I have been told is yours. I will walk you through the upper or middle or lower realm of your mind. I will ask you to be silent while we take this journey. I will recite more Bible verses to you while you are in a silent meditative state. It is my responsibility to keep this space safe and protected from outside entities or negative spirits that may try and sneak their way into your subconscious or even into my own mind. I stay prayerful and focused on the task. I am with you this whole time while your ancestors or guides speak to you and give you advice that I cannot hear (nor be a witness to). This is your experience, and I am a guide.

We may not travel or journey. Perhaps you are a visual person. Then I may use tarot cards or playing cards, or I may pick up bones or thread or any other objects in my meditative space.

You may draw, color, stay silent, yell, scream—it is all specific to you, and I am here to bear witness and keep you safe.

After the reading is finished, the spell is complete and transferred to the chat room or to a special document I will send to you after the reading is complete. I pass along instructions and help you answer questions. This is the time to do so, as once I have disconnected from Spirit I will remember little. We do a final blessing, and I answer any further questions. I tell you the most important part of any hoodoo reading: how to pay offering to your ancestors, guides, and deities that gave you this deliverance. Step-by-step we go over how, when, where, and why you pay this offering. It is never a high price or anything you have to shop for; it must come from the heart.

Finally, we say our goodbyes, and we check in with each other by text or email. My hope for you is that after you read through this book, you will have enough information to be able to understand the basics of hoodoo, learn more about me and yourself, understand how to integrate hoodoo's tenets into your life, and possibly understand what the ancestors, guides, and deities have for you as you connect with them).

Welcome to book two, covering hoodoo foundations. I'm introducing you to my favorite hoodoo historic places, people, and events that I personally work with or were told by Spirit to include in the book. I am That Hoodoo Lady, and I am a *real* hoodoo worker.

THE ELEMENTS IN HOODOO

Once you have completed the conjure and its finished doing its work, you have a few choices:

Destroy the work. Destruction is the act of tearing down. When you tear down something, then you allow it to be free to do other work. When I tear down a box, then the box is flattened down. It can no longer be used for its original purpose, but that doesn't mean it has no purpose. When I destroy or break down a spiritual bag that contains herbs and words or even delete a text that was used as a spell, then it can now go free, and even better, so does the energy (intention, direction, and faith) behind it. Freedom is important. It allows the work to go to someone else and frees up the ancestor to stop working on your request and do something else for you (or others).

Creation or destruction by fire is exactly that: you set something ablaze by lighting it directly from a match or other source. Then once it burns down to ash, you allow the wind to carry it. What if you don't have time for all that? Then can you burn it in a safe fire pit? Can you burn it in an open flame? Can you burn it and then throw it away and take the trash out afterward? All of that counts. There are some that think you have to have a serious ritual around anything you do in hoodoo. Not the case in updated hoodoo. Give yourself the freedom to break away from the mold and the naysayers. Use destruction by fire for those things that you no longer want or conjure that needs to go away. Direction again is a tenet of hoodoo. If it needs to go away, then fire, water, and air are good choices. You can bury it in the earth too if you want it to go away, but the earth is solid and the earth isn't really going anywhere. If you create conjure by adding fire, then what you are burning will change chemically to air. This air will carry the intention and faith upward. I love the idea of igniting something that is a hoodoo chant or a wish for something to be destroyed. If I have a strong emotion that is burning inside me and I need it to swiftly spread around the world, then I burn it. Before I began writing this book, I put my thoughts and emotions into words and applied oil to the paper. I attached it to a Bible verse that I use for anything when I want it to spread like wildfire and then I put that energy out there. I repeated it.

I prayed for it. I spoke into the fire of the fire pit (I use my fire pit for just about everything) and then I left the ash there to be carried away. My Bible verse that I modified came from Acts 6:7: "The word of my soul kept on spreading; and the number of the people that are helped continued to increase greatly in the world, and a great many of the practitioners learned and understand the faith they can have in themselves."

Then there is creation or destruction by water. Water emotes. It can grow, it can shrink, it can fill up things and stretch their capacity. It can move quickly in a stream or river, or it can be solid like ice. When I destroy my conjure in water, I am signaling it to go away. I am asking it to go away quickly—not as quickly as burning in fire, but quickly all the same. If I had a love spell to bring someone to me and that love relationship needed to end, I would use the love and emotion that flows in water to safely and respectfully send that love away. I would package up the spell ingredients (if they are water soluble) and then I would place them into a stream. I wouldn't put them into stagnant water because I want the water to actually move. Ice, still rivers, ponds, and even hot tubs aren't good choices for destroying by water if you want something to go away. But if you want something to stay, then those things would work. If I have a souring spell to keep someone from harming me, then I will add a Bible verse, poem, or written text in a prayed-over and clean vessel, I will add something sour—like lemon juice or bitter mugwort—and then I will add my water and let it freeze. If I want to destroy it, I will heat it up and destroy the energy. If I want to prevent someone or an energy from moving against me, then I will freeze the water to make it solid. I will fill up the item with my intentions, faith, and direction. The same holds true for love spells. If I want a love that is solid, I will put it in a solid place, but I won't put it in a cold place, like ice. I want the spell to be in a place that is warm and fiery and not easy to break, like earth.

INTENTION, FAITH, AND DIRECTION

Hoodoo is the African American/enslaved African folk tradition of giving someone deliverance using several components, and the Bible is one of them. Hoodoo has three tenants that I use: intention, faith, and direction. You can do average hoodoo with any of these but having all of them is what makes the real hoodoo workers stand out. It isn't our tools that make us hoodoo workers; it is our intention, faith, and direction that made our shared ancestors do this work. It wasn't for notoriety or likes or followers and, Goddess no, it wasn't for the money. It was to get us out of something that we needed to be delivered from. Keep this in your mind as you continue doing the exercises and reading through this book. Hoodoo is for everyone if you keep these tenets in mind.

Intention

Intention is the mental capacity or state to perform or do something. If I intended to write this book, then my mind is focused every day on writing the book, perfecting the book, editing the book. There's a separate saying that the road to hell is paved with good intentions—another scare tactic, but there's some truth in it. What we physically do and what we intend to do may be different altogether. In magic you make your intentions known in how you speak in conjure. How you set aside your ingredients. How you cleanse yourself before you begin. It's the gentle words from your guides that help you along, but it's up to you to give your intentions a spark to make them a reality.

Intentions are different from direction. Intentions are more subtle. Intentions are a contract, a commitment, an actionable statement that you will do something. In hoodoo when the hoodoo worker directs their intention of a spell to do this or that for deliverance, then they write it down. As the spell book, the Bible, says, "Write it down and make it plain." I write my intentions down to solidify and obligate myself into fulfilling that purpose. When you intend to become someone's partner you do so willingly and without hesitation (or should). When I intend to get deliverance, I do so willingly and without hesitation. When my intention is to kick a spirit out of a space that they are trying to take over, I put into my spell that by the end of the spell the spirit will be gone.

Intention is not intuition. Intuition is more about your spiritual connection and compass, but having intuition with no intention on how to use it is fruitless.

When I was a little girl, my grandma would test my intuition all the time. She would hold up her hand, like in a magic trick, and ask me to tell her what she had in it. I would then guess. If I got the answer right, then I got to keep what was in her hand. If I didn't, then I would get to try again. Or if she wasn't feeling like it, then I didn't get anything at all.

Did I guess right a lot because I intended to keep what she had? Probably, but I was a kid and didn't think about it too hard. Do the same with your hoodoo intentions. Don't think about them for hours and hours and days and days. If you have an intention of what you want to achieve, then you know it just like when I would know for sure what was in my grandma's hand. If I don't know my intention, then it's best not to play.

Faith

Have you ever done something scary or risky? Something where you have no control or ability to know how it's going to work out? Like jumping off a high step onto ice? You might slip and fall. You might be fine. Running for a bus that just left the station? You might make it, or you might be late to your destination. Paying your rent? Your check may be electronically deposited in time, but then again it may not. Hoodoo isn't about asking for something thoughtless (even though plenty have tried, with mixed results). I whip out my hoodoo spells and rituals when I need something. I need something solved. I need results. I need help. That's when I use hoodoo. I don't ask my hoodoo guides to help me pick a nail color—that's for my Instagram polls or for friends. I use hoodoo ancestors when I'm in the middle of a conflict and I have no way out and I don't know where else to turn. If I'm doing something scary, risky, or unsure (even in a good way), I use my hoodoo for that.

I consider how someone like Harriet Tubman saw faith. She had faith and assurance. Assurance adds more strength and weight behind the words of the verse. Assurance is confidence. It is confidence and a *promise* from the source that something will occur. In Mother Tubman's faith she was assured and confident that she would be freed. Further yet, she was confident and assured that she could free others. Maybe she was scared. Maybe she knew her road ahead would be full of naysayers, but continue she did, because she had faith. She could not see her freedom in the moment, but she knew that it could and would be done for her.

Using faith when you have none is the first step to getting faith. In books on manifestation like *The Secret* by Rhonda Byrne, *Ask and It Is Given* by Esther and Jerry Hicks, and *The Secret for Sistahs: The Black Woman's Spiritual Guide to Releasing Negativity* by Karen Raye Little, you can find other exercises on manifestation and faith. But my summary of faith is this: I have found that I get faith when I reach out with expectations that it's *not* going to happen and I'm proven wrong. I'll give you an example. When I lost my job after just buying the largest and most expensive house ever, I fell into a depressive state. My stomach was in knots. I was worried that with COVID going on and hoodoo readings at an all-time low that I was going to have to sell my house and move, and even worse, admit failure!

Well, after a few nights of binge-watching *The Closer*, *Medium* with Patricia Arquette, and *The Twilight Zone*, I decided to get myself out of my funk. I got some leftover candles (I wasn't picky, and I wasn't buying anything) and prayed over them to grant me some job opportunities. I reduced my worth by stating I wanted opportunities that were several thousands of dollars less than what I would have sought before. I anointed my candle, placed it on my candle plate (yes, it's a plate that I burn my candles on—candle plate), and as the lights flickered I connected with my guide (my dad at that time) and then fell asleep.

I checked my email the next day and *nothing*. Dammit! *Nothing*— really, Dad? So I tried again. This time I put in the intention of getting a job because I needed to make and exceed the mortgage payment (making it more than my original request). My dad reminded me that when I ask for things, say so like its already done. I did that this time. I let the candle burn down, and I walked away from it. I didn't check my email for about twenty-four hours. I did anything I could to forget about it. I walked. I prayed. I listened to chill and not-so-chill music (rest in paradise, DMX), I gardened and weeded, I spoke to friends, I went on LinkedIn and wrote encouraging posts. I acted like I had a job, like I had all kinds of prospects. It was hard. I was biting my nails sometimes. I'm not going to lie to you—I was worried at times. But then my dad's voice would quietly soothe me to be still and have faith. Sometimes I even wanted to yell back, "I'll have faith when I have a job, Dad!" I can laugh now, but it wasn't funny then.

Twenty-four hours later. Nothing.

Forty-eight hours later. Nothing.

One week later. Nothing.

I didn't light another candle. I kept doing what I was doing. Acting as if Dad already granted my deliverance request.

Two weeks later, a recruiter called me. I didn't remember contacting them at all. We spoke, and it was a beautiful opportunity—several thousand dollars more than the job that furloughed me. I was hired within three weeks and have been there ever since.

Does this happen every time? No. There are times when I ask for things or my clients ask for things that even a month later we get no deliverance on. Why does this happen? Did we do something wrong? Could be, but when I check in with my ancestors, they have always given me indications before we start that what I was asking for wasn't in agreement with what they wanted.

If the ancestor, guide, or deity doesn't want what you want for you, they will prevent you from getting it. Guaranteed. If you do keep trying and do get it, then you will regret it (it's been my experience). We have a saying in my family that if you must forcefully pull, push, and kick open the door, then try opening another door.

Hoodoo isn't faith based upon nothing. It's faith based upon everything (science, math, mental well-being, physical safety, love, healing, increase). We believe in these things and therefore we create them even more every day. What my and your ancestors spoke into existence came to be—in us. You are not a mistake; you were manifested! What you manifest you now create.

Direction

I hate to be lost. When I was a child, I had to take the regular public bus, not the school bus, to school. When I was in the fourth or fifth grade, I fell asleep on the bus ride home, missing my stop. The bus driver was super kind and helped me get where I needed to go by providing me a free pass in the opposite direction. The spirits have been there to protect me from such a young age. Hoodoo workers are human beings and have the same concerns and struggles that you do.

Side note: Consider your healer's humanness the next time you schedule with them. No one has all the answers. When we read for you during a session, we see a glimpse—a short, thirty- to sixty-minute glimpse—into our connection with you and your guides. If we had all the answers, our deity (in my opinion) wouldn't keep us here on earth much longer because we wouldn't learn any more life lessons.

As I was saying, I get lost—a lot! I'll be driving around looking for a destination. The wind in my hair, the music just right, and my spirit talking away to me. They love to seduce me while I'm driving (I don't think this is the safest activity, but it happens to magical workers). Anyway, while I am multitasking a thought will come to me. Random but very important, like, *You need to begin using and researching the power of chives in the spell you were doing for Kim* (a client) *yesterday. It's important to use chives and not a fully developed onion.* Then I'll think, *Why chives and not an onion?* Then I'll think, *What about garlic or scallions or shallots? Aren't they the same thing?* It continues as I go through every flowering plant I know of. Then I will think, *Whoops! Did I miss my exit?*

Again and again, it happens with shopping trips, when staying focused at work, and even when writing this book. Direction is a struggle for me and maybe you too. When doing hoodoo however (when I'm not driving or on a bus or otherwise distracted), I make sure that I know where I'm going. What I mean by this is I literally make sure which direction I am going in by looking at a compass. This is important because each spiritual direction has purpose.

Up—When I send a message or a hoodoo ritual up, I want it to go to deities. To my higher purpose. To shared ancestors. I send prayers up. I send blessings up. I send protection for homes, objects, and beings up. I send spirits and conjure guides up after they have helped me. How do I do this? I say it in the spell "I send ___up ___ into the clouds to be carried away." I want my thoughts and feelings to go up.

I want my growth to go up. I want my financial success to move up. I want my love life to keep moving up. I want my deliverance request to be heard and to go up. I want the incense smoke to go up, and I want it to clean and clear things up (see what I did there?).

Down—Down is always written so negatively. I don't get it. Down is a cool place. Down is grounding. Down can be many temperatures. Down is the center of the earth. It's also where I bury objects that have served their purpose. Down is where we may push feelings or emotions when we don't want to deal with them. Down in music is a good place when we're really dancing and into our feelings; we're "getting down." Down can mean sadness or mourning. But also, sadness can be allowing things to take their natural shape. I plant things down so that they can grow up. In that way, I want to make sure that when things are down, I remember if I want or don't want them to see the light of day. I use *down* in this sentence: Spirit, take this ____ (emotion, situation) down with you into Gaia where it can be cared for by nature. When I ask for something to be taken down, I do not want to dig it back up anytime soon.

Away—Away is another direction that can be seen as negative, but it doesn't have to be. I love going away on vacation. I ask for thoughts or feelings or energies to temporarily go away when I don't need them for a specific period. I ask for things to go away when they no longer are serving me. I ask for an emotion (jealousy, lust, anger, hatred) to go away. I can also change my mind, but for that time I ask it to go. Away (like all the directions) isn't permanent. Think of *away* as a synonym for *go* in hoodoo. If the energy is in your home and you want it out, you will say, "Away ____ (spirit name)."

Stay—When my dog Zhanahary tries to jump out of the car before I have hold of his leash, I tell him firmly, "Stay!" That's exactly what I do with hoodoo when I say, "Stay." I might ask my partner to stay. I may ask an emotion to stay. I may ask a shared ancestor to stay. The list can get very large, but it encompasses this direction. Any of my directions are actionable, and that is why I use them. I need deliverance and I need action; therefore, I use verbs—my action words.

It's important when using words like *stay* or *away* that you have the confidence behind the words. You can't be weak when you say, "Stay." You mean it. Deep inside of your belly, or if you feel your energy more in the pelvic/hip area, then that's fine too. A watered-down "Stay" is not effective and the spirit you are conjuring will know the difference.

THE BIBLE IS A SPELL BOOK

Do I use the Bible for hoodoo work? Absolutely 100 percent. Do I have reservations because of how the Bible has been used to hurt and harm my community, race, and gender? That's a tricky one. To me, reading and using the Bible for spell work is the same as being in a committed relationship. When I fell in love and made a commitment to my partner, I did so with full knowledge and understanding of all their faults, mannerisms, and how they could hurt me. I accepted all of that, but I didn't run. I knew that there would be conflicts and complications, and I bravely unlayered each part of my partner, finding the right way to love them and allowing them to love me in their perfect way. The Bible use and knowledge is the same. Get to know all its parts. Read bravely those passages that have hurt and caused dissension and then take the power back by finding what you can love out of those words or, at a minimum, how to reshape and reframe them to meet what you need in a relationship with sacred text. Is the Bible the only sacred text I use? No, I use several types of sacred text, including ones that maybe aren't sacred to you. Like there are certain movies, songs, and poems that are sacred to me. *Sacred* as defined by Merriam-Webster means "entitled to reverence and respect." I have claimed these pieces and added them to rituals, as they have power, intention, and faith expressed fully.

Here's the way I explain my use of the Bible when it comes to healing, protecting, and banishing with hoodoo. The Bible is the largest accident report you've ever read. There were many people there to witness the birth of this accident called our humankind, and each one has a different story. Mark, Luke, and John may say, "Well it all started with this Jesus person." The unknown authors of the Song of Solomon may say, "Well it all started with this love that couldn't be explained or quenched between two souls." Some may say it's a fairy tale or work of fiction, and others say it's a source of actual truth. Hopefully we can agree that we can say it is a collection of these reports that includes ways to conjure, pray, heal, and love through prose or a written language in its ordinary form. It is meant to be understood by the masses at the time it is read.

When you heal using this sacred text, it adds another level of intention, faith, and direction (which I feel is required in hoodoo). Sacred text is written by those that had faith in what they were interpreting for others to hear. This is the magic of sacred text. If you write something on a sticky note and you believe in its truth, then it carries more energetic power. When authors of sacred text tell a story of visions, tragedies, and lineages through time, abandonment, separation, death, and rebirth, their experience helps us as readers recognize ourselves in the story. In recognition we see the humanity. We empathize and learn to be a healer by being healed from pain.

I get challenged sometimes with those who wonder, *Who am I to change the words in the Bible to match my spell work and updated hoodoo?* I think about this quite a bit as a person of faith. When I was first learning about myself and began loving myself as a Black lesbian hoodoo worker, I had to reach into my history to understand that, from the beginning of the earth, our story has been told by the loudest voice in the room. Many times not the most accurate—just the loudest.

I have witnessed atrocities in history that have been skewed to meet the needs of those that will financially benefit from it with no regard for what cultures and traditions are being sold. Families torn apart, generations dissolved, lands taken away, and countries obliterated, all in the name of trade and revenue. My reasons for changing Bible text are not any more or less nefarious.

When I first started to write this book, I had an outline and about fifty thousand words in it. It was a really well-done book, but then as my ideals of the book and my research shifted, so did the work, becoming what you hold in your hands or read on your phone or tablet today.

It does not make the work less powerful or blessed—it just makes it different. The fashion icon Coco Chanel famously said, "before you leave the house, look in the mirror and take one thing off." Editing. We all do it. Before we send an email, we edit and reread. We can only hope that we edit before hitting send on a text message or before posting something on our social media to our followers. If we do not edit, well, the words are out there, and words have so much meaning, as they can never be taken back—whether in writing or when spoken out loud.

The Bible's history is fascinating. The first pieces of work that began the Bible were believed to have been written around 1300–1400 BC. The original manuscript was made up of around thirty-nine books of the testament written in Hebrew, and Greek manuscripts were completed and edited around 200 BC. This included the fourteen Apocrypha books. Apocrypha history can be found in my first book. On or around AD 380, the first Bible was mass produced in Latin with eighty books: thirty-nine Old Testament, fourteen Apocrypha, and twenty-seven New Testament. From there it has been edited and revised and written for different languages until the current day—all in all, about fifty thousand revisions with the last revision being the English Standard version in 2002. This doesn't consider the lost books of the Bible, those that tell stories of the Koran, Hindu mythology, acts and miracles of the Indian god Krishna, the women warriors, and the detailed stories of Jesus's mother, Mary. As hoodoo workers we are open to reading and studying all of the books (including those that may not be ordained by any religious order) to ensure that the text has the right words we need for a specific spell.

The Bible describes several messengers. There are angels, messengers, seraphim, cherubs, and archangels. There are also the authors of the Bible and its characters, which are royalty and nonroyalty. The name of the deliverer of the message changes to match the faith of the author (or the intended audience of you as the reader). For example, in these texts Jesus is called the "ruler of demons" because of the healing work that they witnessed Jesus perform (Matthew 9:34, Mark 3:22, Luke 11:15). Michael is known as an archangel (Daniel 10:13). Cherubs carry swords and are protectors (Genesis 3:24). Ezekiel 1:10 says that angels have multiple faces: human, lion, ox, and eagle. And so on. This is important because I believe that all our shared ancestors, guides, and deities that we conjure and call upon in hoodoo work have different physical appearances but still can be asked to carry out what you need deliverance from. The Tall Man that you will read about later may seem totally different to you than to me. The Blue Lady may be a cobalt blue or a light blue or maybe not be very blue at all. Maybe she speaks to you as a sound or scent and not an image at all.

In the lost books of the Bible, a "certain being" is a messenger but still deserves reverence for delivering messages (II Hermas, Introduction 1):

> "When I had prayed at home, and was sat down upon the bed, a certain being came in to me with a reverend look, in the habit of a shepherd, clothed with a white cloak, having a bag upon their back, and a staff in their hand, and saluted me."

In II Hermas, Commandment VI, we are told of two different angels, no longer called messengers or cherubs but something in between. At this point you will see they are both angels, even though they have separate intentions:

> And I said unto him: Sir, how shall I know that there are two such angels with man? Hear says he, and understand.

> The angel of righteousness, is mild and modest, and gentle, and quiet. When therefore, he gets into thy heart, immediately he talks with thee of righteousness, of modesty, of chastity, of bountifulness, of forgiveness, of charity, and piety....

> Learn also the works of the angel of iniquity. Who is first of all bitter, and angry, and foolish; and their works are pernicious, and overthrow the servants of Spirit. When therefore these things come into thy heart; thou shalt know by their works, that this is the angel of iniquity.

Messengers, angels, cherubs, shepherds, and others can speak to all of us in hoodoo. Without judgment (which is a religious construct) we need to recognize that it is our responsibility to practice with intention, faith, and direction, and—I would add this as well—with inclusion of any messenger, no matter what form it may take.

ELIMINATING THE NAME(S) OF GOD

Some find the name of deities so triggering that it prevents them from being effective hoodoo workers. The research you do on conjure, root-workers, and hoodoo healers will lead you to believe many were Christian and had a firm faith in God, goddesses, orishas, and so on, and that may be true. But as hoodoo is for everyone, you do not need to state the word of God. Just like if you are physically restricted from having certain nutrients—you must replace the names with others. To do this, you will need to become okay with surgically removing those harmful words and pronouns in Bible verses so that you can get working with your ancestors, guides, and deities. Rewrite your history and keep shining as you—beautifully perfect, imperfect *you*!

The hatred or hurt or fear of the Bible is real. Words like *God*, *lord*, *master*, *ruler*, or even *father* are highly active, possessive, controlling names. It gives those reading the Bible several different emotions, from support and love to trauma and anxiety. Whenever I am reading the Bible for a spell or use it to inspire and encourage, I want to make sure that it is not triggering or harmful. If I told you that everywhere in the Bible I recommend that you replace those God-like words that may be causing you tension with words you enjoy, embrace, and love, what does that feel like in yourself? At your core spirit? To many of my clients, it feels good—damn good—and I am here to give them more. So let me give you permission to go through your Bible (please make sure it's yours) and replace those words with ones that represent you. Need suggestions? Here are a few:

- Higher Power
- Spiritual Guide
- Spirit of Old
- Mother
- Light Maker
- Dream Giver
- Life Force
- The Light
- Goddess
- Nature Force
- Beautiful One(s)
- Beloved Source(s)
- Dream Maker(s)
- Miracle Worker
- Giver of Gifts
- Way Maker
- Deliverer

After you find a nice fit, go through a few of those harmful Bible verses and replace their words with your new empowering word. How does that feel in your heart? You may find yourself weeping or crying out in joy. Let those tears flow. It is your awakening and your gratitude of this new spirit of self-love and appreciation. You no longer need to be tied to fear or hatred of self.

Consider this verse taken from 1 John 1:5:

This is the message we have heard from him and declare to you: God is light; in him there is no darkness at all.

Take this verse right out of the Bible and copy it on a piece of paper and then, taking a trusted marker or crayon or similar utensil, strike out the word *God*—yes strike it out through and through from the verse. Let that sit with you. Throw away any guilt or anxiety about this exercise. You are doing what That Hoodoo Lady says, so you aren't *really* culpable yet, right?

Okay, you should have the new name you want to use to replace *God*. I'm going to use *Dream Maker* for myself. So now the verse will read for me:

This is the message we have heard from him and declare to you: The Dream Maker is light; in him there is no darkness at all.

Feeling good yet? For some, we are only halfway there, and I get it and I support you, so let's not stop there! Let's push ourselves to even more hoodoo and Bible magic perfectionists.

BIBLE VERSES TO GO

In chapter 1 I mentioned the importance of understanding and using the Bible as a spell book for you to conjure. The Bible has been used and can be used as a tool for any purpose, just like any text. The words can incite and cause sensitivity, but by taking them back and crafting them to match my own spell work, I have turned this process of memorizing or cataloging my own Bible verses into a portable thing I call "Bible Verses to Go."

This chapter helps you build your own beginning knowledge of Bible verses to add to your own database of text. You can edit and customize these to meet your needs. Some are familiar, as you might have seen them in my first book, and others are added from my own personal work that has helped me. In the appendix I have added some of my favorite verses that I encourage you to cultivate to match your own personal understanding of faith and deity.

In updated hoodoo this can be an app, an online document, or a printed document that you have handy so that you are not tied to technology. I also recommend that you have one verse—one powerful verse—you can use for general protection and purpose that speaks to you. This may require quite a bit of research, and that's fine, because the life of a hoodoo worker is about study. Here are some ideas:

Love is patient, love is kind. It does not envy, it does not boast, it is not proud. It does not dishonor others, it is not self-seeking, it is not easily angered, it keeps no record of wrongs. (1 Corinthians 13:4–5)

Do not be anxious about anything, but in every situation, by prayer and petition, with thanksgiving, present your requests to God. And the peace of God, which transcends all understanding, will guard your hearts and your minds in Christ Jesus. (Philippians 4:6–7)

Therefore I tell you, whatever you ask for in prayer, believe that you have received it, and it will be yours. (Mark 11:24)

So do not fear, for I am with you; do not be dismayed, for I am your God. I will strengthen you and help you; I will uphold you with my righteous right hand. (Isaiah 41:10)

May he give you the desire of your heart and make all your plans succeed. (Psalm 20:4)

HOODOO ALTAR

Clean down a space that you can use as an altar. An altar is just a sacred area that you use to do your hoodoo offerings and lay your conjure upon. It is remarkably similar to if you are cooking, so you may want to do this in a kitchen. You probably wouldn't cook in the bathroom or bedroom. When I'm doing conjure, I have a small area (it can be anywhere, really) where I set my conjure work: candles, flowers, offerings, pictures, herbs, roots, fetish dolls, Bible verses, poems, dedication objects, personal concerns (like blood, urine, hair, nails). I wipe and clean this area, and once I use it for conjure work, I don't use it for anything else. What if you change your mind or move or the altar is disturbed? That happens. I once laid a cup of water for my ancestor, and my dogs drank it right up because it was at their level—whoops! I moved the altar a bit higher and kept going about my way.

Does the altar have to be large? Nope! My favorite altar is in a matchbox. I cleaned it, and put a couple of leaves of my holy basil and a thorn from a rose in it. I breathed my intentions into it and wrote on it "Protect me from evil." I closed it up, struck a match, and once the match blew out, I laid the burnt match on top of the matchbox and set it in the corner of my windowsill. It protects my window to keep anyone from trying to sneak in and look at me while I'm dressing or doing other things. I have curtains too, but this is for spiritual protection when I am at my most vulnerable.

What do I put on my altar? I have several altars for different purposes. Here are a few other examples:

I have an altar to honor my mom. This altar is actually her last wallet before she died. I placed the wallet itself on a wooden stand. I removed her pictures, identification cards, and a lock of her hair. I cleaned the wallet by anointing it with oil (but not so much that it took away her energy). Then I prayed over it, connecting with her and asking her to be with me. I told her how much I loved her and offered her some of her favorite items so that her spirit would stay with me and keep me safe and smart in everything I do (which was her job while she was here physically). From time to time, her altar wants to be moved. I feed her bourbon by placing a clean shot glass near the wallet. When she asks for something different (she loved chocolate-covered cherries), I place them on a piece of fine china (from the thrift store) and keep it cool and dry and protected from insects (ants love to go after sweets). Finally, I go to the altar and say hello to her whenever I think about her.

For my dad I recommend you do something similar. Now of course you won't have a picture of him, but using the information that I gave you about him, you can set aside some space in your home for him. Pick out a song, poem, or Bible verse, and write words of thanks to him. Call his name, gently, and then listen for his response—he speaks so quietly. Await his response—don't rush him.

SACRIFICIAL OBJECTS AND OFFERINGS

When I first started out as a hoodoo worker, I was so diligent in making everything real. I wanted to make sure that my spells were real. My headdress was real. How I cleaned my home to protect it was real. I think you get the point. Part of this includes making sure that my sacrifices and offerings were real too. I wanted to use real animal sacrifices because that's what my ancestors would do and, therefore, that's what I needed to do.

I would polish bones from cows and pigs and chickens until they were pearly white (this takes a significant amount of time and energy). Then I would apply lacquer to protect them from decay. Next, I would pray over them fervently and drill holes into them so that I could wear them, just like my ancestors would have.

Spirit then asked me to research tools and cabins for enslaved Africans, and here's what I found:

Imagine a shack that is as small as one room in your home. Now take away all of the paint, furnishings, and flooring. Oh, and windows—take those too. Now add mud and dirt on the ground and, if you were lucky, straw and rags to sleep on. Your animals were not really yours. They were your superiors, and they probably lived a better existence than you because they were well fed and watered (you had to be certain of it for your own sake) and they received veterinarian care, whereas you would rarely, if ever, be able to see a doctor for anything.

As you lay down after an exhausting and painful day, you would hear the wind coming through the cracks of your hut. The insects could easily make their way in as well. Wood was a luxury many enslaved

Africans would never know about. They would sleep on the ground with a jacket or item of clothing as their pillow. There were dozens of them—yes, dozens—in one room, housed just like they were shipped over. In a pack, smushed together. Always reminded of where they were and who they were. There were babies, children, and adults all huddled together. Warmed by a fire and the knowledge that tomorrow they had to go through the same pain and endure it. Their reward was the leftovers from those enslavers. Scraps from their tables that were stored in a makeshift kitchen, which also served as sleeping quarters. Sometimes they received a rough blanket to share among themselves—just one. If there was a bed, everyone would sleep on it—as many as could fit. If someone was sick, then I can only imagine everyone would get the same illness, unless there was a medicine worker there to boil up healing herbs.

After dealing with unrest and damp surroundings, and fighting off colds, pain, and infection, there would be a horn blown early in the morning, awakening everyone to let them know that another day had come. Another day of the same abuse and torturous field work. Does any of that seem real?

My family came from enslaved people. I know this. I am a direct descendant who lived those hundreds of years ago, where my bed was a cold damp floor, covered in straw, rags, and insect droppings. In a one-room shack where I could hear nothing but the voices, breathing, and moans from others. So many others always near, always watching. Some watching to tattle to protect their own hides. Some watching for a chance to escape. Others watching just because there was nothing else to do.

I bring this up to remind us what hoodoo is about. Hoodoo was gifted to us from a time where we had nothing. Have you ever had just nothing in your life? No sense of self or purpose, for sure, but deeper than that, you didn't know if you would be here on this earth the following day—and maybe you were almost okay with that. Once you allow yourself to get into that mindset of awareness of self, not depression, think about where you came from, really came from. For example, do a DNA test and learn about your ancestry, and then use Google Maps to look at the locations of some of the places it mentions.

I know that my family is from Africa, but I have no idea where. I do not know if I am North, South, East, or West African, and what a shame that is, because it leaves me even more empty inside at times. In those empty places I need to be filled with a spiritual connection that is stronger than burdock root. I want to be certain that even if I don't know where I came from that I do know that it was from strength, wisdom, and destiny. Let's do an exercise together on sacrifice to help us connect with our sacrificial objects that can be used in place of those that many tell us are real.

Sacrifice

Allow yourself to think about the word *sacrifice*. The ritual meaning of the word as defined by *Webster's Dictionary* is an act of slaughtering an animal or person or surrendering a possession as an offering to a deity or to a divine or supernatural figure.

Now think of your deity or supernatural figure that you serve, worship, or even just admire in your conjure and rootwork. Describe them in your own self. Are they happy, loving, kind? Are they judgmental, hard to please? Controlling? Manipulative? Guilt or fear based? Now breathe and think about your history, your ancestry, and what they sacrificed. This sacrifice—is it different? The second meaning of the verb *sacrifice* is deeper. This definition is to give away something (usually something valuable) for the possibility of gaining something else of value (such as self-respect, trust, love, freedom, prosperity) or to avoid an even greater loss. The meaning I want you to focus on in this next part of the exercise is to give away something for a possibility of gaining something. Think of your deity or supernatural force and listen for what you are giving and what you are getting. When you can answer this, then the exercise is complete.

When I was creating those hand-drilled bone amulets, what was I really getting besides Facebook likes? I wasn't getting closer to Spirit while inhaling bone fragments and dust. I wasn't more serene hearing the high-pitched whine of the drill as it pierced the very part of the animal that gave it a structure. I was actually the opposite of what I wanted to be. I wasn't trading anything or even offering anything to my supernatural force. I was in preparation, you could say, but what was my supernatural force really asking me? It isn't like they woke me up that morning with the expectation that I produce five bone necklaces by five that evening. In fact, my deity wanted me to be present. To contemplate. To listen to them and be led by them. To enjoy the life I've been given and to share that joy with others. To try my best to harm only when necessary and even then, to do it very carefully. To react in time. To bring to them what they deserve and desire. To me, that's an #updatedhoodoo sacrifice.

Offerings

Offerings are the items you offer or give to the spirit by way of sacrifice. It isn't always about something that is metaphysical. Think of a ring you may give to your partners in a poly relationship. You offer that ring or token to symbolize your relationship, love, adoration, or commitment. That you will be there for the time that you agreed. That you will respect each other's wishes as a unit. Each member of the relationship having a say in the outcome that is successful or that requires a checkup.

I place an offering to my metaphysical construct onto my altar of choice or even present it as a word spoken or written, or maybe it's a gift. My spirit of choice enjoys lots of different offerings. Sometimes I offer my voice in song in praise and worship. I tell that being that I love them and thank them for keeping me safe day by day and healthy and happy. Other times I offer tears in gratitude when I get things that mean a lot to me. Like when I get that promotion I wanted. When I hear "yes" from my beloved. When I see the smile of my child. When I get to play fetch with my animal. When I see the blueness of the sky or the vastness of the universe. I offer my thanks in the hopes that they hear my offering and receive it in kind.

In church, which I attended with my grandma as a kid, we would have to put money in a collection plate when we were told, and this was our offering. Sometimes my grandma didn't have the money to have food for us for the next week, but she put her offering and tithe into the basket like she was a millionaire. This type of offering takes so much faith and sacrifice. I never knew why they really stressed us doing that as children, but thinking about it now, it makes perfect sense. They did this to teach us humility and to understand how to share. How to share what we had with something or even someone that we would never meet. Why did we give this offering? Maybe we were doing it because everyone else was sure. Maybe we did it because we didn't want to hear negative comments, or we feared that our parents would look poorly upon us if we didn't put that quarter in the bin.

Now I give that offering because I want to be looked upon as a giver. A giver of the resources I have and can share with others because it is my right and also because in my own morality it is my responsibility. It is my responsibility to care for others by sharing my resources, even if I never meet them or hear a word of thanks. I know that my offering doesn't have to be made at a church service. It can be something I hand out randomly to a stranger. It can be sharing a good review of an artist, or it can be community service, like volunteering at a local theater or serving coffee at a shelter. Allowing someone to use my phone when theirs is out of battery. Walking someone's animals if they can't. Listening to my friends when I really could be drinking and watching Netflix. These offerings of sacrifice are all recognized, and all seen by our guides.

Now let us return to how this meets with what we do in conjure and hoodoo. In hoodoo we offer to our deity and supernatural force some type of sacrifice in honor and, in that same respect, gratitude and submission as a partner. We are joined together in covenant, and in that covenant we are giving something for the possibility of getting something in return. The "something in return" is the granted deliverance request that you seek. This is the reason we give objects and offerings.

The type of offering is insignificant, because if you know in your heart your desires in your relationship with Spirit, then you know what they want and they know what you want. Without knowing you I cannot prescribe to you what to give them any more than I can offer to you what you would enjoy.

There are ideas or common themes I can provide for offerings, but I beg you to do the work of connecting with your ancestors, guides, and deities and ask them. After all, it is a relationship that will stay with you from life to life (this is my belief).

Some general offerings for hoodoo work include herbs, coins, food, drink, personal concerns (hair, blood, nails, urine, mucus), and objects (dolls, writings, songs). My deity likes all of these. My ancestors are pretty specific about what they want. My dad enjoys tobacco, but only from a pouch. He also likes rice pudding, caramels (he's actually telling me right now what to write), peppermint candies (those big, round balls of peppermint that are crunchy and kind of explode in your mouth), hats—not baseball hats, but the older fedora type. He likes when I play some Santana for him or R&B. He doesn't like my tears as offering. He likes my laughter instead. He appreciates me remembering the times we had together. He appreciates my learning more about my ancestors from his side of the family.

My mom is completely different. She likes coins from casinos and lottery tickets—she was an avid gambler in life. She likes Newport or Benson & Hedges cigarettes. She likes chicken noodle soup made by Campbell's with Ritz crackers because it was what she would make when she got home at three in the morning after working three jobs. She likes knives with blue handles. She doesn't like tiger's eye stones. She prefers onyx or obsidian. She appreciates my retelling of her stories to others—especially if it scares them or makes them fear her. She doesn't like my telling of her bisexuality, because she didn't associate happy feelings around that. But she does like that I am lesbian, because that is who she identifies with. She likes the offering of her being in this book and will take it and make the book a success and help those that read it.

Now your turn. Think of your sacrifices and offerings that you will prepare and have at the ready. Your ancestors, deities, and guides will surprise you with what they want. They will build bridges. They will form relationships. They will strengthen your covenant (your spiritual contract). These are hoodoo foundations of sacrificial objects and offerings.

Bible Verses for Offerings

I have real-world offerings. I try not to think of movies where people sacrifice their children or blood or animals, but in many cultures, this is 100 percent right. If it feels okay for you, then go for it with responsibility and with an understanding of law and morality. There is always a time in hoodoo to offer up something to seal the hoodoo contract. If deity or guides are giving you deliverance or fulfilling your request, then how will you say thank you? This is an offering. When you are giving offerings or paying tribute or want to have a meal with your ancestor, what common, local foods today are like what this verse recommends?

> *May the Lord, the God of your ancestors, increase you a thousand times and bless you as he has promised! (Deuteronomy 1:11)*

If you want a successful career, to increase your finances, or to add intention to your work, use this verse. For the offering you may give away a symbolic gesture of the increase that you want, like a coin. You can also give something to your ancestor that represents what they enjoyed, like something sweet, savory, or spicy. My great-grandfather loved spicy things. I leave him a jalapeño or cayenne pepper on the railroad tracks when he does work for me, because he made his living moving from train to train, working odd jobs.

What other ways, even as an atheist, could you use this passage?

> *These, then, are the regulations for the burnt offering, the grain offering, the sin offering, the guilt offering, the ordination offering and the fellowship offering, which the Lord gave Moses at Mount Sinai in the Desert of Sinai on the day he commanded the Israelites to bring their offerings to the Lord. The Lord said to Moses, "Bring Aaron and his sons, their garments, the anointing oil, the bull for the sin offering, the two rams and the basket containing bread made without yeast and gather the entire assembly at the entrance to the tent of meeting." Moses did as the Lord commanded him, and the assembly gathered at the entrance to the tent of meeting. Moses said to the assembly, "This is what the Lord has commanded to be done." (Leviticus 7:37)*

As an atheist I would use this to anoint myself in something I believe in. Maybe science. Maybe mathematics. Maybe health or fitness. The offerings that are sacrificial in this story would be garments, oil, and bread (unleavened crackers), all set aside to a guide that means something to someone that does not condone or believe in traditional religion. It could be Einstein and you're leaving him an egg or mushrooms—in my research I discovered that he was a huge fan of mushrooms and scrambled eggs. Another guide that you can use would be Alan Hart. He was one of the first female-to-male transgender people and was also a leader in the study of tuberculosis—he was the director of hospitalization and rehabilitation for the Connecticut State Tuberculosis Commission until he passed away. An offering to Alan could be something from the states he lived in (Kansas—wheat, Oregon—hazelnuts, Connecticut—apples or lobster shells).

NATURAL HEALING

Every wound is not healed with the same plaster; if the accessions of the disease be vehement, modify them with soft remedies be in all things wise as a serpent, but harmless as a dove. (The Epistle of Ignatius to Polycarp 1:8)

Have you ever been to Sedona, Arizona, to see the vortexes? In the canyons and hills that surround the city, there are four well-known spots that tout the full energy of powers that help beings to heal, be themselves, learn about themselves, and meditate. There are also other vortexes. Some also say that a vortex is simply a person, place, or thing that is capable of drawing energy toward itself and its center.

When you witness a vortex for yourself, you may notice a circular spin of wind and air that goes to the center or a situation that draws things into it (ideals, beings, animals, concentrated energy systems).

Just like any New Age metaphysical worker I've been to Sedona to see the most popular vortexes in the United States. Again, these are not the only but some of the most famous. We went to two of the four known ones in Arizona: the Airport Mesa, which was quite a hike to a scenic overlook of the red rocks, and the Boynton Canyon, which is the location that is famous for a balance of gender energies. Its energy is upward and inward, all at the same time. It looks across the valley and has breathtaking nature scenes. I went there on a quest of discovery after being laid off from a job that I was at for almost five years. My ancestors (my dad and the Blue Lady—you will learn more about the Blue Lady in chapter 4) had warned me that change was coming, but I still was a bit shaken up after I received notice from my employer. My best friend offered a trip through the Southwest as a healing tour, and I took her up on it. Besides, it was going to be interesting because I could go the Grand Canyon and walk the Skywalk.

I don't claim asthma, but asthma sometimes has a hold on my lungs, especially at times when I'm more physically active than usual. Here we were hiking up a mountain and having quite the time of it. I was able to connect very deeply to Spirit and ancestors. I saw energies walking around as if lost, and between my friend and I, we released those souls that wanted to be released in love. Spirit work is pretty exhausting, as you will discover if you keep up your conjure. Anyway, there we were enjoying ourselves, and I noticed the familiar tightening of my chest and looked through my pack for my inhaler. I also did some prayer work to remind my lungs that they were actually functioning fine and that I would have medicine to them soon. *Hmm*, I thought to myself, knowing I packed my inhaler but not finding it. My mind raced around the hotel room, the breakfast rest stop, the car—anywhere I could have left it. The more I worried—as with any stress—the more my anxiety flared up and the more I couldn't breathe. We were about a mile away from the parking lot; I couldn't exactly hop back to the car to look, so I reached out to my ancestor.

"Ancestor Gran Gran that always gives me the ability to heal and to remember natural healing work, what do I do?"

Oh, baby, said Ancestor Gran Gran. *You don't have asthma. Asthma just visits you from time to time.*

It was important for me to hear this because what we say to our bodies is what our bodies manifest. This is especially important to remember in any kind of magical work. Our words become actions and our actions carry out what our words tell it to. I then observed my fear and lessening of breath.

She then told me to sit down and look around at the mountain. I did. She asked me to see it as a medicine healer, where medicine is all around me and at my disposal. I did. I saw the trees around me. Rock formations. I did not hear water. I saw birds flying. I concentrated on the air that the birds were bringing into their bodies—in and out, in and out. I asked my lungs to hear what the birds were doing and asked my lungs to feel what the birds' lungs were doing. This worked for a moment, and then I felt myself go back to anxiety. *Damn it, where is my faith?* I thought. *Back in the car in your other pack!* my gran gran joked. *Bad time for a joke,* I thought. Anyway, she asked me to do another sweep around the trail, and I looked at the vortex. I felt nauseous and sleepy. My racing heart began to slow down. I held on to my body. I then saw the most gorgeous juniper tree in front of me. Juniper trees are coniferous. There are almost sixty-something species of them in the Northern Hemisphere. They are evergreens that can grow between sixty to over a hundred feet tall. They have needlelike leaves. Some have a little blueberry-like fruit protruding from their leaves. Some (like me) would think they are cousins to the cedar, but they are not. They can look like they are crawling around the desert or ground as well as growing tall. They are very drought resistant and survive well in arid climates—hence Arizona.

The glorious juniper right in front of me almost glowed as if it were telling me that it was what I was looking for. I walked calmly over to it and did what every very intelligent botanist, herbalist, and the like would say *not* to do. I helped myself to some of its bark. Yes, I walked over to it and asked it to heal me from the asthma that was trying to restrict my breathing, and after it confirmed, I took off a small piece of bark and chewed it.

Disclaimer: You should never ever eat or even touch anything in nature that you do not know as well as your own body, because nature is a beautifully sensible equalizer and will have no problem with harming or killing you if you do not know any better.

Thankfully, my sweet juniper bark did not kill me. My breathing got better, and I caught up to my friend and let her know what occurred and that I needed to get back down the mountain—pronto. Off we went to safety.

Why did the juniper bark work? Was it my gran gran's magic? I can't say. But I can say that in life, and now in death, my gran gran has never steered me wrong. When I went back to a safe place after catching my breath—literally—I did some research. The common juniper is an ornamental tree. Birds, turkeys, and waxwings eat the cones for food. It's a great source of shelter for turkeys in the South and owls in the North. Native Americans of the Great Basin and Pacific Northwest used tonics made from the branches to assist with colds, the flu, muscle aches, and arthritis. The bark (yes, bark) would be used for stomach ailments and to treat respiratory problems. Did I mention our Native American background (specifically my gran gran)? There it was. A beautiful natural remedy.

Natural remedies are remedies for a reason. Using the knowledge of herbalists and natural medicine workers, you'll see there are many natural medicines out there for the taking. It just takes research and time, the same way you would take time with a healer. I recommend (before you are stuck on a mountain in the middle of Arizona) that you investigate some natural remedies that you can use in hoodoo work to heal and provide deliverance. All of our bodies are different—always consult with a qualified doctor and herbalist before consuming or touching any plant, flower, or tree whose properties you are unfamiliar with. There are several excellent books on medicines by enslaved African Americans that I recommend in the research section of this book, but I wanted to share a few natural remedies that I absolutely use in my own conjure:

Camphor—This was used by our shared ancestors to help reduce fevers and it was used in teas for colds, cold sores, respiratory infections, and as an antiseptic. For this reason, in my hoodoo work if I have someone that is having issues with breathing in the right truth or speaking the right truth, I will ask them to sleep with a cotton ball that has camphor on it and to pray for the right words to come from their spirit. If a couple or throuple is coming to see me because they are arguing, I will make an amulet of camphor and sweetener to calm down the arguments, encourage communication, and heal up the pain that was caused by the harsh words.

Fennel—Our shared ancestors used fennel for pain relief for things like toothaches and earaches. It also has been known to help cure colic, gas, and indigestion issues. It is antibacterial, antifungal, and lowers blood pressure. It has been known to help relieve coughs and bronchitis.

Garlic—Garlic is used in hoodoo to ward off negative energies, stop arguments, and clean or protect objects and people. Enslaved Africans used garlic to ward off illnesses. Garlic was worn around their necks to prevent diseases from flowering (which may associate it with being a protective hoodoo tool). If you want to move people away from gossiping or talking about you and to you, then mix some garlic, asafetida, and onions and place the mixture near the gossipers, or in updated hoodoo remotely/virtually place this mixture in a circle around them (physically touching people is called assault and is illegal).

Grapes—Grapes, in the magic practiced by enslaved Africans, are helpful for when your client is suffering from menstrual bleeding and cramps. During slavery, the grapes were mashed and filtered (like a wine) and used like today's douches. Because they are anti-inflammatory in medicine, you can use them as an anti-inflammatory in magic. You can put raisins (dried grapes) in a bag and carry them around your neck or waist when you are entering a place where there will be animosity. The grapes crushed by your feet are a great way to increase the potency of a job or money spell because it is used to help blood circulate and when you want to get things moving— you need to use natural sources that get you up and out.

Walnut—All pieces of a walnut tree, including the walnuts themselves, have been used in folk medicine to purify the blood. They also can be taken to help with constipation, and it has antifungal properties and wards off parasitic infections. This is helpful in conjure as the hoodoo purposes will match. When I need to get my spell "moving" I can use walnut or walnut shells in the work. If I want to prevent damaging people, places, or things, then I use crushed walnuts in the bag or amulet that I make to prevent damaging energies from growing.

In hoodoo the folk medicines are in direct correlation with literal interpretation. For example, if you want to relieve a headache, look for something that looks like a head or brain, like a walnut. If you want to heal a broken bone, use the plant called boneset. To add sexual potency to a work, use something that resembles genitalia. There is a story that John the Conqueror was an African prince in love with a princess. He was tricked by the princess's father and sold into slavery to keep them from marrying. He then outwits every enslaver and eventually wins his freedom. He eventually escapes back to Africa with his princess as his bride. He renounces his powers in exchange for love, but he leaves his heart and spirt in the form of his roots (High John the Conqueror root) to other enslaved people so that they, too, can win any battle they are fighting. High John the Conqueror root is circular and wrinkled, resembling darker testicles.

Moss

I have moss everywhere in my backyard. It clings to all of the rocks and trees. From a distance it almost looks like a fragile, intricate lace blanket. It really is. Mosses are a division of Bryophyta, non-vascular flowerless plants that present themselves as clumps of green coverage in wooded, damp, and shady locations. They are a one-cell-thick distribution of leaves that are branched or unbranched. They do not have seeds, and they propagate by the wind transmitting their spores. Like other forms of life, they have the ability to reproduce asexually—with the vegetation that is produced on the leaves or branches breaking off to form new plants—without having to go through any other type of fertilization. They are excellent at providing insulation to the grounds they cover. Mosses can be monoicous (male and female reproductive parts are on the same plant) or dioicous (male and female reproductive parts are on different plants). They absorb up to twenty times their weight in liquid (very similar to my carpet; if you've ever spilled something on a carpet and then tried to pick up that spill in one shot, you probably weren't successful).

And what do we do with this organism that has all of the traits of a good magical spell of protection, insulation, and healing? We kill it, of course.

You may have seen all kinds of moss-killing techniques, because mosses can encompass a large area of ground if left on their own. They will take over anything. Beautiful to look at, deceptively aggressive. These wonderful tiny beings are also helping scientists to understand DNA, as the organisms show how plants repair themselves through homologous recombination. All of this within one little bunch of plants that lie low to the ground! As rootworkers our jobs are to get to the roots of the plant-based world and use this knowledge of the living organisms around us in a combination of science, faith, and magic for the deliverance of our clients.

Trees

Cultures and trees are so interconnected. When I think of the first drawings made with ocher on caves, I think of these same ancestors telling folktales around a fire. Without a tree we would not have the fire. We could not have the fire without the trees. We cannot have rootwork without the root system of a plant, and I can think of no greater root system than that of trees.

What is a tree? A tree is a perennial plant. It has a primary stem (trunk) that connects with the ground. It typically grows very tall and has branches that support themselves and spread out in some type of formation. Trees typically grow in nature next to other trees. Rarely will you see a tree unprotected by a tree family unless there was some type of interruption (harvesting, landscaping, intrusion) by some type of predator or disease—and I believe humans qualify as predators.

What are some attributes of trees? Strong, powerful, hardy, provide protection from the elements.

What are some of its uses? Trees keep a forest sustainable, and their root systems are the delivery system of the glucose needed to give it nourishment. In forests they also provide nutrients to large masses of mushroom populations (that then in turn distribute through its network more nourishment and growth). Trees are used for the wood and pulp extractions. They are used in construction, as flavoring in cooking, and to make fire. Trees can be fruiting or nonfruiting, giving sources of nutrition for other beings to enjoy, meaning we eat the fruits, seeds, and nuts that they provide. We also eat the trees' leaves. We use the branches, bark, and sometimes the roots. The leaves, bark, and roots can be used in healing rituals.

Before you go taking a selfie with a tree, consider that the tree has lived here for centuries, generations, and millions of years longer than you. How old is the oldest person? Maybe no more than 120. How old is the oldest tree? The Great Basin bristlecone pine tree in California is over 5,000 years old. Trees have a story to tell, and you can hear it by looking at their bark, their twisted trunk, the branches that spread out wide. The diseased limbs. The insects that dine upon them. The animals that cower under them for warmth. The humans that use them for protection and navigation ("turn left at the big oak tree").

The tree deserves your respect and not a photo—it has a story. Ask the tree its name. Ask the tree if it *wants* to be in your Instagram post or if it would rather you sit quietly, respectfully under it and listen to its sage wisdom. Ask it if it cares how many likes or shares it gets—I can tell you now it probably will not care at all. And then query it about how many lives it has saved in the forest. In the park. In this neighborhood. Ask where it came from and why it came here. Investigate its network of other trees and ask its family some of the same questions. Look at the bark of the tree. Is it damaged? Did someone cowardly inscribe some message of "X loves X" into it? If so, place your hand upon those wounds—yes, they are wounds—and apologize for our carelessness as beings. For our lack of empathy and understanding. Give it a drink of water. If it shares its fruits or nuts with you, thank it for sharing its bounties.

Then and only then, take a selfie. Notice how it will require the full attention of the photo. It will be the primary focus. It will give you likes and shares because it is in the tree's very nature to awe and inspire.

Trees are useful in hoodoo for their resilience, their healing power, their wise advice, and their ability to command attention. I use the tree bark in medicinal teas. I use the limbs and branches to make fires that

I use when I do a chant or ring shout. I use trees to protect myself from the elements when I stand under the umbrella of their leaves. I use their leaves to write requests to my guides. I place offerings at their feet. I feed them out of respect because they have served and will continue to serve humanity.

Strange Fruit

There is a song by Billie Holiday titled "Strange Fruit" about the lynchings in the South, producing African Americans as fruit. As an African American I cannot think of trees without associating them with the violence that is carried out on and with them. Their branches and limbs were used to whip and punish us. We were hung from them in the South. We were tied to them and left to the elements.

According to the NAACP, there were 4,743 lynchings from 1882 to 1968. Imagine that this is only those that were reported and documented. Of all lynching victims, 73 percent were Black. The remaining 27 percent were white. These whites were lynched because they were helping Black people when they sought freedom. After 1865, when the Civil War ended and the last state declared slavery was illegal, Black people wanted to vote. To the polls they went, or tried to. When they went to the polls in Confederate states, they were targeted and bullied, punished, and woefully, lynched. Even more tragic, as recently as 2020, lynching is still a tragic outcome of social and racial injustice in the world. Lynching does not happen just to Black people, nor is it restricted to the South. Charles Seguin of Penn State has a colored graphic online of the lynchings across North America. From 1883 to 1941, lynching was one way to murder people, and it touched every state and ethnic group (although a significantly larger number of people lynched were Black). The ratio of Black people lynched in comparison to others was two to one. In an article in Futility.org, Seguin is quoted as saying,

> *Although people knew about these lynchings at the time, I doubt many people today now know that brutal lynchings occurred in places like Chicago, Illinois; Duluth, Minnesota; or in Coatesville, Pennsylvania.*

Many people probably do not realize just how brutal those lynchings were. What we are showing here is a legacy of racism and vigilante violence that stretches far beyond what is commonly remembered.... lynching was "our national crime."[1]

In Portland, Oregon, a thirty-one-year-old Black woman, Titi Gulley, who was experiencing houselessness, was found hanging from a tree in Rocky Butte Park in 2019. The local officials called it a suicide. The family of Titi Gulley called it a result of hatred and murder due to her brave willingness to identify as a transgender female. This is one of six hangings of BIPOC Americans reported in 2019, some experiencing houselessness, some experiencing prejudice by gender identity. The society as a whole is using the beauty of the tree, the sturdy, everlasting plant with its strong trunk and limbs, as a mechanism for carrying out a sentence for those that dare to be brave enough to be nonconforming.

In India in April 2020, a vigilante group hanged three Hindu sadhus because the vigilantes inaccurately thought they were thieves after receiving a series of WhatsApp messages. The victims, Chikne Maharaj Kalpavriksha Giri (seventy years old), Sushilgiri Maharaj (thirty-five years old), and their driver, Nilesh Telwade (thirty years old), were driving, tragically and ironically, to a funeral when they were attacked and murdered.

These are the strange fruits of trees, but the trees are not to blame. It's our society that insists on preventing its members from getting equitable treatment. The immigrant, Black, brown, yellow, and red ancestors have battled and prayed for deliverance. Our time here on earth comparatively is to join this fight.

Hoodoo workers offer deliverance by working with the deities, spirits, and guides of those that have passed before us. We must stay awakened to civil unrest and remain educated on how the acts of violence affect us. It's because of these attacks that hoodoo work exists to continue blessing and protecting our social justice fighters. There's a saying: "When one of us is hurting, all of us are hurting." Religious, racial, and gender tensions and atrocities bring about deliverance requests. As a hoodoo practitioner recognize you are already now a member of a nonconforming practice. A practice that has misconceptions and fear associated with it. A practice that is shunned by a system that dates as far back as 500 BC, where rule over others and the removal of their freedoms is a game and the winner gets the rewards—in the form of human lives.

These rulers desire first what they do not understand and then fear because they cannot understand. Finally, they want to extinguish that which is different or force it to integrate with its own system (all while taking the essence or culture with it as its own). This includes religions that strayed away from those that are now traditional but were not tradition. Christianity and Catholicism are very new religions. Christianity is around 2,000 years old. The African Yoruba religion has existed since AD 1100. Hinduism is the oldest religion still practiced—it began roughly 2,300 years ago. Nature and pre-Abrahamic religions (like Islam) predated these religions by several hundred years. Plants are associated with all types of religious philosophies because of the healing and nurturing properties plants have. Trees (because of the attributes and uses) go hand in hand with any magical ritual if you need fire, protection, nourishment, and healing.

There is no greater need for healing than the healing we need in this world from prejudicial practices and hatred toward each other, and folklore practitioners, in my own belief, are the deliverers of this message. Where there is social injustice, we as hoodoo workers fill the void.

In hoodoo and conjure, understanding the background of trees is necessary when working with BIPOC clients and understanding their connection to trees and sometimes the trauma that comes with them.

I have favorite trees all over the United States. One in Colorado in a canyon. One in Oregon in my favorite park. One in Nashville near a corporate complex. One in California. One in Kansas where my grandma and grandpa first kissed. I do have very positive tree stories. However, when working with your clients, if a tree comes up in their reading, be respectful and sensitive enough to walk through their experience with trees before recommending a spell you read on Facebook. Our very lives as a community are intertwined with trees—and not always in a good way.

My Dedication to a Tree

I look at you tree.
What you say to me is profound.
You have so much wisdom in your bark.
You outstretch yourself wide to anyone that will listen.
You line our neighborhoods, forests, and highways.
Your roots get in the plumbing system.
I don't blame you tree.
I know your spirit and your nature.
You call upon me to witness and honor.
I do so gratefully and without prejudice.
So many years ago, I would hang from you.
My final thoughts were one with you.
Your limbs supporting the rope that broke my neck.
I don't blame you, tree.
I know your spirit and your nature.
I worship you, and I lie down at your feet.
I am safe in your roots.
I am loved by your warm blanket of leaves.
I sniffle and sneeze when you bring forth more life.
I don't blame you, tree.
I know your spirit and your nature.
Let's share the sunlight, rain, and glucose water together.
You take in my pollution.
My harmful words.
My tearing of your roots when I need you to make a house for me
    and my family.
My orphaning you by spreading you in a laboratory or nursery.
My overharvesting of your true form and purpose.
You don't blame me.
You know my spirit and my nature.

TURNING GENERATIONAL CURSES INTO BLESSINGS

We talked about prayers, which brings me to the next thing that people
associate with hoodoo. The Curse. The Jinx. Hoodooing someone (as
a verb). Is it possible to curse, jinx, banish, or bind something using

hoodoo techniques? Yes, it certainly is. You can use any tool for negative or positive purposes. In hoodoo, there isn't this ruling of deliverance or not. Here's a scenario to explain deliverance in hoodoo.

Say you are in an abusive relationship and you need deliverance. The need is there, and you have the intention, faith, and direction. You intend to get out of the relationship, and you have faith that your ancestors and guides will give you that ability, and the direction is *out*! You need *out*. Maybe you need a place to stay, money to move, safety from the person, or a change of job.

There are superstitions around hoodoo workers (and those that wrongly confuse voodoo with hoodoo), and families have generational curses. You may have read of a friend of a friend that was convinced to pay thousands of dollars to remove generational curses from someone. The generational curse invariably caused the family member to have terrible luck—loss of employment or relationships, perhaps even suffered a stillbirth or miscarriage. The faux worker would then ask the client to come back for more blessing work (and to deliver another payment). This is another reason for ethics and morality around any spiritual work, and it is safe to say that this type of practice has harmed hoodoo workers. As a part of hoodoo foundations I want you to understand that there are Bible verses that mention curses:

> *Spirit punishes the children and their children for the sins of the ancestors to the third and fourth generation. (Exodus 34:7)*

> *The Universe is slow to anger, abounding in love and forgiving sin and rebellion. Yet they do not leave the guilty unpunished; they punish the children for the sin of the parents to the third and fourth generation. (Numbers 14:18)*

> *You shall not bow down to them or worship them; for the Highest of High is jealous and punishes the children for the sin of the parents to the third and fourth generation of those who hate me. (Deuteronomy 5:9)*

When practicing hoodoo, maybe you came from a lineage that believed in curses and taught you that you were part of them. That your struggles with addiction, fear, anxiety, loss, anger, and other troubles of being in this human form were caused by others in your ancestry that you had nothing to do with. Maybe you were also raised to believe that you had to remove this by fasting or prayer or self-flagellation (even if not literally but spiritually through extreme restriction or punishment). In #updatedhoodoo I want us to dive deeper into these passages in the Bible. Again, looking at it as a spell book. A book of myth and a book that helps some with understanding that root of their chosen faith. From a spell book standpoint, when items are repeated over and over it is (for an author's purpose) to ensure the message is delivered consistently. To make sure that the readers of the text had access to it when casting a spell. What is interesting in the generational curse passages is that they read almost word for word regardless of author. Is that possible?

Let's look at another scenario. You are with a group of friends at a movie. You all watch the movie and have separate experiences. Some love the movie, and some may not care for the movie at all. When you meet and discuss the movie afterward—maybe over tea or coffee—and you ask your friends about their favorite parts or they describe the plot and they all used the exact same phrasing to describe their experience, would you find that perplexing and suspicious?

I've read that memorizing something requires more than just hearing and reading something repeatedly. Typically, the best way to memorize something is to have an association—a connection with the words. Again, look at the passages from the Bible as a spell booklet. When using the text and separating the parts to make a spell, we have a few things in common:

- The authors want us to understand that there is a deity that is jealous and requires complete obedience.

- The authors want us to understand that there are negative ramifications when followers do not comply.

As a hoodoo practitioner, think of ways that this information can be used in spell work, especially when it comes to deliverance. How would you use this passage (if at all) to support or reject work you would be doing for deliverance? Possibly you wouldn't use them, but if you did, then the first component is to research what the deity's, ancestor's, or guide's understanding of obedience is. Obedience is when someone complies with an order to do something; that is a social influence where something or someone has the authority over someone or something else. Laws request obedience. Rules require obedience. Religions also in many cases require obedience. In spell work the ritual itself can be, to some, an act of obedience on behalf of the deity, ancestor, or guide. But this is not always negative. When your dentist recommends dental health care, they expect that you will continue the steps they prescribe for maximum benefit. In the Bible there is a warning or message that there is a life force or a deity that expects its instructions to be carried out, and if those instructions are not carried out, then the expected results of the spell will not be met. This unmet spell will continue to not work for generations. Almost like the definition of insanity. If my deity has told me to prepare a ritual in a certain way and I do not follow it, then I should not be confused when it doesn't work. Nor would I expect my lineage to have any other experience—it wouldn't work for them either.

I challenge you as you read the Bible to view it as a spell book and use it as you would a scientific or other reference book. Doing this objectively will help you take the emotion and the dysfunctional (to many) understanding from the words, and you can remove the guilt, pain, and anger, leaving you with what the true message is. And understand that repeatable steps are best when building a spell. Do you now see the passages differently? I do hope so, especially as you continue to practice hoodoo.

Enslaved Africans used this to tell of oral tradition of spells and conjure work. They would start with certain roots and herbs, add passages, recite prayers and chants, and have full understanding and faith that their efforts would work. And guess what? They did. Just as the text outlined.

Does this also mean that it could be the same for the opposite goal? Absolutely! When you notice that you have a client or are the client that is experiencing generational curses, then turn the passage to your advantage. Start with the intention to bring about generational blessings. Make repeatable steps that you will follow to honor your lineage, no matter where your background previously began. Start with the passage and its new understanding. The deity has shown you steps, that when repeated, will ensure your lineage is blessed from generation to generation.

Next, add herbs and roots that will bring you joy and happiness. There are several, but I would suggest a few of these to start: holy basil, rue, sweetgrass, and rosemary. Use this in your rootwork (in a bag, as a spiritual bath, in salt or sugar, and sprinkled as offerings to nature). Let your imagination keep you inspired. Bring yourself this joy and deliverance. Conjure up what your new generational blessing will be. The Bible spell book says in Habakkuk 2:2, "And the Spirit of All Spirits answered me, and said, Write the vision, and make [it] plain upon tables, that they may run that readeth it." Write your vision of your generational blessing in plain words. No need to get fancy. Then repeat these words again and again when you are tempted to believe that you are cursed.

Maybe use your favorite song lyrics that inspire you. For example, I like to think of Kelly Clarkson's song "Piece by Piece." She sings that she's going to put her child first (unlike in her experience of being abandoned by her father). It's a love story to her husband, her child, and to herself for being a survivor.

It costs you so much less than hiring a practitioner that may not have your best intentions at heart. Hoodoo practitioners know that they are responsible for their own deliverance, and they make it happen. I believe that you can do this too. Later in the book I give you several examples for how to use #updatedhoodoo to make spells, bags, text messages, and dollies. So keep reading and keep learning more hoodoo foundations.

◇◇◇◇◇ CHAPTER 2 EXERCISES ◇◇◇◇◇

Create Your Altar

There really isn't much to do except to do it. Add your intention, faith, and direction, and make an altar. No need to be fancy, but clean yourself, clean a space, place down your intentions that this will be your altar space, and make it happen.

My favorite type of altar is a matchbox altar. It's as big as it sounds. In a matchbox I place a tiny, tiny piece of herb and one Bible verse that is written on a small piece of paper in the smallest font I can do and then rolled up. I add a dab of blessed water or holy water. Finally, I put in a small object that I like (it could be a kernel of corn or a grain of rice to bring nutrition to the guide I am honoring) or a small object that represents my faith.

I hold my hands around the matchbox, and I say, "You are my altar for _____." I then keep it in a safe and sacred space. The reason to start your altar now is because your altar is an essential piece of your hoodoo, as your deliverance petitions are stored in it. It represents who you are as a worker because how you keep your altar is how you do your hoodoo. If you keep a sloppy or unkempt altar, then you probably aren't dedicating yourself to your deliverance practice.

Intention

This is an easy intention exercise. Ask yourself what you want. Really. Anything. Are you thirsty? What will help quench your thirst? Do you need money? Why? What will the money buy you? Do you want sex? What kind of sex? Be specific. Once you have your intention in order, then connect with yourself in your heart and ask *why*. Intention scripts go something like this:

Example 1: I, _____ (name), want _____ because _____.

That's as easy as it gets. You can also change it around a bit by saying,

Example 2: I'm asking you, _____ (ancestor, deity, or guide), to give me _____ (request) because _____.

Examples 1 and 2 are delivered with the other two tenets of hoodoo: faith and direction. Once you can state with conviction that you are asking for something, then you can move on to the next exercise.

Faith

Start by asking yourself about what you need. In my updated hoodoo the goal of your chants, spells, rituals, dolls, and Bible spells is for receiving deliverance. We first have to know what you are being delivered from before we can be delivered, so what do you need deliverance from? I will start with a very light and possibly whimsical example: I need to keep these mosquitoes away while hiking.

Then I begin with doing the preparation work that we discussed: clean body/clean mind, intention, shield or protection from possession, then develop the words from the Bible spell book. I do this by looking for keywords in my "hoodoo to go" Bible verse database. I have lovingly crafted this over years of doing hoodoo work. I have cross-referenced and cataloged this baby to a T. But as a new hoodoo practitioner, you will need to do your own. Begin with doing a web search on "Bible and protection" because you want to be protected from those mosquitoes. The keywords will bring up different suggestions from your browser, like these:

Bible verse protection for health

Bible verse protection from evil

Bible verse protection by angels

Bible verse protection from harm

Let's choose from these auto suggestions. Bible verse protection for health may help if you want deliverance from the effects of the mosquito bites, so maybe not use that one, but I would add it to my personal "hoodoo to go" search criteria for possibilities when I have any health deliverance requests. I would pop into the results and jot down a few of the recommended verses and then move on to the next search recommendation.

Bible verse protection from evil. Hmm, evil? Is that really what I'm wanting deliverance from? Not really a match. Mosquitoes aren't evil; they are just going about their day and wanting to live and feed. They are known to pass on diseases through bites and the transmission of blood (like malaria and encephalitis)—not evil, but certainly something to be protected from.

Protection by angels is good—especially if your faith is in angelic or seraphic energies. Did you know that there are several angel protectors in religion and in folklore? Any of these angels could be called upon in your deliverance call. Angels have a quiet magic in my experience, but still powerful. They protect by allowing us to have free will but also by giving us guidance on whether to do things that may or may not be against our best path. I keep Bible verses for protection by angels for those times when I want to have the best answers to something (like a test if I was in school). Angels are also great for object protection (like my home, car, or job). Angels protect and guide relationships (in whatever way is best). Angels can prevent harm, and they also can be asked to carry out harm (in the form of protection or guarding). To harm may seem like a negative word, but actually harm is defined as "to deliberately inflict injury." When I do a spell to ask for deliverance, then I am harming the person I am protected from because I am asking the angel to intercede on my behalf and prevent a force (physical, spiritual, or emotional) from harming me—even if that means injury. Injury isn't always a broken bone. Injury could be physically restricting their ability to move toward me. It could mean changing their mind or affecting their ability to move forward (if someone did this to me, then I would find it harmful), but it would be for protection as well.

Angelic protection is something I would add to my "hoodoo to go" database. These are generic enough to use for a multitude of deliverance requests (love, career, and justice work). I would go into the search criteria and add a few of these suggested verses for later use. I would update them to be more fitting to my own beliefs later—the important part is to gather the information for now. (Besides, I certainly don't want to limit the expectations of what angels can do, but maybe their time is better spent on something else.)

The final suggestion, "Bible verse protection from harm," is the best fit of all. It provides deliverance and is specific enough to bring forth what I need. I don't want the mosquitoes to harm me. I don't want them to physically interfere with me. I'm not asking my ancestors or guides how to do it (like to use angelic forces), but I do want them to restrict the mosquitoes and protect me from them so that they don't do me physical harm.

The search results might yield a few Bible verses. I would then look at the recommended Bible verses and choose accordingly. There are less helpful all the way to "100 percent yes, use this one" results. You'll get better at finding the right one. I would pray for guidance as part of this experience, and you may find that they begin to jump right out at you in your research.

Here are some Bible verses I found when I continued looking for "Bible verse protection from harm." Please note that I extracted these verses verbatim from the search—I will recraft the verse later on in the exercise, so feel free to skip over any words that you are sensitive to. The important thing is to distill the general theme and apply it to deliverance from mosquitoes.

> *The Lord keeps you from all harm and watches over your life. The Lord keeps watch over you as you come and go, both now and forever. (Psalm 121:7–8)*

> *But whoever listens to me will live in safety and be at ease, without fear of harm. (Proverbs 1:33–34)*

> *But the Lord is faithful; he will strengthen you and guard you from the evil one. (2 Thessalonians 3:3)*

> *The fear of the Lord leads to life; one will sleep at night without danger. (Proverbs 19:23)*

> *Those who live in the shelter of the Most High will find rest in the shadow of the Almighty. This I declare about the Lord: He alone is my refuge, my place of safety; he is my God, and I trust him. For he will rescue you from every trap and protect you from deadly disease. (Psalm 91:1–3)*

Given all these above, which one would you choose? My choice would be Psalm 91:1–3, which protects from being trapped and from disease.

Direction

Come with me down a path of the cardinal directions that are known to all languages. North, east, west, south. The directions of the world are all around us, and with our guides, ancestors, and deities, they offer us the most accurate way to get deliverance through conjure. Cardinal directions or points are typically read clockwise. North is the polar opposite of south, and east is the opposite of west. They are parts of the compass, the compass being an instrument that helps us find direction. We have so much in common as humans with navigation and geographic orientation. The navigation of our energies and spirits is in alignment with the directions of the compass in many traditions.

One well-known navigational system would be that of the Underground Railroad, which was the collaborative network of humans working together to aid freedom-seeking enslaved people get from the South to the North. For this reason, in hoodoo south is heat and it is a place where your history is but not necessarily where you want to be forever. South is a place to break away from. But before we go too deep into south, let's look at north.

NORTH

In some ancient wisdoms, north is green. During slavery north was a direction for hope and freedom. North can also mean a place for understanding and joy, where you go for freedom from thought. Where you can be present or meditate upon your deliverance request. It is also where you will send, reflect, or banish energies. If I want something to go to north, I will want it for education or knowledge or introspection. I will also use the north when I want to perfect my own understanding. For example, before and during the writing of my book, I channeled my direction toward the north so that I could research and better understand what to write. I kept my eye on the north. On my goal line and what I wanted to achieve. I focused on my intention to write the best book that Spirit desired. My faith helped me to understand that I have never failed at anything Spirit asked me to do. My faith also let me know that those that read my book would get what they needed. Finally, north was the direction of the energy to thrust my request into the atmosphere for it to be received and achieved.

North in Indigenous beliefs is cold and winter. Cleansing, snow, resting periods, hardships that you must endure, and the trials you will overcome. You cannot gain sage wisdom unless you've gone through a trial. When I donate blood, I want to go to someone who has the experience in drawing blood from several hundred patients, not someone making their first attempt. When I want deliverance from an addiction or harmful situation, I am in the middle of the winter, where I am stuck; and if I want to continue to grow and learn, I can conjure this direction. If I want to move out of this place, then I will need to conjure (through my intention, faith, and direction) the strategy of "out." No better direction than the north. North deities require obedience or offerings to perform work for the north. In Direction Deity physiology, deities' use of direction is specific to them. If I honor and respect and worship a deity of the north (let's say Mercury) then I am asking for a period to reflect and understand. Think of the cold winter frost we get here in many parts of the world. In that cooler weather you may feel like just wrapping up in a blanket, with something warm and taking a nap. Our bodies need more rest when its chilly. The direction of the north gives us this relief.

EAST

The sun rises from the east. The east gives you deliverance requests that manifest more understanding and better health and increase. This also means that if you direct your conjure while facing or directing the energy to the east, then it will give joy. Kenya is part of East Africa. Kenyans use ornamental bead work, vivid colors, and are warriors. The colors are varied, but when I think of the east, I use blues and greens and golds. When I look to the hills—to the east—from there comes my help. In religious understanding the east is where the wise people traveled from to find Jesus. When there was the exile of Babylon, the Israelites went to the east. I read about it best when I read this passage: "When you want to see the past and the present, you look east. When you know what you want and want to move toward that, then go to the west."

WEST

The fall is my favorite season. I personally recognize some of the pagan holidays (my favorite is Samhain) that welcome the new harvest. It is a time right before the winter where I can see leaves change before they completely fall away from the tree. I make apple and pumpkin and cinnamon-spiced desserts, and I also use dried apples in my conjure.

On Halloween I do a ritual for the New Year. I have done this for several years and it works every time. I start with my favorite wicker basket. I fill it with the things that I want to happen in the New Year (this is my intention). When my wife and I were first married we spread out a cheese board, apples (harvest), and wine for the gods to hear our prayers. We threw in chocolate to ensure our year together was sweet. I then added a dollar and change we had from our piggy bank and a few sprinkles of salt to make sure we were protected and that life would have flavor. We said a blessing over our life and love and our home and family. We prayed at exactly midnight that our next year gave us the same if not more than what we were given. We took this wicker basket filled with our intentions and the prayers (faith) and took it across the threshold of our home at midnight. We sealed our night by loving each other facing the west.

The west in the Bible signifies the Great Sea. Numbers 34:6 reads, "As for the western border, you shall have the Great Sea, that is, its coastline; this shall be your west border." The west is a gathering place. A place to go to and be from. It is a place to go to when you need rescue and refreshment. The sun sets in the west in the autumn and spring. When doing work at these times, be sure to face the west for best results.

SOUTH

As an African American I am both in love and also very sensitive to the word *south*. South makes me think of summers and gorgeous, lush flowers and scents. Hospitality, being kind to one another. Being dressed up in bespoke outfits and large hats. Mint juleps and cornbread. The South also brings to mind antebellum, enslavement, prejudice, racial tensions, inequality, and restrictions. When I think of the far south (Mexico), I think of migrant workers harvesting plants and fruits, laboring for pennies a day. I think of Texas where a man was killed by being dragged through the streets, bound to a truck. In Indigenous tradition the south is emotional and the summer (heat). It's about how we deal with each other. When I do work from the direction of the south, I want to bring heat. Not always anger or frustration but sometimes action—I want things to move with the speed of fire. Not the glacial speed of ice.

Moss Spell

What kind of deliverance request would I use for a moss spell? Well, any request that needs lots of coverage, like a good piece of gossip or a rumor. Moss will spread anything you want—not quickly, but it will blanket it. So, if you want your cancer to remain in remission, I will put this request onto a large blanket of moss. If you want steady income, I will bring this request to moss. If you want protections from systems that are outside of your authority but have a huge impact on you personally, I will ask moss. Why? Because of moss's natural ability in the forest to insulate, protect, and spread.

Before interrupting the moss blanket, ask permission and take as small of a sample as you need for your work. Or even better, take a picture and do not disturb this network of spore-bearing plant systems.

Using this sample (and the sample should be very small—a dime-sized amount is plenty), thank the ancestor, guide, or deity and touch the stems and branches that make up this system. Talk to the fibers and give them your request. Place your hand upon the moss blanket that your sample came from and thank it for being here on the earth as a perfect example of how the plant life is so resilient when left alone. Ask the plant system to carry your request across its root system for as far as it reaches. Remove your hand. If you have some, leave a few drops of water as payment for the amount you took.

Words you may say:

Moss, my friend and plant family,

I come to you with this urgent need.

I know that you can carry out this message to Mother Gaia through your root system.

I need help.

I need _____ (enter your plea for help).

I need protection.

I am believing that you will carry this message to whichever life source will help me with my request.

(Now pour the water onto the moss sample.)

I thank you and offer this nourishment to you.

(Place the moss on your altar.)

End with your own benediction that speaks to your faith. For me I might say, "In God's name." You may say, "In Hecate's name," or "To the science that supports it," or something else.

Then you leave the moss (keep it moist) on your altar while it does its work. When the work is delivered or you feel satisfied, then return the moss to the forest you found it in or return it to a damp, darkened area. Never take it to a sunny location.

Water

I want to show you the first thing my grandma taught me about how to clean things. Take a clean glass. Pour some tap water into it and put your good thoughts, your most sacred words, your love, and breath into it. Speak into the water and thank it for giving itself to you. Then drink the water and allow it to soothe anything that ails you or fails you. Hoodoo is simple and profound. It takes water to clean things thoroughly, including ourselves. I drink water when I feel ready to take on a new hoodoo project. When I am building a new spell. When I am praying for a client. When I need clarity. I bless my water and then drink it down. I also use my water as an offering to my ancestors, guides, and deities. If I need refreshment, why wouldn't my ancestors? Respect goes a long way in hoodoo.

The water exercise is known among many spiritual workers. As you continue to learn that simple deliverance can be done with just water, I hope you are inspired to do more exercises.

Dr. Masaru Emoto's study can be found on several sites, but I located this one: https://thewellnessenterprise.com/emoto. You may purchase a copy of his book, *The Hidden Messages in Water*—and I encourage you to do so—from any reputable bookseller.

Second glass of water Bible verses:

The Spirit of the Universe appears to you in the past and said, "I have loved you with an everlasting love; I have drawn you with unfailing kindness." (Jeremiah 31:3)

And over all the virtues put on love, which will connect them all together in perfect unity. (Colossians 3:14)

Love always protects, always trusts, always hopes, always perseveres. (Corinthians 13:7)

Third glass of water Bible verses:

They said to Moses, "Take vengeance on the Midianites for the Isra-elites. After that, you will be gathered to your people." So Moses said to the people, "Arm some of your men to go to war against the Midianites so that they may carry out vengeance on them. Send into battle a thousand beings from each of the tribes of Israel." So twelve thousand beings armed for battle, a thousand from each tribe, were supplied from the clans of Israel. Moses sent them into battle, a thou-sand from each tribe, along with Phinehas son of Eleazar, the priest, who took with them articles from the sanctuary and the trumpets for signaling. They fought against Midian, as they were instructed by Moses, and killed every soldier. Among their victims were Evi, Rekem, Zur, Hur, and Reba—the five kings of Midian. They also killed Balaam child of Beor with the sword. The Israelites captured the Midianite partners and children and took all the Midianite herds, flocks and goods as plunder. They burned all the towns where the Midianites had settled, as well as all their camps. They took all the plunder and spoils, including the people and animals, and brought the captives, spoils and plunder to Moses and Eleazar the priest and the Israelite assembly at their camp on the plains of Moab, by the Jordan across from Jericho. Moses, Eleazar the priest and all the leaders of the community went to meet them outside the camp. Moses was angry with the officers of the army—the commanders of thousands and commanders of hundreds—who returned from the battle. "Have you allowed all the partners to live?" he asked them. "They were the ones who followed Balaam's advice and enticed the Israelites to be unfaithful in the Peor incident, so that a plague struck the people. Now kill all the children. And kill every partner who has ever had sex. Save for yourselves every virgin." (Numbers 31:2–18)

You and Eleazar the priest and the family heads of the community are to count all the people and animals that were captured. Divide the spoils (human beings and animals) equally between the soldiers who took part in the battle and the rest of the community. (Numbers 31:26–27)

And Jephthah made a vow to the Spirit: "If you give the Ammonites into my hands, whatever comes out of the door of my house to meet me when I return in triumph from the Ammonites will be the Lord's, and I will sacrifice it as a burnt offering." Then Jephthah went over to fight the Ammonites, and the request was granted. Jephthah devastated twenty towns from Aroer to the vicinity of Minnith, as far as Abel Keramim. Thus, Israel subdued Ammon. When Jephthah returned to his home in Mizpah, who should come out to meet him but his child, dancing to the sound of timbrels! Jephthah's only child. When Jephthah saw her, Jephthah tore Jephthah's clothes and cried, "Oh no, my child! You have brought me down and I am devastated. I have made a vow to that I cannot break." "My parent!" the child replied, "you have given your word to our Deity. Do to me just as you promised, now that the Deity has avenged you of your enemies, the Ammonites. But grant me this one request," the child said. "Give me two months to roam the hills and weep with my friends, because I will never marry as I will be burned." Jephthah allowed the child to go. After two months, the child returned to Jephthah and Jephthah fulfilled his offering by burning Jephthah's child. (Judges 11:30–39)

Self-Love

When is the last time you loved yourself? I was reading for a group of souls recently, and I came into conversation with an ancestor and a client. The client looked perfectly happy. Well spoken, beautifully dressed, not pushy or forward. However, their ancestor yelled at me to really look at them for who they are. They shouted at me to tell the client a few things like "When will you get a newer pillow? How many glasses of water are you drinking?" It's okay to say "No, I'm busy" or "I'm staying home today to love myself."

In 1 Corinthians 13 (that some people use for weddings and ceremonies but gloss over "the goods") it says: "If I use human and angelic words and don't have love, then I'm just making noise. If I understand everything and have all the knowledge in the world and just as much faith but do not love, then I have nothing."

As you read these words, I want you to know that in intention, faith, and direction, many may have told you that you have to have those things toward a certain being or deity, but that is only part of the picture. The larger part is that with all of the knowledge and abilities that your hoodoo guides will give you, and even those that I share in this book, it means nothing if you do not know in your heart and soul that you are worthy of love. Not just any love but self-love. The kind of love that helps you hear the right things when you are connecting to deity. The love that encourages you to keep going when you feel like giving up. The love that helps you with discerning if that future lover is truly worthy of your time. I could go on with other examples in career, family, relationships, communications, and challenges. They all revolve around one thing and that is having the bravery to step aside from what some may tell you is love and find it for yourself.

It starts with water, continues with words, and ends with wine (or dessert).

Every now and then my mom would gather us kids, and we would take the family car to the grocery store in the middle of the night and purchase fruit. Fruit was a big deal to me and my brother because we lived on government subsidies, and having a meal that was filling to all five of us was to have a meal full of fats and carbohydrates because they gave us satiety. Eating vegetables in my household meant opening a can of peas or corn and putting a tiny amount near a mound of mashed potatoes and buttered bread. That held us and kept us growing and able to not fall asleep in classes the next day. Maybe it didn't give us the most nutrition to sustain our academic needs, but it worked.

So off to the store we would go, usually after my mom finished her second job (so that meant late at night). We would head to the fresh fruit section, which was just being refreshed for the next day. I saw rows and rows of colors. Green, yellow, orange, red, purple. All of the choices. Each of us would get one or two dollars to spend on whatever kind of fruit we wanted. I rarely got red apples because they were ordinary to me. Instead I found rare fruits. Cherries, watermelon, cantaloupe, tangerines, pears, and limes were my favorite. I learned that limes and salt and pepper were delicious. I learned that I liked only the rind of the watermelon, so I stopped getting that. Instead I would choose oranges and plums and would gleefully take those to class with me for the week. If I cut them very small, they would last until the following weekend. I can imagine what it was like to savor each one of these delicacies and how I would prepare them and lovingly save them in plastic containers to keep them fresh.

This was my mom's way of showing us how to love ourselves. I learned several different ways to self-love, including masturbation as I grew older, but fruit has been one of my favorite splurges.

In our shared ancestry we may have been told that our deities required obedience. Wasn't it in the Bible in Colossians 3:20? Children must obey their parents. It was repeated again in Ephesians 6. Speaking of Ephesians 6, right after obedience in regard to children to their parents, there is the cringe-worthy verse that reads, "Slaves obey your earthly masters with respect and fear just as you would your chosen deity." It goes on to say that this is because you will be rewarded in the next place for what good you do here. Yikes! How many enslaved people heard this rhetoric in Sunday service after being beaten, tortured, and sexually assaulted by their enslavers or by the designated speakers for the enslavers in the form of ministers?

In magical workings we know that obedience to ritual and ceremony can be flexible. For updated hoodoo it certainly is. If I need salt in my ritual and I can only find white table salt and not pink or gray salt, then I use what I have. If I am doing a ritual using paper and I have paper bags and not notepad paper, then so be it. Obedience is subjective. The only thing I want you to know in hoodoo is that our shared ancestors learned that love meant being obedient to yourself in love. Speaking up for your rights because you loved yourself enough to do so. Living a magical life and finding more ways to use the Bible as a spell book was because you loved doing so for you, not because a religious leader told you to. Inclusive prayers for yourself and your community are important as loved members of the world we live in, because we have visions of the world that we want to see.

Let's look at how to ritually love yourself. I have a few ways that I enjoy. As I mentioned, it takes water, words, and maybe wine or dessert. Let's start with water. At the beginning of chapter 1 I mentioned that before you use any sacred text or object, we need to be clean. I take showers for many reasons: because it is hygienic, because I want to smell good to my partner and those I encounter in the day, because it feels good to me. Those are all great reasons. In metaphysical ceremony we wash our body out of respect to the practice. I want us to go deeper.

In updated hoodoo I challenge you to wash your body for yourself because it is one way (of many) that you practice self-love. To do this properly you will clean the shower or tub or bucket that you will bathe in. You can do this with vinegar or salt or water or a mixture of all three. As you clean, recite this (or a similar contextual reference).

I am cleaning you because you will come in contact with my body.

My body is a vessel of love.

My love is of myself as a reflection of faith, intention, and direction.

My body is a divine work of the universe that I take space in in this moment.

Once the area is clean, it's time for you to get in and get clean. Make it a special time. Light your favorite candles. Turn on your favorite music. Use your favorite essential oils. Wear your favorite robe. Add some almond or other sweet oil in the water to moisturize yourself if you choose. Pick some flowers or leaves that inspire you and adorn your cleansing place with them.

After you have cleansed yourself, pat your body down and admire yourself in the mirror. Notice how your body's skin changes when it is wet or dry. Look at all the parts of your body that make you extraordinarily you. Notice your arms, legs, stomach, neck, face, and hair. If any parts are not there, honor what occurred that took those parts and realize you are still a whole person. See how your hair texture may differ from your head to your underarms to your genitals to your arms and legs. Touch your skin and watch if it changes color or stays the same. Discover your warts, pimples, dimples, folds, and curves, and tell each place that you touch "I love you!" This may take a while, so put on your robe if you need to, but stay naked if you can. Touch the soles of your feet and pay attention to their wrinkles and each and every toe. How many steps have these feet taken for you? Squeeze them and tell them "I love you."

Work your way up from your feet to your ankles to your calves. Squeezing and touching and speaking your words of "I love you" with the same emotion you would to a lover you were just enjoying for the first time or to something you held precious that you never wanted to leave. Keeping your mind on your body, lie down on a flat surface (like a bed or couch or outdoors if you dare and feel safe). Close your eyes and go inside yourself, starting at the inside of your body with your feet. Think of all the muscles, tendons, nerves, and cells that make you complete. Tell all the components inside your body that you love them too. Don't forget your organs (your skin being the largest one), and move into your brain, lungs, and heart. Don't forget your eye sockets, your nasal passages, or the bones in your fingers. The fatty part of your bottom. It's all you, and it is all about you. Continue this self-love as long as you'd like. Moving your fingers up and down and back up again. Your hair and its follicles, your nose, your ears—no part of you should not be investigated and loved.

Now put on your clothing. What outfit of yours says how much you love yourself? Wear that. Take care in your application of any makeup or any moisturizing of your skin. Don't rush getting dressed; love yourself while doing it. Put on your shoes. Love your hair and put it in a style that you love. Look in the mirror, telling yourself in the reflection that you are loved, and tell yourself how much you adore you and how grateful you are that you chose this body to share with you.

Prepare your ceremonial meal. With the same enthusiasm that you may feel when you share a meal with a celebrity, a beloved ancestor, or a loved friend, make this meal from and for things that you enjoy. Not caring about any other person's allergies or preferences. You are what matters today. After the meal is prepared, whisper words of love to it. Here's something you may want to say:

I am worthy of all of this love that I have to offer.

I accept and love myself exactly like this.

Damn, I love me!

My body is so beautiful; I love it so much.

I am such a masterpiece.

I am everything I thought I could be.

My mind, body, and soul do so much, and I love all of what I represent.

Enjoy the meal you prepared and take your time to enjoy every morsel (or as much as you want to be satisfied). Once the meal is complete, leave a small amount and offer it to your altar as a self-love sacrifice with a small glass or cup of water.

After the meal is over, enjoy any after-meal experience you want. To some this may be an alcoholic beverage; to others it may be dessert; to others, more meditation; maybe even a nice lingering masturbatory celebration of self-love. Choose what you want to do without prejudice or guilt. Look at yourself in the mirror, and smile again.

> Dare to love yourself
> as if you were a rainbow
> with gold at both ends.
>
> —*Author and poet Aberjhani, Journey through the Power of the Rainbow: Quotations from a Life Made out of Poetry*

In hoodoo how you love yourself shows in how you can and do the spell work required to cause true deliverance. With the same deliberate ceremony for your self-love, I encourage you to choose portions for experiencing and loving your guides, ancestors, and deities in the chapters that come.

Don't forget to say "Damn, I love me!"

NOTE

1   Matthew Swayne, "Map Shows Lynching Went Far Beyond the U.S. South," Futurity, May 16, 2019, www.futurity.org/lynching-map-united-states -history-2064252/.

3

ETHICAL HOODOO

How was chapter 2? Let's recap what we've learned so far:

- Trigger words. Research yours and allow yourself to change your tools to align with your values. Include sacred texts such as the Koran, Bible, Torah, Gospel of Buddha, and Masonic Rituals.

- The intention, faith, and direction are the tenets of hoodoo. They are your North Star when you create your rituals. They can be taken individually, but all three are required for my way of building my spells and rituals because they ensure you have real power behind them.

- The Bible is a spell book (just like other sacred texts listed in the first recap item) and is to be used in hoodoo accordingly. Search for and find text that works for your spells and, without judgment, leave anything that doesn't meet that goal. Change words, phrases, and agenda to match your intention, faith, and direction. This is hoodoo for everyone. Adding crystals, tarot cards, or picking the perfect herb is nothing without intention, faith, and direction.

◆ Build your altar, pick your offerings, and sacrificial objects, in no particular order, but build them. Your altar is your home base. Without it your offering and objects will not have a foundation.

◆ If you have a generational curse, then turn it into a blessing. This may be something as simple (but complex) as an addiction to a substance like candy. Why remove these? It's easier to do your work for others if you have done your own work. Feed yourself first as a hoodoo worker so that you are nutritionally solvent to feed others.

If you have any thoughts or questions around these points, then go back and read through the chapter again when you are in a prayerful and thoughtful state. Continue working through chapters 1 and 2 until you are ready to understand how to practice by learning about my walk in hoodoo.

CODE OF ETHICS

When I read for clients, I let them know about my ethics first. My ethics are the morals that tell me as a being what behavior is acceptable. I do not read or have sessions with everyone. I am very choosy and let my guides tell me who to see and who not to see. If you have never given a psychic reading, giving a reading means you sit down in front of someone and you hear their need for deliverance. Sometimes the person tells you everything. Other times they expect you to be a mind reader, and they say nothing except "Tell me what you see for me." I'm fine either way. I'm here to help them as their reader. Then I tell them after communing with the energies that I connect with what the energies' response is.

This becomes a cycle, a dance if you will. A beneficial conversation where we open the session, obtain trust, connect, and share messages from Spirit. Then, just as quickly as you can say sixty minutes, it is over. This whole formed, perfect relationship is over. But just like any communication, there has to be rules of the game. What do we do and when? What makes us comfortable in this sixty-minute relationship? What are deal breakers? These are the basics of a code of ethics.

Each one of us has morals that are unique, and some are universal. As a hoodoo worker you will be asked to do many things. What kinds of things? Let me give you some examples of what I've been asked to do in a hoodoo reading. After reading these things ask yourself, would you give answers if you were told to by a spirit? This becomes your ethical baseline. Here are some situations I've been presented with:

- Can you make my partner come back to me?
- My house is possessed by a spirit or entity, and it is hurting us. Can you help?
- I want to get revenge on (insert situation). Will you help?
- Can you tell me when my family member will pass away?
- Will I get the job?
- Can you harm or kill someone?
- Can you make sure my employer's business fails?
- Can you make sure I don't lose my house?
- Will I ever find anyone to love?
- What gender will my child be?
- I have this particular (ache, pain, cyst, infection, headache, allergy, insert another symptom). What do you think it is?
- Will I win the lottery?
- When will the money, insurance settlement, inheritance, etc. be given to me?
- When will I get a new house, car, business, (object or thing)?

What are morals? Morals are tied directly to your ethics. Morals are your sense of what is right and wrong. Ethics tell you what is evil or negative and what is good or positive. Morals can be standard ways to act in a society, like "We speak to each other truthfully." Ethics are "I respect you as a person." You may decide not to read for someone because their request goes against your ethical framework or because they go against your personal morals.

I believe in ethical and moral readings. I don't want to tell you anything that is illegal, harmful, or downright wrong. Even more than that, I am bound by my own spiritual understanding of what I can and cannot do as a hoodoo practitioner. I feel that I know my ancestors and my guides and that they all have bound me in truth to do what work is for me. For example, I worked in the corporate world. There were people I interacted with that sometimes weren't the easiest or most professional to work with. During those times I had an option to do darker hoodoo where I would harm them. Believe me, I have the ancestors that would do it! Instead, my dad, very quietly, told me what to do to give me deliverance without losing myself—yes, me—in anger, fear, and vengeance. This works for me.

However, this does not mean that you do not need to do work that matches your own ethical and moral appetite. Walk through my code of ethics as an example for ideas. When you are working with your guides and your clients' guides (because I don't think I work with the client, I work with their people), come up with guidelines that match your code. When you do your work (start with your own personal readings), what are ethics you can go by? Here are some starting questions to answer for your code of hoodoo ethics:

- Do you do readings that harm?
- Do you do readings that will call upon being possessed?
- When do you do readings?
- Do you read for people of all gender identities, sexual orientations, faiths, or religions? If not, whom do you exclude if they do not match your own morals?
- Do you refer clients to other hoodoo practitioners if you cannot read for them?
- What are your policies for promptness to appointments?
- Do you allow same-day readings or emergency readings?

- Do you allow reschedules and cancellations? If so, how much notice do you need? (Consider using hours, like twenty-four-hours' notice.)

- Do you require deposits for work? This is especially important when making hoodoo work that requires materials.

- Do you do substitutions if the herbs are not available? How do you make sure this is okay with the client?

- Do you do readings on clients that are under the influence of mind-altering substances?

- Who is your ideal client, and what do they need to know to feel safe in hiring you for their hoodoo needs?

- Do you do work that brings deliverance when someone wants to win back a lover, partner, other intimate relationship?

- Do you do vengeance work?

- Do you do work on the behalf of the client that will cause separation, divorce, financial hardships?

- Do you do work on behalf of the client that will cause personal harm?

- Do you do work on behalf of the client that will diagnose or treat medical or mental health concerns (see my chapter on legal responsibility)?

- Do you allow recording of your sessions?

- Can the client share their recordings with others, or are they still classified as your property and require approval before sharing, posting on social media sites, etc.?

- Do you allow photographing of your hoodoo works (bags, spells, amulets, table setting, washes)? If so, do you allow the client to photograph just before you start or when the work has been given "energy or love"?

- Do you want client testimonials to be available on your site or social media?

- Do you keep all client information private? If so, how?

- Do you always receive financial reimbursement for your work?
- Do you guarantee results?
- Do you offer refunds?

My code of hoodoo ethics was built from my own experience as a professional tarot reader, event facilitator, and hoodoo/conjure worker. I answered all of these questions for myself and blended them with other hoodoo ethics that I have taken from other practitioners that I trust and respect.

It's okay to keep building onto your hoodoo ethics as you grow and as your comfort level increases. Ask your clients what they want and see if your hoodoo ethics conflict with that—that is always a good start. Better yet (and even beforehand) ask your *ancestors* and *guides* what should be included in what *they* will and will not do with you and for the client.

Here is my code of hoodoo ethics. As a purchaser of this book, you are free to use my ethical code. If you did *not* purchase the book, then please do *not* use it.

THAT HOODOO LADY'S CODE OF ETHICS

Sessions are informational in nature and will not take the place of a diagnosis or treatment from a qualified professional (such as a licensed therapist, lawyer, accountant, or physician).

My client information is kept confidential, and I do not discuss the nature or conversations of our readings.

I will notify the proper professional authority (licensed therapist, healthcare professionals, or police) if I feel that our conversation will cause harm to other people—even you.

I may request to record our appointment to provide you a copy for your own personal use that will be held on my secured server for a period of seven business days. You will receive a link to this address. I am not responsible for unauthorized access to this audio recording.

If you wish to make your own audio or photographic images at our appointment, feel free to do so. These are yours for your own personal use. If you distribute them to others, I require that you obtain my permission prior to distribution.

Violence, threatened violence, or other illegal conduct is not permitted, and I will report it to law enforcement authorities.

I will do my best to treat you as you would like to be treated. As part of this process, I require honesty, respect, and professional courtesy during our appointment.

I charge an hourly appointment rate, and I require payment at the time of service. A sliding scale fee is available and must be discussed and agreed upon before the appointment begins.

Home blessing and ritual rates are commensurate upon the size of the property and the complexity of what is encountered when I do a scan of the spirits and entities of the home. Also, there may be additional fees for subcontractor healers as I feel appropriate.

You are never required to purchase additional consultations or products as part of our consultation services.

Meetups, classes, and seminars may have their own fees and will be posted well before the class's start date. Payment is required at the time of services (as applicable).

I make every attempt to be physically and mentally present and request that you be as well. I do not conduct appointments under any influence of drugs or alcohol.

I request that clients mute or turn off any electronic devices (I make exceptions for the purposes of personal listening as described above).

I do not conduct appointments under any influence of drugs or alcohol, and I will not continue consultations with clients that appear to be under the influence as well.

I request that our consultations begin on time unless arrangements have been made twenty-four hours prior. Failure to make our agreed-upon appointments may result in a failure to continue receiving readings.

I request that I have accurate information on all clients for my accounting and administrative use in a secured, confidential location.

I may refer you to qualified professionals and resources to continue your journey and path.

I may cancel the appointment and offer a refund at any time during the appointment if this is the best option.

There they are—my code of ethics as a hoodoo worker. Think about what your ethics are and answer for yourself before you consider working with a client. Before sitting in a café and putting out a sign that lets people know that you are ready, make sure that you, inside of your heart and body, are ready too—to read and do things that are outside of your comfort zone, to help make the best sixty-minute relationship ever for the both of you and whichever guides work through and with you. Once you have done this and built your own personal code of ethics, feel free to write it here on these pages.

My personal code of ethics as a hoodoo worker:

I am most comfortable when this can happen in a reading:

My wants for the client are:

I am comfortable with doing:

I am not comfortable with the following:

Insert any answers to the questions you have thought about or answers to questions I posed to you in the notes section or a separate document that you can use in the future. Congratulations! You now have a personal code of ethics.

MY FIRST TAROT READING

When I first started out as a hoodoo worker, I began as a tarot reader. In my training, after reading cards for months on my own and to my tarot teacher (yes, I went through a course with a professional), I was finally ready ... to read tarot for free. I sat in a café with a small sign that read "Free tarot readings with Sherry." I'll never forget the terror I felt when I had someone sit down in front of me. They were probably as nervous as me, and they uttered those words, "I want a reading." I was so excited. I was finally doing it! I remembered everything in order:

- Make the client comfortable.
- Empathize.

- Protect yourself by putting up your shield.
- Remember the card meanings and help them to understand the meaning as it applies to them.

And so on it went.

I had so many rules in my head that I'm sure my client felt they were going for a doctor's examination or a cross-examination. In the years that I taught tarot and became the co-organizer of the largest tarot meetup in North America, I learned to relax on the rules and instead look into my own sense of self and connect with the cards. When I did that, I noticed the cards really spoke to me. I could hear each little image give me information that didn't resonate with the descriptions of cards that I read. They got louder and louder the more that I listened. These pieces of paper written over in ink were helping me to understand what was happening to the client. It was something that I'll never forget because it taught me the importance of listening to myself and that part of me that I couldn't put my finger on at the time—maybe you've felt the same thing?

I continued with the reading, but in my next readings, after I had connected with my client, I learned to listen to myself and that very quiet voice that I would hear. I didn't know what it was because I hadn't connected the voice with the same voice I heard when I was in the church. It sounded like me, but I knew it wasn't really me. I needed to figure out which voice was mine and which was external to me. That is another lesson that any hoodoo foundations worker must learn—that we all have these intuitive voices in our head. Some are us, some are external to us, some are speaking to us from another existence that is larger than us. To know yourself, figure out deep inside of your heart and mind and soul, your very being, who are you? Do you have prejudices or judgments that will interfere with a reading? Do you have a handle on your emotional stress or health conditions? Is your home life interrupting your ability to read? Are you distracted or are you present? The largest question ever is: Can you read for this person and give them your entire self for the entire duration of the reading without bringing in personal judgments and opinions? If so, then you may, and I mean may, be ready. Your ethics will tell you. Your morals will give you more boundaries.

RESPONSIBILITY OF A HOODOO WORKER

Being a healer is a great responsibility. A healer is someone who can make someone feel better by means other than traditional medicine. Many of y'all do this already with foods, kind words, song, art, poetry, dance, and just being there for a friend or loved one when they need help. I do it with hoodoo. There you are. You are a healer. Now that you know you are a healer, it is all in how you heal. But being a healer in the community and spiritual realm is different. There is a responsibility when you are a healer that I do want you to acknowledge and keep close to your heart. When you heal in the name of an ancestor or guide, then you are responsible—yes, responsible—for the actions and results of that healing. That may frighten you if you have a solid sense of awareness of the weight of my words. For example, if someone hires me to help remove them from a situation that is no longer serving them, I connect with that person's guides, ancestors, and deities, and together we build out a plan. The guides, ancestors, and deities might ask me to prepare by cleaning myself with sugar or herbs or a specific root of an herb like ginger or verbena or lemon balm. They may require that I go into a trance and work with the client's spiritual ancestor. They may require a specific offering, such as a personal effect or a particular object. I listen and carry this out to the letter. Then I check in with my client to make sure they are satisfied and comfortable with the results. If there is more work to do, then I continue with the deliverance spells until we have received satisfaction for the client or they request that I stop. What if this doesn't work out? What if what I expected doesn't happen? Sometimes healing isn't about the client getting what they want; it's more about the client being healed of the issue and pointing out they are healed *because* they didn't get what they wanted.

After the healing, I give offerings to the guides, ancestors, and deities on behalf of my client. That may be a simple thank-you or it may require physical chants, songs, drums, cymbals, scents, or objects that will satisfy their request. I do this until the guides or deities are satisfied.

Practitioners tell each other all the time that we get the clients that will give you answers to what your guides, ancestors, and deities need *you* to hear. Be ready for that. Be ready to hear that you and the client will both learn from guides, ancestors, and deities, and the sixty-minute relationship will hopefully make you both better.

Warning: Healing is a duty and a gift. It is a contract with the guides, ancestors, deities, and the client. There are consequences to healing for the healer as well. If not done correctly through vigilant ritual work and protection, you can yourself become harmed or injured. Yes, injured. I have had nightmares, been physically scraped, bitten, burned, and hit by energies and forces during a healing. I have also seen others attempt to do hoodoo as a healing without working with the correct guides, ancestors, and deities, or not understanding their energies, and they end up hospitalized, or worse, with unknown illnesses that baffle doctors. I have seen witches and hoodoo workers that have died as a result of a wrongly worked trick or conjure.

It is serious work and not to be done by anyone that is unsure or hesitant. If you do not have the time to do the work, then appreciate those that do by working with true professional healers. If you are still unsure of your healing ability or even plain don't want to accept you are a healer, then thank you for being honest. You do not have to heal because you *can*. I *can* climb the tree in my front yard to cut down some limbs, but that doesn't mean I have any desire to. I'd rather hire an arborist.

In this book I will give you the hoodoo foundations that you need to become an excellent hoodoo practitioner of #updatedhoodoo. To protect you from making the mistakes that I shared above, I will go step-by-step with you as you learn more about me. Then I will learn more about you, and together we will learn the basics of hoodoo.

DIVERSITY, EQUITY, AND INCLUSION

Many of us have two different ways to make a living in the spiritual world. We have one muggle job (or many), and we have one spiritual job (or many). In my muggle job I am a leader in the corporate world. In this corporate role we drafted a diversity, equity, and inclusion (DEI) statement so that future clients and prospective new team members would know how we stood as a company and to provide a safe space for all beings. A DEI statement consists of how a company's values and experiences advance diversity, equity, and inclusion in their work. In the old tradition of hoodoo, I couldn't really say that there would be a DEI statement I could write in good faith. This is because most hoodoo workers came from a background of using the Bible as a spell book (check—I do that) and they use prayer, spiritual bathing, and other tools to obtain deliverance (gotcha—me too).

However, where I begin and others end is that in That Hoodoo Lady hoodoo foundations, I believe that all are included, regardless of culture, faith, body image, gender identification, sexual orientation, place of origin, or spiritual craft acceptance. You may find some practitioners not going this far. They may teach you hoodoo … if you have an African American lineage. They will teach you hoodoo … if you come from a heterosexual background. They will work with you as a client … if you believe in Jesus and the monolithic belief system that there is one God that is part of the Holy Trinity. There are other ways I differentiate Hoodoo Lady foundations from others, but this hopefully gives you an idea.

If you are called by your ancestors, deities, and guides to practice hoodoo, then I am not to get in the way. I am to help you in hoodoo foundations so that you and your guides can begin a relationship and you can have a strong foundation in the tenets of hoodoo that I believe, which is that hoodoo is for deliverance using intention, faith, and direction. No special tools are required except for an exceptionally gifted spiritual foothold in what makes African American hoodoo special and important. Why do I qualify with African American? Because it is different. In conjure and folklore magic there are many types of practices. There is Slavic folklore magic, kitchen witch folklore magic, Afro-Cuban folklore magic, animism folklore magic, and more. The similarities are that the folklore magic practitioners may utilize faith-based magic for a purpose, using everyday items and tools. I do this too, but I do it from my own background and culture—which includes my experiences as a Black person from North America, specifically the South and Midwest (Mississippi, Georgia, Texas, Oklahoma, and Kansas). Pride for this background is built into every spell, bath, herbal bag, and cologne. That is part of me. When you build up your hoodoo experience, you will need to take stock of your culture and experiences and merge those like a stew into your DEI statement.

Begin with something as simple (and complex) as your identity. Who do you identify as? I provided my background at the start of the book, but from a DEI standpoint I value culture and ethnic diversity. I will work with anyone and help introduce them to hoodoo, with a caveat that they build a fundamental knowledge of the Black experience as North Americans. This is crucial because it helps us to speak a similar language if we know each other's backgrounds. I won't be able to hear yours, but I want you to introduce yourself to your hoodoo spiritual practice. You do this by continuing to read through the chapters and using them as chances to integrate the ancestors, deities, and guides that I write about into your daily life. Begin simply by saying hello to those that I offer. Then allow yourself to meditate or reflect upon your own special upbringing. Imagine how you would have handled situations that I identify or how your experience was different. As there will always be differences, find the commonalities, and more importantly, find acceptance that the differences with the unique lenses are natural. You will never be me, and I will never be you, but together we make requests to our shared ancestors, deities, and guides for the same cause—deliverance.

Next in the diversity statement is simplicity. As hoodoo was created by enslaved individuals in the American South, the language in the DEI statement should be very easy to understand, maybe eight to twelve words per sentence.

Who do you value? Why do you value them? Is your language positive and affirming? These are important in a DEI statement and how you work with clients. I can imagine our shared ancestors wanting freedom from exclusion and persecution and needing to feel at home where they landed. If you practice hoodoo with a bunch of restrictions, then how does that resonate with diversity, equity, and inclusion? If it doesn't, you may want to look at your hoodoo statement again.

In conjure workings where you are possessing or calling about the possession contract with a spirit, then you come up with the same type of agreement. You are making sure the spirit knows the rules and that you have your own boundaries that you declare in the contract. This can happen before you meet or even agree to speak with the spirit, or it can be after being introduced. Like when you first start reading for a client, their ancestors, guides, and deities will introduce themselves, and you will give them your DEI statement, and they will share theirs. In the introduction you both describe yourselves and help each other understand each other's values and what is and is not acceptable. In hoodoo we are all equitable, meaning that hoodoo is not bound to any belief, deity, or faith. It works for any and all of us. As long as you have the intention, faith, and direction, then you are practicing hoodoo. Practitioners of hoodoo start with a respect of our North American roots of slavery and racial tensions and Southern religion and faith roots.

When working with spirits be inclusive, but that doesn't mean you should allow them to walk over you or to disrespect your boundaries. As a powerful and spiritual life force, you have free will to work (and not work) with any guide you wish. From any culture you wish. For any time period you wish. If that guide requires a level of commitment or obedience that you disagree with, then attempt a compassionate solution. If that cannot happen, then stop the conversation and move on. That guide is not for you, and that is okay. It happens in physical relationships, and it happens in spiritual relationships.

I have guides and ancestors from all walks of life. I have read about inspirational historical figures and physical locations. I respectfully initiate a discussion with them in my journey time, and if we come to an agreement, I ask for their assistance in deliverance requests. I ask for their permission to use certain herbs, roots, and prayer practices that are different from my own. I try very hard to appreciate their practice by acknowledging that they are not my own, always giving them credit and bringing them an offering to honor their work—no matter how small. I show you ways to do this in the book, but it bears mentioning here. Before you work with another ancestor, culture, or faith, do the following:

1. Introduce yourself and explain your deliverance request.

2. Learn about that culture and that guide's experience, from the joys to the pains.

3. Come with respect and honor in your heart. Never appropriate or "try on" something for fun. A culture isn't a costume. It is a lifestyle and a journey that are lifetimes in the making.

4. Provide an offering after they have met your deliverance request, whether that's an offering of a small token, like candy or tobacco, or speaking words of thanks or fulfilling a contract. Offering is required to show respect to the guide, ancestor, or deity. Some require more than others. But all deserve a thank-you for working with you. If you have nothing else, you have your breath and your full heart, so say, "I appreciate you." Many guides, ancestors, or deities that I introduce you to in this book ask for nothing more.

Every being according as they have purpose in their heart, so let them give; not grudgingly, or of necessity: for Spirit loveth a cheerful giver. (2 Corinthians 9:7)

Inclusiveness in Hoodoo

What does gender have to do with hoodoo? Nothing, really. If you are a hoodoo worker, you are a hoodoo worker. You are not a (insert gender) hoodoo worker; you are a hoodoo worker doing the work of deliverance with an ancestor, guide, or deity on behalf of a client or group or community that has requested it. As a hoodoo worker works with and uses the Bible in their toolbox as a spell book, the social ramifications and demands of having genders in the Bible necessitate a conversation about gender. This is because to be a successful and inclusive hoodoo worker, it is best to meet people where they want to be met. Not where *you* want to meet them or where you think *they* should meet you. This means understanding that language is important. If your client does not feel comfortable with certain gender references or deity references, then learn that before starting any session work.

It's like baking a cake (that now comes with negative connotations in the LGBTQIA community because of recent controversies involving discrimination by bakeries). When I bake a cake for someone, I want to bake one they like. So I will begin by asking them very simply, "What kind of cake would you like?" Then I listen, make sure I understand how to work with the ingredients that they request, and then I make the cake.

In hoodoo it is the same way. I worked with a client that wanted spell work that was inclusive of Hecate. I do not work or know much about this Greek goddess; therefore, I did research before our call. I first checked in with my ancestors and guides to see if they were comfortable with me doing this spell work. If they would have not allowed it, then I would have let the client know that I could not work on their deliverance request. Fortunately, my guides pretty much said, "Groovy," and so off I went, learning what I could to respectfully integrate Hecate in the deliverance reading.

I love working with any client where our ancestors, guides, and deities collaborate. This means I work with anyone: Christian, Jewish, pagan, straight, polyamorous, gay, lesbian, atheist, socialist, conservative, independent, Indigenous, mixed race, cis, nonbinary, binary—I have worked for and with them all.

The only person I will not work with is someone that my ancestors, guides, and deities say that I should not. That's my boundary. That's my line in the sand. You, too, will have your own line in the sand.

I do recommend that you have a couple of Bibles that are marked up for gender and deity: one that has gender-neutral pronouns and terminology and another that is deity-neutral. It just makes things more fluid and inclusive for you as a reader and healer. If you do not have a physical Bible, even better, but you may want to create a separate spreadsheet or cross-reference where you have options for gender identifiers that are inclusive, replacing pronouns with ones that your clients may prefer. How do you know what they prefer? Ask. I have not found one client that did not help me navigate the waters of gender identity and inclusiveness with me as long as I was respectful.

Same for religious beliefs. If someone has a particular deity that they would like added to their spells, then use the one that gives them comfort, even if they are most comfortable with no deity. It's like making a gluten-free cake for a friend. You wouldn't shove gluten down their throats, I hope. You would adapt and give them something that they would find delicious. Your spells should be deliciously palatable.

If the Bible verse in its present state offends or does not speak to you, it's not worthy of *you* yet! Not until it is totally unique and custom for you. Pronouns. Why do these pronouns mean so much to some people? It's just a part of speech. It is only a substitution for a noun. That's it. So any noun can be substituted for another pronoun. There are first-person pronouns like "I" and "me." There are second-person pronouns like "you." The ones that seem to cause people to go a bit to the left or right are the third-person pronouns like "she" or "he." When you see a third-person pronoun in the Bible, you can replace it with a few things like the person's name you want to include in the spell, or use "they" or "them" or "all" or "any." Use it in action in a Bible verse that may cause some stress, and see how we totally make it accessible and less harmful.

I appreciate the following verse because it is inspirational as a spell verse. I can see this being used in spells to battle impotence, to increase sexual fidelity, to reassure, to comfort, to use as part of a blessing of a community or even a community garden—so much to use with this verse.

He remembered us in our weakness. His faithful love endures forever. He saved us from our enemies. His faithful love endures forever. He gives food to every living thing. His faithful love endures forever. Give thanks to the God of heaven. His faithful love endures forever. (Psalm 136:23–26)

Taking out your handy marker, first mark out any of the pronouns that do not fit for you. Next you can remove any names or references to the word *God* if that does not give you comfort or safety. Now that we have those out of the way, proceed to work through the intention of the verse. For me I would use this to bless a community garden for my friends Stuart and Marcy. I would take this verse and modify it in this manner:

They are remembered in any weakness. The garden is blessed in our faithful love that endures forever. It has saved us from any natural insect enemies that try to destroy it. Our faithful love of this land and the nutrition it provides to those that we make it in will endure forever. Our Natural One provides food to every living thing. Our Natural One's faithful love endures forever. Give thanks to Our Natural One for this ever-enduring fruitfulness and strength to keep this garden forever. (Psalm 136:23–26)

THE DECEPTIVE POSSESSION OF VENGEANCE, ANGER, AND FEAR

Do you ever feel just angry, depressed, or downright frustrated at the news these days? Every time I open the news app on my phone I almost cringe in terror at what horrible thing will be written. I have begun having anxious thoughts when I see certain names in the news. Just those pronouns or titles cause me to want to close my browser permanently and get away from any news or social media apps. When I feel this way, it is easy to want to stir up a spell or two and put those apps in "their place." I want to further banish or remove their very existence to prevent them from crossing paths with my own. But how honest or feasible is this as spiritual workers? Our global goal is to ensure that the healing powers of our herbal and spiritual medicines are delivered to those that need it—these mystical powers that are fueled by faith, intention, and direction (the tenets of #updatedhoodoo and #hoodoo-foundations). Conjuration, as explained in my first book, *The Hoodoo Guide to the Bible*, is described as compelling someone to do something as a verb or calling upon a spirit or deity or entity in a ritual. When you are conjuring someone, you are using the energy from one emotion and mixing it with the ancestor's, spirit's, or guide's needs, and then the possession is the output or extract of that.

My example of the news—let us pick that up again. I'm in the middle of my day, and my energy or emotions at that time may be happy or content or even sad. The conjure message of the media outlet or triggering individual has been possessed with a different energy—an energy to steal you of your own emotion and replace it with their emotion and intention. This is the damage of not being prayerful and grounded in our work as practitioners. When we are in the everyday world, we are still vulnerable to everyday energies that are not coming with the best intentions, or even more than that, are in direct opposition to what our own intentions are. When those polar opposite intentions clash, then the most powerful, or driven energy will win out. If you do not have a strong hold of your emotions and energies, then you will fall victim to the conjure.

The conjuration of the world right now is this sense of all or nothing. You are either with me or against me. You are either voting with me or against me. You are either culturally diverse or you are complicit. As individuals and human beings and representatives of our lineage, we carry the stories of those that are in our bloodline. They carry their own possession abilities. You may have noticed these just in your day-to-day. You may have found yourself bound or tempted by a certain object, addiction, or sensibility and wonder to yourself, *When did I start thinking that?* If you do a bit of ancestry work, you may also find that generations before you have had those same traits. Scientists call this your DNA. Religious folk may call it a generational curse or blessing (more about that later), but for now, let's say it's conjure. It is when you are compelled to do something because of something outside of yourself. Conjure is always for some purpose: to heal, to protect, to encourage love, to eliminate fear, to balance our emotions. But conjure can also be used for other reasons: to cause change, to compel each other to act, to instill fear so that we are safer, to restrict ourselves from doing something harmful, to incite anger, to encourage us to destroy. All of those things are part of the energy or spirit that possesses us.

When I am possessed by the social media app that I cannot stop scrolling through, what am I being taken away from that Spirit may want me to do instead? Is it work? Taking care of your responsibilities? Enjoying your life? Finding deeper meaning in something by studying a new talent or skill? Is the possession also something you are perfectly okay with accepting because it gives you something? Maybe it makes you more content, keeps you busy, or frees you from addiction for just one more second, minute, or hour. Possession is not always a bad thing.

CREATING AN INCLUSIVE PRAYER

In the Bible as a spell book, there are verses that teach us how to pray. Psalm 17:8 says to Spirit, "Keep me as the apple of your eye; hide me in the shadow of your wings." Romans 12:12 says to your ancestor, "Be joyful in hope, patient in affliction, faithful in prayer." Deuteronomy

33:12 says, "Let the beloved of the Universe rest secure in it, they shield us all day long, and the one the Universe loves rests between their shoulders."

When I was a kid, my gran gran taught me to pray by saying the Lord's Prayer, but maybe that doesn't resonate for you when you are doing conjure, and that is okay. Then I would encourage you to take this moment to consider the purpose of a good prayer when you are doing your rootwork. When we are doing #hoodoo and #updatedhoodoo, we are asking for deliverance, for a goal to be achieved, for healing, for social justice—we are pleading and maybe even begging, but more importantly, we are talking to the being, the very light source that makes us alive in this space, on this earth, as a member of our communities.

A prayer is a conversation. It is an opportunity to talk with your guide or to a spirit that speaks to you. It is a time to listen and reflect. It can be a request, or it can be said in thankfulness. The Bible has a ton of prayers in it you can use to understand prayer work. Remember, you do not have to be a specific religion to pray. You only need to understand what you are wanting out of the prayer and to be sincere. Here is a definition of prayer for those from any type of background:

Start with the wish or want. For example, you want your family to be happy. You may say (without prefacing with a deity), "May my family be happy and know joy at this time." Amazingly simple, right? What if you wanted to add an occasion or special event? Then you could say, "On the day of our wedding, may we as a family be happy and know joy." If you do have a particular religious culture, then now is the time that you can add that faith base into the prayer, making the prayer something like, "Higher Power, on the day of your wedding, we ask you to bring this family together in joy and happiness." Easy, isn't it?

Here's another idea. If you are doing a spiritual blessing on a home that you are protecting from negativity or influences that are against the nature of a home being a place of comfort and rest, then you start in the same manner: start with the wish, then add an event or occasion, followed by adding a faith (if you so choose).

Here are example house blessings:

Prayer 1 (no deity, no event): Keep this house in perfect harmony and protect it from any negativity.

Prayer 2 (add the event): We are so excited and grateful for this new home. Before we enter it, we ask that this house be protected from any negativity and that it is full of perfect harmony.

Prayer 3 (add the deity or ancestor): I am asking that the spirit of our grandmother enter this house before we move into it. Keep it, Grandma, in perfect harmony and peace. Protect it, Grandma, from any negative forces. Make sure that we have comfortable rest and enjoy each moment we are given.

Prayer 4 (add a Bible verse—Proverbs 24:3–4): I am asking for protection of this house and property. I am asking our ancestor John Brown to keep this house and the land it stands on protected and secure. I know that it is written that with wisdom a house is built, and through understanding it is established. Through knowledge its rooms are filled with rare and beautiful treasures that are filled with the spirit of my grandmother.

Once you have added all these layers you may think you are done, but really you are just beginning. Now it is time to add the anointing to the prayer, which is necessary to transmit your energy into the object that binds the prayer to the intention, faith, and direction that makes hoodoo work like no other magical tradition. Next we will look at examples of using anointing with prayer.

ANOINTING OIL

Prayers and oil go hand in hand. You can use any type of oil you have around, like vegetable, sunflower, olive, or almond. Oil is used because in the Bible, oil was an essential part of anointing an object, person, or place. Anointing really means just to smear or rub with something. Anointing a forehead is placing oil onto the forehead. Anointing in religions relates to doing something for a religious purpose or event. When people are prayed over for healing, their head is touched with blessed oil or anointed with water.

When you are in a traditional religious setting and someone says that they are "anointed," it means that they are touched or blessed with an object or spirit. You may hear "that singer's voice is anointed," meaning they have a powerful voice that can touch others with song. Another phrase may be "the message today was anointed." This could mean the actual deliverer of the message was touched by an energy or spirit or that the delivery of the message touched those that heard it. When I was growing up, I always thought that everything I did had to be anointed. I identified anointing with blessing or spiritually blessing something. I do this now with my hoodoo oils and sprays. I touch or dab the specially prepared oils and alcohol-based sprays onto objects to deliver the energy that I want (protection, love, healing).

In hoodoo when you anoint something it is the same. If I bless a home and make sure it is protected from negativity, I will anoint it with oil that I have specifically prepared for this purpose. This is the root-work. This is the conjure or the work. The conjure is making a force or energy appear when it is called. When you call upon a force, you are asking for and receiving agreement with that work. When I conjure an energy, I must be certain—very certain—of the energy I am call-ing. Therefore, it is important to research every energy you call into an anointing, conjure, or work. The energies I speak of in this book have been vetted for you. I have asked my ancestors, healers, and guides to give me energies that can be shared and will do the work with you and not against you.

But even then, I recommend you practice one prayer to protect your-self before doing any work. Start with something simple and then add more as you feel you are asked to.

Protection prayer 1: Protect my body, my energy, and my work as I do this on this day, for this purpose. Keep my mind on the work. Keep my body focused and present. Thank you.

Protection prayer 2 (based on a Bible verse, Psalm 144:1–2): Blessed be the Highest of High, my rock, who trains my hands for war and my fingers for battle. You fill me with steadfast love, and you are my for-tress, my stronghold and my deliverer, my shield, and in whom I take refuge. As I do this conjure work, a work that is for protecting and blessing this home, I know that you are keeping my mind and spirit as one. Thank you, ancestors, for keeping me in perfect peace. Amen.

Protection prayer 3 (based on nature): As the birds fly in the sky, as the earth moves mountains, as the crickets make a joyful sound, I ask their protection and energy as I do my magical work. Protect each spell. Protect my words. Protect my presence and mind. Protect my body. Protect my essence. I want this to be great work. I want this to be a gift of nature and of the earth.

As you are reading the stories of these historical people, places, and events I want you to step into them and imagine how they will help encourage you and help you conjure up the energy you need to focus on. Reading their stories, whether they are fact or myth, always gives me the encouragement I need to be strong in the practice that I love, which is hoodoo.

CREATING A PERSONA

I loved watching cartoons when I was in my elementary school years. I would sit in front of the TV and watch them for hours on end. On the weekends or even after I came home from school, I would be in commune with my bowl of cereal and milk, some orange juice, and the TV. The TV didn't really have a remote, so every now and then my exercise would be to get up and change the channel once one block of cartoons ended and another began. When it was Saturday and my viewing time ended, the real world would start again. There would be news stories. The news stories would trouble me. They would concern my family. Gone would be the laughter and joy. Back to being an adult and having responsibilities, bills. I knew then I never wanted to be an adult like those in my family were.

Before COVID, as an adult I clung to this pastime by participating in comic events and comic conventions, where I get to take on the persona of a character from one of my favorite comic books. I get to dress as something totally different from anything I ever would be in the real world. When I put on that makeup, when I put on that wig, when I put on that outfit, when I put on those shoes, I become that person. I become a character, and I get to go around the convention that entire day as someone different. It's an amazing way for me to express myself and to take on a new human form in spirituality. When I am in this persona as a ship's captain, a fairy, a science fiction character, or an angel or spirit or energy force, it is the same as a type of possession. It's remarkably similar to when you are possessed by an energy source like an ancestor, guide, or deity, or an assistant. Spiritual possession does not always have to be a negative thing. When I go to comic conventions, I always have control over when I take on a full comic book character. It is the same with my persona as That Hoodoo Lady. It is for a particular time and place, and I take it off when I am done using the character. It protects me from others who want to harm my true self by spiritual or physical attack. I encourage you to have the same separation when you are spiritually doing any type of deliverance work. I want you to consider finding out who your spiritual character will be, and when you are ready to start doing magic work, you put on that spiritual character just like you would if you were at a comic book convention. Think of the character's motivation, background, characters, family history, ethnicity, hair type, and home. Make the character real, and then it will become who you associate yourself with for this healing work.

When I started my journey into tarot reading, I noticed that after I read for someone, I invariably took on their pain/trauma/tragedy experience as if I were in their minds or had their experience. I told my tarot mentor of my worries, and she laughed kindly and said, "Oh dear, you're taking on that person's energy because you are an empath—you are soaking it up like a sponge." Empaths are like tofu in cooking. Tofu is a bit flavorless unless you allow it to soak in or take on the flavors of other ingredients. As a spiritual and energy empath you feel and take on others' energy, and it can drain you and give you their individual experiences very vividly. When I go to a large event, like a concert, I enjoy the concert and can be euphoric, but I can also take on the life force of the concerts. When the concert is in an uproar, then an empath is in an uproar. The morning after you may feel tired and nauseous or have a headache like you have a hangover.

I have the persona of That Hoodoo Lady because of my experience as a beginning tarot reader. The individual, an adult survivor of sexual trauma and child abuse, asked me to read for him about a totally different situation, but the abuse kept coming into my mind and heart. I could hear the perpetrators thoughts. I could hear his understanding of what he was doing to my client, and I could feel the guilt and the shame that the perpetrator felt. I did not know how to turn it off, so it stayed with me, that pain, for the entire reading. I was not experienced enough to ask the client the right questions to confirm what I was feeling, so I assumed it was not part of the client. I felt it was part of me (incorrectly). There I sat in the reading like tofu—taking it all in. The Tall Man thankfully interrupted my thoughts and immediately severed the connection with my client. He gave me the information that I needed to share with my client about his reading so that the client was happy, and we ended the session. That night and the next day and the day after that, all I could feel was the experience of being sexually abused at the hands of this perpetrator.

◇◇◇◇◇◇ CHAPTER 3 EXERCISES ◇◇◇◇◇◇

Element Conjuration Exercise

There is nothing really new under the sun, so I've read, and this is another example with a twist. This exercise is my own hoodoo version (that is not scientific) of the very scientific, very thorough study done by Dr. Masaru Emoto, the Japanese scientist who revolutionized the idea that our thoughts and intentions impact the physical realm. I honor you, Dr. Emoto, for sharing your wisdom and foresight.

There are five elements in this world that a conjure worker uses when working with hoodoo:

Earth—our physical space, our ground, dirt

Fire—our actions, fire, movement

Air—our thoughts, words, breath

Water—our emotions, water, rain, snow

Spirit—our deities, orishas, goddesses, light sources, energies, nuances

The purpose of this exercise is to conjure water using words, visual cues, sound, and emotion. It is the beginnings of understanding the three most important tenets of hoodoo: intention, faith, and direction—the next step.

For this exercise, using water, see if you can note any differences when water is exposed to different conjure techniques. You will need three small glasses of water and an audio or video recorder.

First glass of water—Hold this glass of water and drink from it. Allow yourself at least two to five minutes to truly experience the water. Notice the temperature and how it tastes and feels in your mouth. How does it feel across your tongue and teeth? Does it quench you? Does it satisfy you? Are there any components in the water that you can taste, like chemicals, or does it taste clean and clear? Speak into your audio or video device, recording the results of this first experiment.

Second glass of water—I want you to cup this glass of water in both hands. I want you to (for a solid two to five minutes) tell this water your most joyful, loving, and kind words you can think of. I want you to thank this water for quenching your thirst, for nourishing your body, for giving your life. Anything that comes from your lips as long as it is something that will give this water joy, love, and kindness. Even if you can only think to repeat to the water "I love you" over and over. Set the water down. If you want a Bible verse to repeat into the water, I have offered some choices in the notes for this chapter. Speak into your audio or video device, recording the results of this second experiment. Now proceed to the third step.

Third glass of water—Take this glass of water and place it in front of a TV, radio, phone, text message, email, or photographic or printed material that gives you anger, fear, or resentment. This may be the scariest or most frightening exercise, but just know that you are doing this for your growth, and allow your ancestor and guide to come with you on this journey. Maybe it's a TV series that you find disturbing. Maybe place the glass of water in between you and the social media app that angers you. Perhaps put it in front of a YouTube video that causes you distress. Let the glass stay there between you and the offensive object for anywhere from two to five minutes. If the object is audible or visual, be sure that the sound or video is on so that if you can hear it or see it, the water can too. If you want harmful or inflammatory Bible verses to repeat into the water, I have provided some exceptionally harsh ones in the notes section. Record the results of this last experiment into your audio or video device. Now proceed to the final step.

Comparison and conclusion—Like any good scientific experiment, we now get to review the results of our experience. You may be surprised by the things you didn't expect to learn.

1. Viewing the water: Does the water appear different? If so, how?

2. Tasting the water: Does the water taste different? If so, how?

Listen to your three recordings:

1. How did each glass of water change?

2. How did they remain the same?

3. What do you think is the reason for the change (if you noted any)?

4. What do you think is the reason for there being no change (if you did not note any)?

5. What are your conclusions from this exercise?

6. Do you think this exercise would be different if you used another element?

Ethics

Consider creating your own code of ethics as a hoodoo worker. To do so, insert your answer here for each of these situations:

As a hoodoo worker I am comfortable answering:

___Can you make my partner come back to me?

___My house is possessed by a spirit or entity, and it is hurting us. Can you help?

___I want to get revenge on (insert situation). Will you help?

___Will I get the job?

___Can you harm or kill someone?

___Can you make sure my employer's business fails?

___Can you make sure I don't lose my house?

___Will I ever find anyone to love?

___What gender, date of birth, physical characteristic will my child have?

___I have this particular (ache, pain, cyst, infection, headache, allergy, insert another symptom). What do you think it is?

___Will I win the lottery?

___When will the money, insurance settlement, inheritance, etc. be given to me?

___When will I get a new house, car, business, (object or thing)?

___I will answer anything that they ask for.

The answers to all these questions make up your code of ethics. Put the answers in a place that you can display to yourself (also to your clients if you choose to have any in the future, but it's more important for you to see it)—to remind yourself what you stand for.

Persona

I want you to consider taking on a different persona for your own protection and for the protection of your clients. I want you to understand that when you do your spiritual practice and spells, you are in collaboration with spiritual forces and those spiritual forces will become part of you. This is the reason that you also do not engage in communication with energy forces that you do not know or have not worked with or that have not been referred to you by a trusted source. I want you to make the persona as different from your real self as possible. I want you to limit how many pictures you have of yourself with that persona's name until you have a grasp on protection, mirroring, and banishing energies that do not serve you.

If you do not want to have a persona, then that is your call. If you do want to have a persona, then reach out to your personal ancestor, guide, or deity and ask.

Cleaning your body and your mind. Give honor to the ancestor on your altar. Do this by giving them their favorite food and drink. Place their image onto the altar or an object that represents them. In a prayerful state, ask them for your persona name. Sit quietly until it is presented to you. If none comes to you, then don't force it. Come back later. You do not want or need to rush this. Once you have a persona, then consecrate the name. Try it out for a few weeks or months. Keep it to yourself for a while. See if it feels good before going out and sharing with the world. And for goodness' sake, don't go telling every one of your TikTok followers, "Thou shalt call me Super Diamond 2000 from now on because Jesus said so!" Be chill about it. It's a birth of a new you, not a new bracelet to show off. It needs honor and respect. Separate the persona from yourself. It will have a separate social media. It will have a separate phone number. It will have a separate space to practice than you. It will have a separate altar if you use one for your personal work.

WORTHY HOODOO FIGHTERS

I don't know about you, but when I think of ancestors, I think of my mom, aunts, and grandmas. When I was growing up, my mom scared the living shit out of me. Her stories were kind of legendary. She was a tax collector in the state we lived in. She went after delinquent companies on the city's behalf, and she was excellent at it. She used to explain to me that she *was* the PIC (person in charge) of her area and that even as she crossed the street, she dared buses, cars, and scooters to touch her. No one did. One day she moved from a shared apartment with her brother. Angered that he asked her to be a bit neater, she retaliated by taking not only her own belongings but also the light bulbs, paper towels, plates, napkins, and even the toilet seat! I can't imagine my uncle coming home to a dark home that was stripped bare.

Introducing yourself to a hoodoo fighter, deity, or ancestor is like starting any new relationship. It can be scary at first, which is why I provided you some helpful and comfortable examples in chapter 2. I work with my dad, Michael (you'll learn more about him later), the Blue Lady, and the Tall Man frequently, and I asked them to be receptive to working with beginning hoodoo workers just like you. They said yes, and now it's up to you to make the connection. Let's start with an easy one—my dad.

My dad (or Norvette or Burney—he goes by any of these names) wants to be here for you with open arms. If you make a connection with him, I will start by going through steps one and two in chapter 2 about working with an ancestor. Next burn some tobacco for him. If you are allergic to tobacco, then use something sweet, like rice pudding, butterscotch pudding, or butterscotch candies.

If you are going to do work with a guide, deity, or ancestor *and* you've done steps one and two in chapter 2 to protect yourself *and* you have anointed yourself with oil or water *and* if your spirit and soul feel this guide is approachable and available, then proceed. If you cannot say yes to all of these things, then I 100 percent recommend you don't start your work until you can say yes.

I don't mind working for clients and getting spiritual cleansing work, but I don't recommend working with unfamiliar spirits. It's not something to play with, and I've seen firsthand the physical, mental, and spiritual scars that can happen when someone goes against my advice. Make this a good experience and not a reason to find a qualified hoodoo practitioner to help you clean or cut ties with some spirit you knew nothing about and should not have connected with. Leave that to the movies and those that have a bit more experience. Don't worry; you'll get there with time and understanding. Most hoodoo workers, after that time and understanding, have learned not to try, even if we can.

In no order, here are my guides. Some identify as male, some as female, and others are genderless. Read their stories and learn their history. These are some of our shared ancestors and fighters. They cross races, culture, and religion. This is important. You will be spending a good amount of time with them. These energies may be female or have feminine attributes. They may be nurturing. They may be prophetic. Warm and friendly, or vindictive and spiteful. Agree with me or not, these are energies I see that mostly identified as a female (whether they identify as or are born female). Read about these glorious heroes and learn their stories. Connect with the ones that speak to you and leave the others for someone else to embrace.

Below, I have given you their stories, showed you how to use them in a simple spell, and told you what sacrifices and offerings they may enjoy. Feel free to add your own observations and customize them in the notes space so they work for you.

THE STORY OF THE PINK LADIES

The pink ladies was a magical quilt that my gran gran would use when we got scared in the middle of the night as children. The large pink-and-white quilt had the Sunbonnet Sue pattern in nine squares equally spaced in three-by-three formation. It was heavy enough for the winter but light enough that you could use it during the summer and not sweat. (You'll read more about my fascination with quilts in a later chapter.) I can't tell you how many times Gran Gran would lay the quilt on my bed and I would feel its protective blessings over me. It smelled of mothballs and a sweet scent that I couldn't place—and probably never will. She kept it in a steamer trunk at the foot of her bed, and it came out only when it was needed. You see, as a child, I had frequent nightmares of things that were going to happen. I would see tragedies (house fires, kids kidnapped, children being abused) and would wake up crying and go into my gran gran's room. She would take the pink ladies quilt out of its trunk and put it on me. Then she would whisper a Bible verse in my ear, rub sweet blessed oil on my forehead, and put me back to sleep. I would dream wonderfully after that. This, my friend, is hoodoo. The oils, the Bible verse, and the blessed quilt. Hoodoo uses all these elements and more, but to get good at it, you must start with Bible knowledge.

Gran Gran was born in a time where her only means of receiving education was through the church or by word of mouth. She was born in Kansas in 1899, one of several children of Black, white, and Indigenous ancestry. No one in America was focused on providing her with a better way of life. She had to make it by relying on her community and her family. Her parents before her never stepped foot in any school. Her parents worked in the fields or cooked and cleaned for whites. Their parents before them were stolen or traded to whites or South Americans for sugar, grain, or money.

My ancestors had one thing in common: a desire to live without fear of an oppressor—someone who held their lives in one hand and a Bible in the other. Before we as a people had a Bible or Gnostic texts or Satanic Verses, we had a polytheistic belief in several gods and goddesses that provided for us, kept us safe from the elements or from animals attacks. They required in return offerings, faithfulness, and respect. If you disobeyed them, then you were punished. If you pleased them, you were blessed with whatever you wanted or needed, not just for you but your family and your family's family. We've always been creatures of faith in something larger than us.

Gran Gran is my very own ancestor. She was and is this mythical and present epitome of a strong, confident being with supernatural powers and beliefs. She raised two Black girls all on her own and lived to see ninety-nine years of age. She outlasted any naysayer and kept her head held high. Her consistent wish was that we would survive under the scrutiny of others by having a deep faith and knowledge of using the Bible to get what we needed.

In my first book, *The Hoodoo Guide to the Bible*, which I call the Red One, I give definitions of hoodoo, conjure, and rootwork. Definitions are important. They ground us. They give us a starting point, like in running. Once the starting pistol goes off, you are starting from somewhere, right? Maybe it's a line in the sand. Reading through the Red One is the line in the sand, but it's not the only one. I'll give you enough knowledge to get started today with my definitions.

MY DAD, THE IMPERFECT HERO

Who shall ascend the hill of the Lord? And who shall stand in his holy place? He who has clean hands and a pure heart, who does not lift up his soul to what is false and does not swear deceitfully. (Psalm 24:3–4)

Parents can be difficult. My mother and father divorced when I was ten years old. After their divorce, my relationship with him suffered. It was like when they signed the divorce papers, I lost my father, brother, and sister. After those papers I saw him on fewer and fewer occasions until finally I didn't see him at all. I had phone calls with him, but he never lived up to my expectation of what a father should be. When I became an adult, I learned so many lessons from my father about what imperfection and perfection are. I hope his story helps you.

My dad was easy and quiet. He didn't have a formal education. I don't think he ever made it past the ninth grade. His mom, my grandmother, was a devout Christian that was at every Sunday service with her two children by her side. She single-handedly raised her kids in a time when not having their father around meant they got overlooked for apartments and she got overlooked by hiring managers. Being divorced (or deserted they would have called it then) was a shame, and being a divorced Black mom meant you signed up for a lifetime of poverty. My grandmother turned to the one career she knew would always be plentiful—sex work. It's rumored that she and my grandfather met because he was the owner of an establishment and she was once his worker (the nice way to say it).

They married, and heaven knows how it all went down, but in the end there was my dad, Norvette, and his sister, Janette (Jan). After the divorce (and with no establishment protection) my grandmother Annie and the kids lived in the Midwest and South in cities in Kansas, Texas, Mississippi, and Oklahoma. I cannot imagine the fear of not knowing if you would have anything to share with your children at the end of the day, but she was more successful than not, and my dad and Jan made their way through primary school. Annie using her sexuality as her means of income was what her Spirit of Old gave her. She kept the children as safe as she could. Around the time my dad would have been going into middle school, my grandmother began losing her sight. I'm sure the years of lack of nutritious foods and lack of being seen by a qualified physician were part of the reason this happened to her at such a young age (she was in her early thirties to forties). She was completely blind before I was born.

My mom and dad met in Kansas when Mom was in high school and Dad was working a part-time job in places where kids hung out (like a soda shop or café at a filling station). They started as best friends, and that led to love. My dad was gentle and soft-spoken, and what he lacked in formal education he more than excelled at in spiritual and metaphysical gifts. This was in the 1960s where you didn't just go around telling people that you had psychic visions or dreams that came true, but my dad had those things.

He would dream in detail about what was going to occur. He would see the people, their clothing, their eyewear, the building, its occupants, and even hear their voices, and it was never wrong. To his mother, this talent or gift was God-given and should be used only in the church. But Dad saw more things than just what he saw in those church services for those church worshippers. He saw his friends and their lives. He saw his mother and saw her losing her sight to diabetes. His saw his future wife and his future children. He even saw his own death. Armed with this understanding I could only imagine the terror that every day must have been for him. Just imagine if you dreamed about something cataclysmic and then it started to happen on what was supposed to be a normal day. Do you tell everyone what's about to transpire, because your dreams are always right, or do you tuck it away inside your heart and head and see the vision unfold right as you saw it days, months, or even years ago?

Because of his lack of public schooling, many of his friends thought of him as simplistic (never knowing his psychic gifts). They helped him get odd jobs that didn't pay enough for his basic needs, and they covered for him by reading and sometimes writing for him when he needed them to do so.

I remember one time my dad sent me a letter when I was living with relatives in Oklahoma. I was a teenager that knew just about everything (of course I did; I was fourteen), and my dad was trying to tell me how much he loved me. His letter was delivered, and I remember (now with embarrassment) that all I could see were the grammar and spelling errors and that he wrote out a Bible verse at the very end, asking me to keep it close. I did not see any of that. I only saw his errors and flaws—what I understood were errors and flaws—but not his humanity or struggle. We never spoke of our psychic gifts—I don't know if he ever shared them with anyone (except my mother).

My mother was the breadwinner of our family. She worked as a manager in the secretarial pool for the government. She told us about the struggle getting up that high, especially as a Black woman working for the military. She knew that she would never go any further because of her race and gender, but she also knew that every paycheck kept her family whole for just one more month.

My dad stayed home and watched us. Every now and then he found work at printing shops or as a mechanic at gas stations overhauling engines, lining brakes, among other tasks. He kept the family station wagon and would take Mom to and from her government job.

One day while my mom was in hospice care, she told me a story about my dad's ability. It was my first time hearing of his gift.

According to my mom, Dad was driving her to her first interview for a government job. She had never worked for the government, but she was an excellent assistant, and her typing scores were through the roof. She was organized to a fault, driven, and professional. She was dressed for her interview in a crisp suit consisting of wine-colored blazer, white shirt, and print skirt. Her pantyhose had a run, but she made sure to use nail polish to make sure the run wouldn't get bigger. Besides, she didn't have the cash to buy new pantyhose unless she got this job.

As they were driving, my dad told her, "I had a dream about the interview. You will meet a man in a plaid suit. He will have horn-rimmed glasses and a small face with cropped black hair. When you see this man, he will hire you no matter what. You're getting this job today." Mom (I can only imagine) looked at him and dismissed his vision, and then went into the building. She sat and waited in the reception area until a young woman called her name. The woman led her into a drab gray room where a thin white man with glasses, a small face, and cropped hair greeted her. He extended his hand to my mom. My mom turned pale, screamed, and ran away.

I don't know how she saved face, but she did eventually see the man again, and she did lead the typing pool and was the manager of secretaries for years to come. All because (in my mind) my dad shared his dream with her.

Now we can always wonder what would've happened had my dad not shared his vision or whether there's a totally logical explanation for why he saw what he did. Maybe he saw the gentleman on a street corner weeks before and the image stuck and it was a lucky guess? Who knows. But what I do know is that my dad was and is (even in death) a true hero to me for sharing his gift and helping me by allowing me to call upon him in his new form as an ancestor.

The message my dad always told me was that when you're open and allowing the spirit's message into you, it was like holding yourself in a hug. He also told me that it is almost impossible to speak your truth and tense up at the same time (the sphincter exercise). Finally, once I could be just me, all of me, he helped me stretch and grow as wide as I needed to in order to connect with my ancestors.

MICHAEL: A GENTLE SOUL FINDS HIS PLACE

When the righteous cry for help, the Spirit of Old hears and delivers them out of all their troubles. The Spirit of Old is near to the brokenhearted and saves the crushed in spirit. Many are the afflictions of the righteous, but the Spirit of Old delivers him out of them all. (Psalm 34:17–19)

Michael and I met when I dated his father, Dennis. Dennis was about fifteen years older than me, and I was experimenting during a phase where I was dealing with father issues. The best part of our dating experience was meeting his adult son Michael.

Michael was going to college in Colorado, studying liberal arts. He was still figuring his way out in life. He had blue eyes, blond hair, and clear skin. He was quiet, but when he spoke he was surprisingly eloquent, kind, and thoughtful and resisted being the center of the discussion.

Michael was looking for his first job and had a very difficult time doing so. I worked in nonprofits back then and volunteered to help him because he found job searches excruciating. We went through the normal job search tactics. He wanted to start his career in social work or community building. His dream job was to work at a place where he could help LGBTQIA youth. It is important to note that at that point I hadn't started my own journey with vocalizing my true sexual identity, so I was not an advocate or even helping then. I admit and have to accept that although I was helpful on the surface, I secretly held so much judgment and actual jealously of his ability to express himself in this manner that I wasn't the best advocate.

I just represented myself as the religious and backsliding girlfriend of his father and just another in a long line of adults giving him opinions that he probably did not want or need. In hindsight my heart is just aching for what I could and should have said. But many months after I started dating his father, Michael invited me over to his apartment for tea. He had not found the right job. He was so depressed about this. He was in and out of relationships that would turn abusive or possessive. I kept pushing down his throat that if he just manifested his true destiny that everything would be okay. His father and his mother pretty much did the same thing, but we were all blind to his pain.

When I entered his apartment, I noticed that his carpet was a starched oatmeal color and there were celebrity posters on the walls and CD cases in towers. There were flickering fluorescent lights that lit up the entryway. Michael let me in after I knocked several knocks several times. He looked a bit disheveled when he let me in. His always-neat hair was now kind of ruffled.

He led me a few feet north past the kitchen that had enough room for a half oven/stove top combination opposite an olive-colored refrigerator freezer that looked like it was straight out of a '70s family television show.

I'll always remember the care he took in serving me tea from a formal white teapot and two mismatched saucers and cups with tiny silver spoons. The pot was not boiling, but the red coils of the stove gave it away that we were to have tea. Over tea I got to meet the real Michael. Sensitive, precious, lovely, and lost. I really learned what it was like to be alone in a world that is so large and open to some but shut away from so many others. He revealed so many secrets of being the only child of a wealthy Jewish family and the shame of being gay all at the same time. Spiritual leaders, psychologists, camps ... his parents tried it all. After years of therapy while he was in junior and senior high, he connected with a gay therapist that introduced him to other teens like him at a place called the Center. Here he was able to join a community and pick a new family. He was coming up in the world, and he wanted to share his joy with me.

Everything in my soul, my walls about sexuality and gender identity, broke down, and I cried with him as we learned about each other. I wish I could say that I told him (finally) how proud I was of him and that he wasn't an embarrassment to anyone. I wish I could say that I didn't gulp down my tea (because I had to pick up my daughter from my sister's home that night and it was getting very late). I wish I could say that I gave him a hug and stayed there and let him tell me any and everything. But I can't. I didn't. Instead, I went to dinner with Dennis days later and told him about my experience with Michael, and then we glossed over it and continued as if it didn't happen at all. I went on with my life, and weeks later stopped seeing his father. One night Dennis called me, very upset. He didn't hold back anything when I answered. "Sherry," he said curtly, "when is the last time you saw Michael?"

Where is this coming from? I thought. But I thought about it and then said, "When I told you a few weeks ago. Why?"

With even less emotion he replied, "Well, you won't be seeing him anymore. He hung himself in the park last night. Park crews found him this morning." I dropped the phone. I cried. I sobbed. My soul ached. He kept calling my name in the handset, and I never picked up again. *I was* right *there, and all I had to do was save him*, I thought. Of course, now I understand that suicide has so many faces and it is not as simple as a phone call or hearing from a singular person, but it does require help—help and deliverance from a caring and supportive set of resources. A team to help the person recover and maintain their mental health to their vision of success. But to me, I only knew that for the next month or so after this I could see Michael climbing the tree and dying by suicide. I saw it all and felt so much guilt. I begged Michael to forgive me. I prayed for understanding. I asked for insight and forgiveness from any deity that would listen.

In this guilt, in this moment of clarity, I read this verse:

The Universe loves us all so much that it gives us beloveds to love. Whenever we believe in them, they never die. They have eternal life through us. The Universe doesn't condemn us—we live on in eternal life and we are saved through those that we help. (John 3:16–17)

It was my time to help Michael by learning about his struggle and becoming an advocate. I read up on the truth behind the Bible verses that were used to persecute others. I prayed and found that I, too, was chosen to live a different life as a lesbian woman. I had to go through the outing period. The persecution. Risking and not finding work. Being ostracized from my family and told that I was going to hell or a darker place and that I was a sinner. In that false state and with the words of a ludicrously fearful and small congregation (false evidence that appears real) I, just like Michael, stood in the face of that and boldly said, "Liars!"

Michael is a hero for so many reasons. In a practitioner's life there's usually a catalyst to understanding their gift. Michael was one of mine. Seeing him after his departure from this world helped me to understand that seeing him afterward was right and okay. Seeing the act was important because it was Michael showing me, but it took away the stigma of suicide being a choice of someone who is weak and powerless. Michael took the choice that he felt gave him back his power once and for all after being split in two by bickering parents. From time to time, I see Michael in my dream state and when I'm working with clients that have suicidal thoughts or have communication with those that have passed on by way of suicide.

Bible verse for those that have passed on due to suicide:

When the righteous cry for help, the Spirit of old hears and delivers them out of all their troubles. The Spirit of old is near to the broken-hearted and saves the crushed in spirit. Many are the afflictions of the righteous, but the Spirit of old delivers all of them—all of them. (Psalm 34:17–19)

Something to know and to help your clients know is that we are all created with a destiny and we have free will to take our intention, faith, and direction wherever we want it to go. The hoodoo foundations that you learn are not constrained by any faith or understanding. If the ancestors, guides, and deities are helping you, then continue to do work for justice.

There are some important things to know that people who want to hold us hostage through fear are hiding from us:

The Bible says nothing about gender conformity. There is no deity designed for a specific gender that is loved or cared for. The focus is on the spirit, and the life force has no gender; it is what it is.

There's a story in the Bible about Jacob and his brother, Esau. Esau had a face full of hair. Jacob's face was smooth. Jacob stayed in the tent (where Jacob cooked) and Esau hunted. Their father loved Esau more, and their mother loved Jacob more. Jacob transitioned to Israel and became the leader of a nation. Jacob is a representative of a nonconforming leader.

Deborah was the judge and lead in a male-associated role. David was beautiful and had relationships with Saul and Jonathan. Tryphaena and Tryphosa and Euodia and Syntyche were representatives of a living church, even though they held roles that they would be banned from because of their gender assignment.

In hoodoo there are nuggets and jewels of stories to help inspire those that are gender fluid, and as the Bible is a spell book, it is our role and responsibility to use it to research and be ready with language, sacred text, and alternative language that will uplift and support all of us beings when they come to us for healing. Period. We are not meant to judge but to bear witness that through an ask of deliverance, it will be given.

Call upon Ancestor Michael when you need protection, deliverance, and help against an unknown or unforeseen issue. This spell does not take the place of seeking medical, legal, or mental resources but is used as a buffer of #hoodoo deliverance. Coming out can be difficult, but there are so many resources out there to support and help you or those you know that are experiencing this.

You can start with ItGetsBetter.org, PFLAG, Translifeline.org, and the TrevorProject.org. If you want more information about understanding the truth in biblical meanings and distortions of text that support bullying, anger, and hatred toward the LGBTQIA family, then I recommend listening to the Raven Foundation Season 2, Episode 28: How a Mistranslation in the Bible Harmed Our LGBTQIA Siblings, and I recommend reading *Transforming: The Bible and the Lives of Transgender Christians* by Austen Hartke.

THE BLUE LADY

Another hoodoo guide of mine you can use is the Blue Lady. The Blue Lady is my guide when I need help with people that are crossing over. Yes, crossing over into a new life or a new relationship. The Blue Lady also signifies death. She will tell me when there is a death coming, and she will help me speak to those gracefully and gently about health issues that need medical or psychological consultation.

In folklore there are several stories elders tell us to warn us about death and to keep it away. Here are some of my favorites:

If you dream of picking beans or fruit, then death is coming.

If you dream of a bed, then death is coming.

If you want to cause someone to meet death, then put a picture of the person on a wall and drive a tack into it.

If you sleep on feather pillowcases, always check them for hoodoo. Slit open one side and look for a wreath made of the feathers. If you find it and burn it before the wreath is complete, then you break the spell. If not, you will pass in your sleep.

The Blue Lady is beautiful and kind. She is the High Priestess in tarot. She can be Santa Muerte. She can be the Yoruba orisha Yemaya. She can be the North Star Mother Harriet Tubman. She can be a great-great-grandmother. It is all dependent upon your background. My story is how I see the Blue Lady.

Once upon a time I woke up from a deep sleep. It was one of those sleeps where I've had one or two more glasses of wine than I should have. My dream was magical and nightmarish all at the same time. I couldn't wake myself from it. The dream began with me on a yacht in the middle of the ocean. I had on a fitted white jumpsuit and no shoes, with perfectly pedicured feet. My hair was in silvery locs in a bun high atop my head. I walked peacefully around the deck of the boat, letting my fingers slide on the wooden rails, enjoying the sea breezes and the sun's warmth.

I sipped cool champagne. My steps were in perfect harmony. There was not a shore in sight. The water was clear enough for me to see the fish and rocks and kelp below. It was so deep that I didn't see a bottom. It lured me to touch it, and I did. I bent over the side rail and put my whole face in the water and looked around at what was there; my eyes didn't sting. I breathed in the water and didn't drown. The water became a metaphor for visions—the visions of what I needed to see in the days and weeks to come. I saw myself in all stages of my life (twenty-five, forty-five, fifty-five, and sixty-five). My face and body grew older and wiser at the sight of the Blue Lady. She showed me even more. I was around seventy, teaching at a university with bright, open minds encircling me on the grass on the campus grounds.

The Blue Lady whisked me away to my next life with my wife in our future home. I was laying on a chaise lounge that was elegantly placed on a marble floor. I investigated the glass doors that overlooked our patio and felt myself breathing in and out. My breath got more difficult, and I realized I wasn't breathing anymore; I was gasping. I reached out for my wife and tried to call out to her. My voice didn't escape from my throat. My fingers, hands, and body were rigid, and I couldn't move. My wife was reading a book on the opposite couch, just a finger distance away from me. Glasses on and dogs around her feet, yet she couldn't hear me. No one could. I was struggling. Drowning. Watching myself go to another place.

I landed at my home in my bed, surrounded by warm, thick blankets and soft, fluffy pillows. Everything I needed to be safe, but I knew I wasn't alone. To my right was a female form. Shapely. Not large or small. She was average height with no real form to her. She looked at me with dark, oval eyes, no nose, and a thin-lipped smile. A strangely familiar tune began to play. She hummed it. I hummed it. I began gasping for air again. I knew her. I had seen her before. She asked me, "Are you coming with me?" I shook my head firmly. *No!* I said to her with my inner voice, but I heard it resonate through all the walls. She looked at me with disappointment. Her smile fell to a small frown as she looked at me once more with sincerity. Pleading with me that I wasn't seeing the larger picture. She took one more look at me for just one quick second, and I almost changed my mind in remorse and called out to her, but then I knew it was too late. My opportunity was over, but I knew I would see her again—and welcome her. My breath became normal once again as she walked out the door.

The Blue Lady is to be called when you are doing hoodoo work that requires a transition or when you need an advocate in your corner. She is a guide that possesses you. If you call her, then she will enter your physical self and work with you to make the transition happen.

I use the Blue Lady's guidance in this way, but she's also helped me with healing requests as well as when I need to learn. The Blue Lady works with those that are studying or need assistance with tests and homework. I've seen her help with legal and justice work but only with family law, integration, or separation work where families are involved. Have you ever seen those faith-based objects in the form of a blue angel? Many recognize the Blue Lady in hospitals, mortuaries, cemeteries, faith-based schools, and mental health facilities. Calling upon the Blue Lady means you want a sincere deliverance of health, education, death, rebirth, life, transitions, removal of illness, relief from pain, and reduction of struggle or strife. She stands next to you unafraid and unashamed of you. She supports you and comforts you. She has helped me through some of my darkest hours by being there. Other times—as in my vision—she is there to remind me of my own mortality when I am not taking the best of care of myself. She is one of my most precious and severe guides. Honor her well and she will help you through some of the more challenging deliverance requests that you make as a hoodoo worker.

THE TALL MAN

In my first book, *The Hoodoo Guide to the Bible*, I have a full chapter on the Tall Man. It's worth repeating here, and it's worth it to honor him as he is wide and deep and deserving of my appreciation for everything he has done for me in my hoodoo practice.

The Tall Man is a guide from North America. He is very tall (almost six and a half feet) with olive skin, braided long white hair, and a deep baritone voice when he chooses to speak. He is calm, quiet, and powerful. Strong without being controlling. He protects my magical works and warns me of danger in a quiet way, very much like my father (the Imperfect Hero). He enters a home first before I do any spiritual hoodoo cleansing and gives me an all clear when he has made it safe for me to enter.

He delivers me from regular nightmares and lucid nightmares (those that I experience while doing magical work in daylight but have to be in a trance state). He enjoys tobacco and sage, and I can smell his scent in the forests of the Pacific Northwest and in the piney trees of Colorado. He walks with me (but always ahead of me), and I can see his footprints on muddy hikes. When I was hiking the Silver Falls State Park in Oregon, he left me orange peels so that I would not be lost.

When I was blessing a home where a tragedy occurred, he protected me from the residual spirit being that wanted to woo anyone into attempting suicide. He teaches me how to shield myself by telling me to plant my feet firmly in honey-dipped onions when I am feeling a cold coming on. He encourages me to walk faster and for longer distances when I am feeling alone and afraid on any journey.

He tells me about my client's past traumas and protects me from feeling any abuses they may have experienced by shielding me under a blanket of multicolored feathers from peacocks, doves, and hummingbirds. The Tall Man is open to being a source of protection and strength to you as a reader as well once you have been introduced, which I am doing for you right now.

He appreciates many things. As offerings he likes pineapple, honey, and tobacco brought to him in a wooded or forest area. He appreciates oranges and orange peels left near tree trunks. He likes onion halves left near fence posts. He likes it when you leave out water for birds to quench their thirst. Most importantly he loves the quiet of a gentle breeze.

When you call to the Tall Man, it is important to do so in nature. That does not mean going out into the wilderness. I have communed with the Tall Man in a backyard or even by touching a tree in my neighborhood park. When I feel his sage hands on my shoulders and his breath on my neck, then I know he is with me. The hairs on my neck will rise just slightly, and his voice will say, "Beloved." Then our conversation will begin.

When you have left the Tall Man an offering, then expect him to greet you in a similar manner, and wait in silence until he does. If he does not come right away, then make sure you are physically and spiritually present with no outside influences, music, or distractions, and try again. He may visit your dream state. You will recognize him, as he has a long, thin face that shows the age of his hundreds of years walking the earth. You may notice him on the side of a highway when you are driving late at night and feeling too tired to continue.

When you do see him, acknowledge him and thank him for his visit. Keep your deliverance request brief (he will already know what you need), and listen for his instructions. He does not like repeating himself, so write down his instructions, and then leave him another offering. His magic is medicine—never forget that. He will insist you use real roots, herbs, and objects to accomplish your goals, but that does not mean having to pick or pluck items from the root. A simple internet search of the herbs he wants you to use is sufficient. Keep those images in your mind—go into your virtual medicine lab and bring his medicine to life. Place them where he wants, send them to whom he has said, or drink them down as a virtual tea. His healing will be quick and exact. Do not ask him for anything you think you want. Only ask for what you need.

The Tall Man's Bible verses include:

Our Earth is our refuge and strength, an ever-present help in trouble. Therefore, we will not fear, though the Earth give way and the mountains fall into the heart of the sea, though its waters roar and foam and the mountains quake with their surging. (Psalm 46:1–3)

Be strong and courageous; do not be frightened and don't be dismayed, for the Spirits and Ancestors beyond are with you wherever you go. (Joshua 1:9)

They give power to the weak and strength to the powerless. (Isaiah 40:29)

That is why, for my community's sake, I am glad for weaknesses, insults, hardships, persecutions, and difficulties.

For when I am weak, my Guides are strong. (2 Corinthians 12:10)

MIRIAM MAKEBA: CIVIL RIGHTS LEADER

"Girls are the future mothers of our society, and it is important that we focus on their well-being."

—*Miriam Makeba*

African-born civil rights leader Miriam Makeba has inspired so many in her seventy-six years. I was first introduced to her when I started choir in junior high school in Kansas, of all places. See, I was raised in Kansas with my grandparents. Her song "Meet Me at the River" makes me sway to the beat of Africa and a gospel swing. "Meet me at the river, stand upon the rock, and call my name out loud." Her testimony in song told her story of being a powerful activist clothed as a singer and actor.[1]

When I ask people to embrace the work of hoodoo through intention, faith, and direction, then I'm asking them to join me in a river with their own ancestors, deities, and guides. They embrace us and they care for us. They ask for so little. They ask for us to come to them with a deliverance request. They ask us to respect them enough to give them a small offering of what they like and love. They want us to learn about their history, which for some is African American history or the history of them as their identified sexual identities or their cultures. They want us to experience their lives by loving them enough to understand their lives when they were here in the physical world.

Ancestor Miriam Makeba was a singer and musician who was born on March 4, 1932, in Johannesburg, South Africa. Her family was very poor. Her country was in an economic depression as a whole, where everyone was struggling to make sure they had food on the table. When she was an infant, her mother was sentenced to prison for selling alcohol in the neighborhood.

Much like we would associate someone as a Wiccan priestess, a hoodoo priestess, or other folklore teacher by their practice, Makeba's mother was a practitioner of herbal medicine, divination, and counseling in Zulu traditions. Makeba loved her traditional kwela music, marabi, and African jazz. Makeba started to sing with her cousin in a band called the Cuban Brothers, and she did this for a while before she began to sing for the Manhattan Brothers.

She toured around South Africa for three years and then sang for another all-female group (the Skylarks). She received accolades around the world for her musicality. She performed for former US President John F. Kennedy at Madison Square Garden in 1962. Among her other admirers were Marlon Brando, Bette Davis, Nina Simone, and Miles Davis. But still her government rejected her. First, refusing to issue her reentry into the country after she tried to reenter after a tour and then finally denying her a passport to return at all.

However, she also was successful in her own social justice causes. She was the first Black musician to leave South Africa because of apartheid. We know *apartheid* as segregation in North America. There were times when she would perform for the South African government and receive no compensation. In 1963 she testified about apartheid at the United Nations (UN), and her South African citizenship was taken away from her.

In relation to what I stated in chapter 1 about Black hair and wearing natural styles, Makeba sported a natural afro, and she was so happy when she saw other Black women imitating this style. She embraced civil rights activism and spoke out about injustice. She addressed the UN General Assembly twice, speaking out against apartheid as Guinea's delegate. In 1986 she was awarded the Dag Hammarskjold Peace Prize from the Diplomatic Academy for Peace.

She returned to South Africa to sing upon Nelson Mandela's request only after he was freed from prison. She became a UN goodwill ambassador in 1999. This was over thirty years after she had been rejected by the country she loved so much.

When you pay homage to Ancestor Makeba, and to honor her battle with alcohol, it is important to use your voice and your music to share with her and to be free of substances. Do not leave her any alcohol on her altar. Award her not with accolades or awards. She's held them all. She doesn't ask for more applause. But she does ask that you have the freedoms of others in your sight. You can ask Ancestor Makeba to help you in social justice causes. You can ask her to help you with battling addictions. She will help you with fighting diseases (as she battled cancer herself). She didn't think of herself as political, but she did think about what hurtful things were done to her and, more importantly, to her nation and the country she loved.

When you introduce yourself to Ancestor Makeba, she may reply back to you in song or in the chirp of a bird. She is a wonderful ancestor for those that love their homes and their world. I can speak to Ancestor Makeba and ask her to continuously help our world. Our world is so large and sometimes so divided. It can be unbearable, but it is full of ancestors like Ancestor Makeba. For those of you that practice hoodoo in social justice who want a fighter on their side, Ancestor Makeba is that and more. No matter our differences, Ancestor Makeba will bring us together in our ritual and in our lives. She is waiting by the river.

JOHN BROWN: AN ABOLITIONIST DECLARATION

We all need allies, and John Brown was an ally in the fight against slavery. He was a fighter and fought aggressively against anyone that was an enslaver and the very government that supported this practice. This was during pre–Civil War times in the United States, and even though he was a white entrepreneur, he did not let this stop him. He was called to action after a Presbyterian minister and antislavery activist, Elijah P. Lovejoy, was murdered in 1837. Brown vowed then to destroy slavery however he needed to. During his childhood, his family used their home in Ohio as a stop on the Underground Railroad to help keep enslaved people who escaped safe, even if it meant they stayed for more than a night. Brown also had family traumas of his own. His first wife and two of his children died of illness in the 1830s, his business and finances went downhill, and new business opportunities did not bear fruit.

Some would say that John Brown was a radical. He believed that enslaved people should be freed and that they should have the ability to vote. He worked with the uberwealthy mercantile class and sometimes his business practices weren't always the most spotless. After years in Ohio, he moved away with his new family to New York, where he could help more Black communities and Black farmers own their own land.[2]

He became more zealous, and he started to involve his sons in his abolitionist activities. In Kansas they helped to free even more enslaved people and hoped to make Kansas the first free state for African Americans—this was realized in 1858. Proslavery activists were not having it, and they attacked in 1856. Brown and others retaliated. Brown worked with Harriet Tubman and Frederick Douglass, and together they began the work of militarizing their efforts. Ancestor Tubman and Ancestor Brown began planning an attack on Virginian enslavers using armed freed Black people. He wanted to start a civil war. He mounted an attack against descendants of George Washington. They were successful in kidnapping Colonel Lewis Washington and several other proslavery fighters. The wars went on until 1859, when he was captured by the Marines under the control of Brevet Colonel Robert E. Lee at Harper's Ferry. Brown was hung on December 2, 1859, at the age of fifty-nine. At his hanging was proslavery activist and assassin of Abraham Lincoln, John Wilkes Booth.

I use John Brown when I am making Away and Down statements. It is rumored that before he was hung, he cursed the state of Kansas and those that hung him, saying that until slavery was abolished, everything Kansas did would fail. There's no better guide I can think of to use when I need to banish or curse something. I use John Brown's name when I want deliverance for clients that are allies of social justice causes. He can get loud and grumpy if you do not give him the respect he deserves, so be sure to call him only for serious concerns. Don't bother him with simple things like, "Ancestor Brown, my hair needs a lift today." He may have you substitute your hair products for hair remover just to play a joke.

THE GARGOYLE: A GIANT PROTECTOR

Around AD 600 there was a creature by the name of La Gargouille who terrorized the town of St. Romanus of Rouen for centuries. Eventually the townspeople captured it and burned it at the stake. Unfortunately and amazingly, the entire body did not combust. Its head stood firm and proud with a tongue sticking out to tease them about its immortality. The people took the creature's head and mounted it onto buildings and places of worship to fight off and scare other demons and dragons and those that would want to continue to attack their town.

These beings are called gargoyles, and they are fierce protectors. They are mounted onto buildings like castles and cathedrals, and they can look like many things. They can look like goats or birds, usually with human features and dragon attributes merged into one, but they will never escape the capture of being mounted to their buildings. Some people think that they are a supernatural jack-o'-lantern like those we see on Halloween.

When they aren't protecting buildings, they are used as water spouts in fountains, with water spewing from their mouths. *Gargoyle* derives from the French word *gargouille* meaning "throat," which is reminiscent of the sound of the water that comes out of the downspout of the statue. Gargoyles are a physical warning for religious followers of Catholicism that if they don't obey the church's strict laws and reject God then they, too, will become gargoyles.

The gargoyle was used for the wrong reasons at times, and I welcome you and encourage you to call upon the gargoyle and give it an even higher place in history. Gargoyles can be watchful protectors, can scare off those that try to harm you, and can ward off negative energies, of course. On the other hand, gargoyles are mysterious and entertaining; they are sticking their tongue out at a society that tries to trap them. They can be humorous and whimsical. They are a thumbed nose at a society that no longer cares. I believe that one day, with a little faith, the gargoyles will come down from the castle like we all are challenged to do—to make our path on our own terms.

In conjure there are energies we encounter that will be frightening and cause us to tremble. It's a spirit that you sense in a dark building, or it's something that attacks your ankles or wrists when you are trying to protect a family from it. The gargoyle can be your symbol to not take things so seriously and to believe that you can succeed as long as you have faith in the deliverance work and you have exercised the tenets of intention, faith, and direction.

IN MEMORIAM

Honoring those that have left this earth in a tragic manner is unfortunately a sign of our times—and has been for our birth and chosen ancestors and guides. You may have other beings whose lives are now a testament to the brief and important work that is before us as hoodoo workers. As conjurers. As those people that will change and cause change to our world. Their souls are not tortured anymore, and we can call upon them and ask for their help and guidance in our own social justice causes. I believe this is one of the main reasons for using our hoodoo practices—to bring about the change and realignment of our communities to what they can be, which is a refuge for all of us that are different. Our voices are getting stronger and louder, and we will not be silenced.

The Bible verse Amos 5:24 speaks of this in full:

> *But let justice roll down like waters, and righteousness like an ever-flowing stream.*

How do you call upon these departed ancestors? Before you go out and protest, I recommend you do two things:

First write the names of your ancestors in temporary ink on your body (arm, leg, face). If you do not want to use temporary ink, then dip a cotton swab or toothpick in oil and use that.

Next, get yourself a bag (a small bag is fine) to hold the herbs. Take herbs that calm if that's what you want to channel. Calming herb examples include hyssop, basil, or a member of the mint family (chocolate mint or peppermint are good choices). Mint spreads the words and the calming herbs to reduce inflammatory emotions that arise. If you want to channel anger, then use spicier, fiery herbs and vegetables.

I would use cinnamon, garlic, or peppers (cayenne, chipotle, jalapeño). Be careful to not burn yourself in the process. Keep these ingredients contained in the bag. They can irritate you if they touch your skin. If you want to channel love, use sweet ingredients: rose, grasses, jasmine, honeysuckle, salvia.

Note that when I've spoken to spirits that have crossed over, even tragically, I have never heard them wanting retaliation or vengeance. But they have offered themselves for justice, peace, community, and protection work. Approach these ancestors with the reverence that they deserve as I tell their stories. They may not work for any or all of you. They may be of a different culture or belief system than you. Spirit and energy are interchangeable and universal. Hoodoo is for everyone.

On March 16, 2021, a shooter took the lives of eight innocent people. They were doing their jobs at the spas where they worked. Reports indicate this was a hate crime, that the shooter targeted these souls because they were Asian.[3] Rest in power:

Delaina Ashley Yaun Gonzalez, thirty-three years old

Paul Andre Michels, fifty-four years old

Xiaojie Yan, forty-nine years old

Daoyou Feng, forty-four years old

Soon Chun Park, seventy-four years old

Hyun Jung Grant, fifty-one years old

Suncha Kim, sixty-nine years old

Yong Ae Yue, sixty-three years old

A ninth person, Elcias R. Hernandez-Ortiz, thirty years old, was shot and injured in the mass shootings.

On April 15, 2021, Chicago's Civilian Office of Police Accountability released body cam footage of a shooting. Not just any shooting, but the shooting of thirteen-year-old Adam Toledo. There were disputes that the child was armed and a threat to the police. This video proved them wrong. It shows him complying with the arresting officers' demands, raising his hands in the air—just before he was killed by a gunshot to the chest. His death sparked a debate on social media. Posts ranged from blaming his parents, his race, and his alleged affiliation with gangs, to even his nickname for his murder. Regardless of what the court of public opinion thought, to his mother, Elizabeth Toledo, and his friends, and family, he was a teenager, son, nephew, and friend. On the GoFundMe page to fund his funeral expenses, his mom wrote of Adam:

> *I'm going to share a little about Adam he was a son, a brother, a uncle, a nephew, a friend, a child with a big loving family and many friends. Adam loved to play with Lego's, saying funny jokes to make others laugh, he was a child that brightened up the room when he would walk in.*

> *Adam had many dreams that he will never get to live out. Ironically one of his dreams was to become a police officer.*

Eighty-two-year-old Mohammed Saleem was a victim of a terrorist attack. On April 29, 2013, in Small Heath Birmingham, UK, on one of his five daily walks to and from his home to the mosque to pray, he was brutally stabbed to death. He was described by his daughter as being gentle and kind. Saleem was a grandfather to twenty-two children. Saleem's death was ruled an act of terrorism by the West Midlands Counter Terrorism Unit.

A twenty-seven-year-old African American, transgender woman, Bree Black, was shot to death in Pompano Beach, Florida. There were a reported one hundred potential witnesses, but little information was shared with police (even a month later) to help them bring the murderer(s) to justice. The Human Rights Campaign stated that Bree was the twentieth transgender person to lose their life in a hate crime attack that was targeted at the transgender community.

It tears my soul that those taken from this physical world through violence include those that identify as nonbinary, gender nonconforming, and transgender. There are websites devoted to telling their names, like the Anti-Violence Project (AVP). These sites are important because they highlight who the person was, and not their death story.

The page spans four years (starting in 2017). Some of their names are shared below:

Summer Taylor	24 years old	Struck by a vehicle
Angel Naira	36 years old	Shot
Jessi Hart	42 years old	Unknown; identified as "suspicious"
Mel Groves	25 years old	Shot
Poe Black	21 years old	Stabbed
Whispering Wind Bear Spirit	41 years old	Shot
Bee Love Slater	23 years old	Burned
Sasha Garden	27 years old	Unknown; identified as suspicious, trauma

An ancestor reached out to me when I was up late at night writing this chapter. She introduced herself as just Tamika, followed by suggesting that I look up "Black woman, missing, Natalee Holloway." Her name then popped up right next to an article about Laci Peterson. Peterson was a pregnant white woman murdered by her husband. She had gone missing in 2002. The media attention was almost immediate, with article after article pleading for people to look at her picture and help find her. Tamika's story was not so publicly shared. Twenty-four-year-old Tamika Huston went missing in 2004. Her aunt, Rebkah Howard (wife of NFL player Desmond Howard), asked the media to tell her missing niece's story: "I was sending [press] releases, I was calling producers, I was calling news desks, every network, every website I could think of, and I hit a brick wall.... Her story is just as compelling.... The only difference is that Tamika's Black; Natalee Holloway is white." They gave the story very little attention. Tamika's dismembered body was eventually discovered many days after she was reported missing. Tamika insisted that she did not want you, the reader, to pity her but to share her story and the stories of others. She kept mentioning over and over that she is not dead in spirit as long as her name is known and spoken on other's lips. I put her name on my altar and tell her story to any that will hear it. Tamika's story is finally being told on a national stage. Derrica and Natalie Wilson, founders of the Black and Missing Foundation, tell Tamika's story in the *Black and Missing* docuseries that aired on HBO in November 2021.[4]

You can honor these ancestors (unfortunately new names are added almost daily) by reciting a Bible verse, spraying protection and blessing water, and lighting candles for justice work over the creators and owners of websites and organizations that are dedicated to the murdered, like Say Every Name (https://sayevery.name), the Southern Poverty Law Center (https://splcenter.org), and Missing Murdered Indigenous Women USA (https://mmiwusa.org).

◇◇◇◇◇◇ CHAPTER 4 EXERCISES ◇◇◇◇◇◇

My Dad, the Imperfect Hero

Before my dad died, he had a vision of his death. I really think he understood it was time to go and he went around making sure to say goodbye. As a conjure worker we can help each other let go. Letting go can mean physically releasing yourself from a situation that is no longer in your interest, or it can be letting go as in a death or a transition.

Letting go gives you space to allow yourself to be possessed or allow yourself to commune with your ancestors, guides, and deities so you can work with them and they can work through you. To do this, you must trust them and allow yourself to let go of fears. Fear is false evidence that appears real. When we are given someone else's narrative of ourselves that isn't the most positive, then it is common to turn inward and stop trusting. But with the hoodoo practice of learning about yourself and others that deserve your respect and honor, you will get more comfortable with letting the imperfections that you have be the most beloved part of yourself, like my father did.

Do the following exercise:

1. Hold out your arms.

2. Stand up.

3. Try to hold your breath while simultaneously holding your arms around yourself.

4. Sit back down.

Repeat the exercise, this time trying to open your arms wider and wider while trying to tighten your sphincter.

Then repeat the exercise one more time. This time, lift your voice to say "Meeee!!" while opening your arms.

Note the differences in your feelings and experiences. Which one was easier? Which one was more difficult? The more difficult exercise helps you understand how much you can release and multitask. The other will help you with understanding how easy or hard it is to project your voice and yourself to an outside force, like a guide.

Michael's Spell

Intention: Reduction of fear; comfort

Faith: Through courage of the spirit that takes care of you

Direction: Inner strength; self-love

Ingredients: Tea, cups, water, Bible verse, intention, faith, and direction

Brew your choice of tea in everyday, nondescript cups. Earl Grey would be Michael's choice. Play some Depeche Mode or a similar '90s band and begin reciting the following Bible verse:

> When the righteous cry for help, the Spirit of Old hears and delivers them out of all their troubles. The Spirit of Old is near to the brokenhearted and saves the crushed in spirit. Many are the afflictions of the righteous, but the Spirit of Old delivers all of them—all of them. (Psalm 34:17–19)

From the Torah (Exodus 3:14–15) you can use

> I am becoming who I am becoming. This is my name forever.

If you choose not to use these verses, Michael suggests using the lyrics to "Personal Jesus" by Depeche Mode.

Allow yourself to recite the name Michael, and think of how Michael begins to look to you. As you connect, allow the verse to protect you as you enter this conversation, and give him your request for deliverance. Close your eyes, dim the lights, and allow this hero Michael to speak and have tea with you. When the tea is cold and the song is complete, then so is the spell.

Take your tea bag outside, and leave its contents near a tree. Say, "Thank you for listening," and leave knowing that you have been heard, loved, and supported.

A note about Michael: As a member of the LGBTQIA community, Michael reflects how to be an open and affirming guide. He passed away almost twenty years ago, but his light is still shining through this writing, through your reading of this book, and through your practice of his spell.

If someone you know is struggling emotionally or having a hard time, you can be the difference in getting them the help they need. It's important to take care of yourself when you are supporting someone through a difficult time, as this may stir up difficult emotions. If it does, please reach out for support for yourself.

Text GO to 741741 to reach a trained crisis counselor through Crisis Text Line, a global nonprofit organization. It's free, 24/7, and confidential.

Tamika Huston Spell

As I shared in Tamika's story, Tamika spoke to me, immediately wanting to take part as a shared ancestor. She didn't want to be a cautionary tale but rather a source of empowerment for women in abusive relationships that want to be freed. Her story is tragic, yes, but in her story is the knowledge that her story doesn't have to be yours. According to the National Coalition Against Domestic Violence, twenty people are abused by an intimate partner every sixty seconds.[5] In hoodoo I cannot promise you that your deliverance spells will give you protection against physical and mental cruelty and protect your life and those of your children and pets, or promise that they will protect your finances, or do other things. That would be negligent, but I can tell you that faith, intention, and direction have changed the lives of many people in situations that they needed to overcome.

One Bible verse I use when I think of Tamika and how strong her spirit is when you want guidance to find a way out is this: "Behold, I will create new heavens and a new earth. The former things will not be remembered, nor will they come to mind." (Isaiah 65:17)

Start with a picture of you—the you without any of the scars of the current harm. Even if you need to draw it or take a photo of what you want, or create this image in your mind. Then think of the love that you want for yourself and need and deserve. Allow any tears or fears or joys to happen. As this cleanses you, reach to your ancestors, guides, and deities and say this chant with the knowledge that you will be able to be a new self. The former things will not be able to touch you. You are taking steps to become a new you. You *are* a new you. You are strong enough to get away. You are strong enough to take all steps to get to safety. You are strong enough to leave. Say to yourself, "Ancestor Tamika, give me the strength to *go*! To survive. To make a way out of no way. To make my story a new story. To create a new earth and life for me and my family." Make a donation in Tamika's name to a homeless or battered women's shelter. Build your safety plan.[6] Love you. You can do this!

Rescue Me! Spell

There are times when you just need a quick way to get out of a situation. This is the fastest way I know of:

Get your favorite hard candy (mint, fruit-flavored, etc.) with a hole in it (like Life Savers).

Copy or handwrite the Bible verse Psalm 35:17 on a piece of paper, roll it up, and place it in the hole of the candy.

> *Lord, how long will You look on? Rescue my soul from their ravages, My only life from the lions.*

Hang it on a string from your bedroom window or from the nearest window that can catch daylight.

Every day chant the Psalm when you wake up before doing *anything* else.

Keep it hanging until it has been delivered. Eat a candy (from the bag or roll of the one doing the hoodoo) every day until your request is delivered.

Once it is delivered, take the candy down and offer it at the crossroads or throw it away.

NOTES

1   Miriam Makeba Official Website, www.miriammakeba.co.za/.

2   Fergus M. Bordewich, "John Brown's Day of Reckoning," *Smithsonian Magazine*, October 2009, http://macshistory.weebly.com/uploads/2/7/2/9 /27291669/john_brown_-smithsonian_article.pdf.

3   Emily Puckering, "NYC Building Staff Fired For Failing to Help Asian Woman During Attack," *22 Words*, https://twentytwowords.com/staff-failing-help -asian-woman/.

4   Gina Tron, "How Did a Beloved Dog Convince Tamika Huston's Family That She Was in Danger?" Oxygen True Crime, November 24, 2021, www.oxygen .com/true-crime-buzz/tamika-hustons-murder-overshadowed-by-runaway -bride-natalee-holloway-is-black-and.

5   Statistics, National Coalition Against Domestic Violence, www.ncadv.org /statistics.

6   Personalized Safety Plan, National Coalition Against Domestic Violence, www.ncadv.org/personalized-safety-plan.

PUTTING IT ALL TOGETHER

Now we get to the content that some of you may have been asking for since chapter 1. When do I get to write a spell? Here it is! Congratulate yourself on making it through the work of chapters 1 through 4. If you haven't done it—why not? I am providing you with these items in stages so that you can understand how and why I became a real hoodoo worker. I want you to be the best hoodoo worker you can be, and studying and researching our shared ancestry, guides, sacred text, fighters, and more is what it took. It wasn't fast-forwarding and writing a spell. It's so much more than that.

For those of you that have done the work, continue with this informative chapter.

THE WRITTEN WORD

The combination of all four elements in magic (earth, water, fire, air) and the addition of your personal spirit as the fifth gives hoodoo its power. If I want something to go away from me, I will put it in a source that moves away from me. If I want something to stay, then I will have the object stay near me (on my body or on the ground where I live). If I want something to go away, as I mentioned, then I will put it into a source that moves it away. Sources that move things away include rivers, streams, lakes, the toilet, and your sink in your house. Remember that the landfills, oceans, and atmosphere will be recirculating what you put out there. All this magic goes somewhere. In hoodoo, unless you must physically require an object, then recycle something (like a used newspaper or letter or sticky note); do not use new paper. There are around three trillion trees in the world. That sounds like a lot, but because we humans use around fifteen billion trees a year for toilet paper, timber, farmland expansion, and other human needs, it is not going to last forever. The forests and trees will thank you for paying them homage.

When I write home clearings and blessings to remove negative energies, in my protection prayer I find and use Bible verses that protect me—the human—and animal beings in my home before, during, and after the clearing is done. I start the blessing with salt and water that I have prayed over, and I circle the home, sprinkling this solution or spraying it into the air from a spray bottle. It does not have to be a fire hose of water; small amounts work well.

I burn some incense. I play my favorite songs that keep me safe and comfortable. I carry in my mind pictures of the protective energies. I shout and chant, rattle and drum my way through the entire home.

If I am doing conjure work for my relationship, then I start with the love and emotion that the energy gives me. I use herbs that signify love for me. But what if you don't like herbs (or are allergic)? You can always use other objects that speak to you—for example, flowers, jewelry, hibiscus flower, apple, cinnamon, orange, or body fluids (saliva and ejaculate). Say I want to make sure that my relationships between me and my lovers are solid and secure. I would collect objects from my lovers (hair, nails, ejaculate on a cotton swab, etc.). I would ask each lover to sign a piece of paper (newspaper, love letter, etc.) and place them in the ground, preferably somewhere near where we are, with the intention of keeping us in the home. When we depart, I will dig up these blessings and burn them if there has been a breakup or store them in a jar if I am taking them with me (if we are moving). That also reminds me: when doing conjure outside, have some type of marker so that you know where it is buried if you ever need or want to dig it back up.

Fire is powerful and destructive—simply great for making things dissipate. It destroys, it causes change for better or worse, and it matches your intention perfectly. When I put a piece of paper in the fire, it burns, and then that burning of the paper changes the paper into a new form called ash, and the ash floats into the air. That air then goes up into the sky, where it is consumed by the atmosphere in the clouds, and then it turns back into water.

When using fire in hoodoo, it is sending messages directly through that transference of energy for all five elements (earth, water, fire, air, and spirit).

Voting/Election Work

Voting is important. It is free and shapes the world you live in. Many of our shared ancestors fought and died for this right to exercise our feelings and desires in deciding which candidate gets our vote. Bless and pray for those candidates that deliver your shared deliverance work. Banish and fight against those that disagree with what your shared ancestors desire. Note that I did mean to say "what your shared ancestors desire"—what the ancestors want for the world we live in, not what you wanted. There is a substantial difference.

I start with a clean body, mind, and spirit. I gather my ingredients and tools, including my Bible verse(s). I write out my request on a piece of paper (also called a petition paper). It can be amazingly simple paper—a paper bag, sticky note, wax paper, copy of the voting ballot, or an email from your candidate are good examples. Write on the paper "You have my vote, go do my work," turning it in a clockwise direction after you write each statement, until the page is filled with words.

If I were doing the voting work against a candidate, I would chew a piece of gum and stick it to their political flyers. I would say over and over, "Your campaign is stuck and goes nowhere because it is written..." (then add my Bible verse). I would continue doing this for as many as thirteen days (about two weeks), but at least five. Then I would keep checking the polls and watching my hoodoo work.

Banishment and Protection Texts

In Africa, where all civilization began, Sumerians wrote down symbols and lines that became objects that became words that became our beginnings of magic in written form. When someone knew your name and wrote the symbol to represent it, then it was believed that person now had power over you. People would write on slabs of clay. The Persians and the Assyrians duplicated this, and this became writing. Holy people, like priests, were the only ones that could write without persecution because of the power that writing held. The Palermo Stone is one of the first known written documentations of history using a system of characters that represent what we think of as an alphabet. It covers a time period from around 3150 to 2283 BCE. The Kish tablet may be the oldest known writing effort (by the Sumerians), dated at around 3500 BCE.

In 1984, not so long ago, Friedhelm Hillebrand typed hundreds of random words and phrases on a typewriter. Once he counted them he found that nearly every message was made up of fewer than 160 characters. To him, this was the standard length for a perfect sentence, and it became the standard length for text messaging, which was a feature on phones that mobile manufacturer, Nokia, debuted in 1993. The phones did not have a keyboard, so messages needed to be entered using numerical keypads. In 1995, predictive text (which was called T9) added more intellect around the experience of using the short message service (SMS). Who would have guessed that roughly entered slashes and dots and circles pounded onto clay slabs by descendants of old would one day be something that would carry the power of starting and ending relationships.

> "Behold, I give unto you power to tread on serpents and scorpions, and over all the power of the enemy: and nothing shall by any means hurt you." (Luke 10:19)

Using Fiction and Nonfiction as Sacred Words

When you've tried to use the Bible and you've tried to redirect or shift the language, you may still want and need more sacred words. I get my sacred words from anywhere and nowhere in particular. My wife is a woodworker, and she blessed our niece with the most adorable toy box, handcrafted with love. To dedicate the object, I wanted to come up with a special blessing that was free from any religious overtones, because her family is choosing the more spiritual and less religious tradition. Here is what I wrote. Feel free to use or even modify this when you are blessing an object:

Creator and Author of the human race; Giver of all spiritual Graces, Ancestors of my niece, send down. May the Spirit of us all give and grant a blessing from on high upon this (this toy box), that, fortified by the might of celestial protection, it helps bring a smile to everyone that uses it and encourages us all to play as you would have it glory, both now and ever, and to the ages of ages. We call it so.

There is also poetry as a way of blessing objects—for example, if you wanted to bless an upcoming adventure or trip by car or boat or plane. You can take a poem about said car and then shift it by adding the intention, faith, and direction that it needs. I'll be using the Walt Whitman poem "Song of the Open Road" and modifying it to have a hoodoo flair. Original Text:

Afoot and light-hearted I take to the open road,
Healthy, free, the world before me,
The long brown path before me leading me wherever I choose.

Henceforth I ask not good-fortune, I am good-fortune,
Henceforth I whimper no more, postpone no more, need nothing,
Done with indoor complaints, libraries, querulous criticisms,
Strong and content I travel the open road.

—Walt Whitman, from "Song of the Open Road"

Updated hoodoo text modified version:

I take to the open road with a heart full and grateful from all ancestors around me, I've been given this body, this health, this opportunity, and the world is opening just for me on this journey to go wherever I want.

I'm not asking of you, my guides, to do anything special on this trip, because I know that you are always with me and have given me what I need to make this trip successful.

I'm only looking forward and not relying upon any past thoughts or worries. I have everything I need, and this trip will refresh and give me the adventure that is well deserved and blessed. With your protection, I am strong and satisfied to travel this open road.

What makes a fiction or nonfiction text a sacred text? The definition of a sacred text can be many things. *Merriam-Webster's Dictionary* defines *sacred* as "devoted exclusively to one service or use" and defines *text* as "the original words and form of a written or printed work." An important note: the Bible itself has been edited, modified, and translated several times in its over two thousand years of existence. As written in an article by Business Insider, there is no first edition of the Bible; for the first two hundred years of the Bible's existence, it was written out by hand.[1] This is important because the definition of *text* in *Webster's* definition includes "as the original words and form of a written or printed work." Consider there is no "original" draft of the Bible when using the text as a basis for conjure work. This also explains why I make no qualms about editing the text to meet my needs. This has been done, even by the editors and publishers of Bibles over the texts' lifetime. As hoodoo is an oral tradition, with some written guidelines shared now in this century, it would be safe to assume we have no "original" text of spells, conjure instructions, and guides. Only our faith, intention, and direction as we see it to do the work makes it sacred. You using it in your practice makes it sacred. You giving it reverence makes it sacred. If you use this book as a reference to study with and to bring about ritual practices or conduct spiritual aspirations, then this book will become part of your sacred texts.

I enjoy listening to all kinds of music and I especially find opera, country music, and hip-hop to be my favorites. I can get into the classics too, like those from the 1960s and 1970s. There's one about love that always makes me so happy when I hear it—"Longer" by Dan Fogelberg. Fogelberg sings that he has been in love with his partner longer than there were fish or birds flying or seasons or elements. I loved it so much that it was part of my wedding ceremony, as I hummed it to myself as I proceeded to the altar to be handfasted to my bride. It spoke to how much I loved her at that moment (and still do), especially with its focus on the elements.

It has intense and very directed intention, faith, and direction. The author of the text takes you on a journey where you see the romance go from the whimsy of a first-time love through the passage of time to an everlasting love. The intention is clear—the commitment of the relationship for a very long time. The direction is clear. The author wants to stay with this person forever, and they want the intended audience (listener) to know how much they love this person. The faith is a prayer. The text is a prayer, a wish, a demand to the deity and guides above to make this dream a reality because of the enduring power of the truth and honesty in their words. This makes the text special. If said as part of a blessing over the bedroom where they sleep or before there is a commitment ceremony or as a text message to the lover, it is powerful and direct.

Fiction is also a powerful medium. There are fantastic, animated depictions of our human existence that are almost more realistic than our worlds. Fiction is nothing but imagined narratives. The Bible (in my experience) is the imagined narrative of stories that some use as truth and others use as guideposts for how to live life. When friends of mine that do not subscribe to my beliefs read things that are fiction that inspire them, then it is just as powerful to them as it is to me when I read narratives from someone's experience that cannot be proven—therefore is in itself not fact but fiction.

I remember listening to a certain song in the 1990s that made me pull over my car and cry. It was the Cranberries "Zombie." It is the battle cry of the band that is in memory of the killing of young children in the 1993 Warrington bombings in Ireland. Over 3,600 people died in the more than thirty years of conflict and war. More than ten thousand bombs rained down on the victims during this time. You can hear the pain in the writer's words. When I want to have a song that I can use to incite the emotions of a war-torn society that needs healing, I will use these words and modify them to shape what the end result will be. I will recite the words and add the scent of smoke and the pain of tears. I will call to my ancestors to ask for the cries to be silenced. That the bombs will cease. I will take these words and burn them to ash and spread them across poppy fields or honor those that have passed by giving them a resting place in a cemetery of their choosing with the help of the Blue Lady. I will give the Blue Lady an offering and ask her to help ease the pain and reduce the fighting around our countries that has not let up, but it must let up because the number of human and natural world victims is climbing.

Here's another example: I am watching an animated horror film and it tells a story of a dark presence that is taking over a family and terrorizing them. The author created the story and it is not an accounting of anything that happened personally to the writer, but it is a tale that is known in folklore—the dark creepy house with creaking stairs and bone-chilling screams by some unseen energy. The author then proceeds to tell how the protagonist battles this force and wins in the end. Glorious! However, this is a work of fiction, right? Yes, but in most of these tales, the author will use some type of ritual or supernatural force to validate and then prevail over that energy. That makes it something that is more along the lines of a sacred text. It inspires. It builds confidence. It helps the reader know more about the ways of those that operate on faith—something that can never be proven but just is. It doesn't matter the intention of the work, only what it does to the reader. I hope that my book is an inspiration and is held sacred—sacred because it builds up my own understanding of what this world is capable of. This world that can be scary and negative but also gives so much pleasure and community.

The first time I read *The Alchemist* by Paulo Coelho I was transitioning from a married mother of three to a single mother of one after I came out to my family. I left my entire existence to live a life that I knew now was my truth. I needed to find others that also had this same battle within and hear that it was achievable to see the other side. I found this quote from this now sacred text of mine:

When you want something, all the universe conspires in helping you to achieve it.

—*Paulo Coelho, The Alchemist*

This is what I hope hoodoo does for you. As you build your life and your rituals around finding texts that speak to you, you will see that our universe will not stand in your way anymore. It will give you more and more information, opportunities, and advantages. I encourage you to find the novels, folklore, and oral history that speak to you and inspire you and add these to your sacred texts. This is known as documenting a Book of Shadows. A Book of Shadows is a special collaboration of rituals, spells, tools, and techniques that you have used for your magical practice. My "hoodoo to go" is a Book of Shadows. Others may have a heavily adorned book that is passed down from generation to generation.

In my favorite science fiction series *Firefly*, two characters, River and Book have an exchange where River has Book's Bible. Book is a preacher of the old ways and River is an experimental super soldier that has been traumatized by those that her parents trusted with her education (very long story). River attempts to destroy the Bible by tearing out pages from it. Book, rushing to put it back together, tries to explain to River what the book can mean to many:

Book: River, you don't fix the Bible.

River: It's broken. It doesn't make sense.

Book: It's not about making sense. It's about believing in something, and letting that belief be real enough to change your life. It's about faith. You don't fix faith, River. It fixes you.

HOODOO UPGRADES

Hoodoo upgrades mean taking what our ancestors did and making it current for today's hoodoo worker. Adding shortcuts, using our technology, removing past judgments or fears that don't serve us, updating our hoodoo pantry without having to grow everything ourselves. These things are covered in hoodoo upgrades.

Foods, Beverages, and Liquors

When I was growing up, part of my experience with magical rituals included some type of food or drink. When there was a funeral or mourning ceremony, we ate after the service, sharing stories of the departed while enjoying something hot and comforting (and probably cheesy or buttery). This is the upside of food and memories. I love times with family and friends. I enjoy alcoholic beverages, and from time to time even enjoy some marijuana-infused brownies or cupcakes. Sweet, salty, fatty, and sour are all parts of my lifestyle that I enjoy. As a hoodoo worker and lover of hoodoo foundations, will you take a journey with me on some of our favorite foods so that we can share an understanding of why they are important and how to use them in hoodoo?

My favorite parts of holidays are the food and the fun times, laughing over things like cakes or a cocktail with pomegranate or hibiscus tea. Even things as ritualistic as a wedding cake have a fascinating (and sometimes tragic) history. Let's start with interesting.

The first wedding cake was said to have been made in Rome, where the term "break bread" may have originated. Bread was broken over the bride's head to ensure good luck in the marriage. Some origin stories state the new husband was told to do this to show dominance over the bride. Cakes weren't flour based like we know them now. Cakes were made from barley or millet and mixed with dates and currants (think seeds and syrup). In Africa, cakes were made from plantain and kola nuts. African Americans in the South mixed these two traditions of sweet flour into inspirations called tea cakes. African American tea cakes do not resemble the English ones. They are a dropped cookie with a soft, cakey texture. You could make a lot with a few ingredients: fat, lard, or shortening; sugar (or something sweet like molasses); eggs; milk; and flour (you could add vanilla if you had it, but I doubt my great-great-grandma had anything like that back then).

In England, cakes were stacked one atop another as high as they could possibly go. The story is that if the couple was successful at kissing over the stack of cakes, then their marriage would be fruitful. Also in England was the tradition of a bride's pie. A glass ring would be placed inside of a pie and each guest would be offered a slice. If a guest refused, then bad luck would fall upon the couple. The wedding cake as some of us know it did not start until around the 1920s and consisted of cakes that were set on broomsticks used as pillars. Only the very wealthy could afford the sugar in the cake and icing. The cakes each had layers and icing (very common in today's times as well). Fruits, vegetables, proteins, nuts, and grains were included in the original first cakes for all to share. The cake was then presented (and represented) the newlyweds.

During slavery, weddings were mostly frowned upon by the plantation owners. Other enslavers felt that the enslaved Africans were less likely to run if they were married to and responsible for another. The wedding would consist of maybe the plantation owner reciting some verses from the Bible and maybe allowing the couple to hold hands. Then, after the ceremony (if it could be called this), the couple would have to go back to the fields or to the house to continue their chores and back-breaking work. However, when celebrations could occur, the offerings were cornfield peas (black-eyed peas that were traditionally planted in between rows of corn), rice, watermelon, and okra. There were other foods that enslaved Africans lived on at that time. Foods like fufu (a dough made from starch mixed with hot or boiling water and served with soups), grits (ground corn served hot), and gruel, which was a mixture of millet and sorghum. Interestingly the foods that those in North America lived on were sometimes shared with the working animals on the farm. The foods had to be easily transportable and full of fats, and it contained scraps of the foods not eaten by the enslavers. Their diet consisted of mainly carbohydrates, rabbit, squirrel, cow, or fowl, and fat supplemented with a few fruits (the watermelon that they grew and an apple or orange for the Christmas holiday).

The beverages that were available to enslaved Africans were limited as well. Coffee was tied to slavery because of the coffee trade from Brazil and other countries. For example, in the 1800s roughly two million enslaved Africans were brought to Portugal and Brazil to work the coffee farms. Once they arrived, their life expectancy was around seven years. Coffee was traded worldwide through Europe, the Middle East, Asia, and the Americas. Kidnapped or sold Africans were forced into labor in what was called the triangle trade. The same occurred for the sugar trade. The merchandise was very important and lucrative, but the cost of human lives was not. Some who sold and traded enslaved Africans systematically underfed, overworked, and beat them, and if given a chance would rather see them die because it was more cost effective to bring in new "resources" from Africa than to keep the existing ones alive. The conditions of coffee and sugar farmers is something that hoodoo workers need to be aware of when doing any kind of work with them. Alcohol was also part of the triangle trade.

Africans were captured and sold and then delivered to enslavers worldwide. Sometimes alcohol was used to lower the Africans' defenses and make them less prone to fight back. Enslavers and traders also used alcohol as a bartering tool in the slave trade. Some historians argue that Africans rarely indulged in alcoholic beverages and rarely used them in any ritual ceremony. They chose ritualistic use of tobacco and other psychedelics from roots or plants over using fermented mashes of fruits or berries. Once captured and brought to North America, enslaved Africans were prohibited from owning or operating alcoholic beverages or distillery machines. Indentured Black, white, and Indigenous folk could not drink, purchase, or have possession of alcohol unless their enslavers allowed it.[2] This did not prevent poorer whites from trading alcohol to enslaved Africans in exchange for goods and services. Enslavers used alcohol to encourage enslaved Africans to work harder and longer hours during harvest time. The enslavers also enjoyed using alcohol as a way to gamble—drinking contests among enslaved Africans were a pastime for enslavers.

Give strong drink to the one who is perishing, and wine to those in bitter distress; let them drink and forget their poverty and remember their misery no more. (Proverbs 31:6–7)

Rituals using these objects can be powerful with the knowledge of this history. When we as beginning and advanced hoodoo workers use these foods, beverages, and liquors, we do so in honor of the lives, souls, and practices that they originate from. Entire cultures have been torn apart and ravaged by substances. But it isn't too late to change the narrative of what these objects do to us and for us. When used as part of a ritual service, for example, they can help consecrate other tools and even bring a different element into the ritual. See chapter 6 notes for the ritual and spells.

Herbs, Roots, and Plants: Fresh or Dried?

What is an herb versus a plant? An herb is the above-ground part of a plant. The roots are the below-ground part of the plant. Sometimes we eat the herbs or leafy part of the plant and its stems, and sometimes we eat or work with the plant that is below ground (like potatoes, onions, garlic). We also can use both (shallots, celery, turmeric, valerian).

Here's something about working with fresh herbs or dried herbs in your baths (really any hoodoo): in general, I use about twice the amount of fresh herbs than dried herbs. To me dried herbs last longer here in the Pacific Northwest, but if you are in an already dry, climate you may want to get basil, mint, or other fresh herb plants from the grocery or plant store and snip away as you need. I prefer having the fresh plant when I can so that I can put my own energy into them. Either way, be sure to bless and anoint your herbs before using them. I have luck with herbs and retail herb products because I trust my vendors; however, if you get your herbs cheaply (and who doesn't), then make sure the herb is exactly what you expect. I've seen High John the Conqueror root being sold that was really chopped up pieces of broom. I've seen grass chopped up and sold as chives or lemongrass. It's very sad, but it is out there. Start with herbs you know, can see, and even smell to be sure they are ones you are expecting. Allergens may be another reason to be careful with fresh herbs. I have had allergic reactions to the fresh herbs that I haven't had with dried, because the fresh herbs are so pure and natural. Any herb should be spot-checked for allergens and quality before you throw a whole batch of it into your rootwork.

When working with roots, wash and triple wash the roots to remove any remaining dirt or insects (as these are naturally found on fresh ingredients). Be careful when rinsing to not squeeze the roots or the flowers or leaves. In these pieces is the medicine and you'll basically be rinsing it down the drain. To start with, use culinary herbs before you move to more exotic ones. I have herbal book recommendations in the "Suggested Reading" section. I've been using *Rosemary Gladstar's Medicinal Herbs: A Beginner's Guide* and Karen Harrison's *The Herbal Alchemist's Handbook: A Complete Guide to Magickal Herbs and How to Use Them*—and not just because Karen's a personal friend and mentor.

Here are some of my favorite accessible herbs, roots, plants, seeds, and grains for hoodoo:

- Mint
- Garlic
- Basil
- Thyme
- Rosemary
- Turmeric
- Parsley
- Dill
- Cilantro
- Sweet potatoes
- Onion
- Peanut
- Rice
- Black-eyed peas
- Pinto beans
- Chives
- Mugwort

Sugar

I use sweetener in so many things. In my drinks, desserts, condiments, breads—it's just everywhere. But in truth, in hoodoo there are two reasons to use sweeteners. To sweeten or encourage a situation or to stick a situation or cause it to slow down. When you read online about honey jars and the like, these are hoodoo methods that our ancestors really did not use. How do I know this? Because I have been poor. Very poor. When you are very poor and you are eating syrup sandwiches because the government subsidies provided you with white bread and syrup and the rest of the rations are gone for the month, then you aren't going to waste the syrup you have on a ritual to ask for something like a new love life. You have to scrape by using whatever items you have on hand. Our ancestors were making their way with very empty stomachs. There was leftover fat from others' meals that had to be stretched to feed everyone in the cabin—you can't then turn around and use that in a ritual.

But, for some of us, our existence is different. We spend our time and extra income on physical supernatural objects, and that is the way of their path; however, in updated hoodoo this is not what we need. What we need is hard work in prayer, cleanliness of mind and spirit, being present when we attach and allow energies to possess us. These things cost, but not money. They cost your time, energy, and frame of mind.

Sweetening is easy. It requires sweet words. Sweet songs. Sweet poems. Sweet herbs and flowers and plants. Even if you can only afford to take a picture of what you need. The intention, faith, and direction is there, and so is the magic!

> You have not bought me sweet cane with money or satisfied me with the fat of your sacrifices. But you have burdened me with your sins; you have wearied me with your iniquities. (Isaiah 43:24)

Coffee

When I was a kid, if I ever had bad dreams my grandfather would give me a cup of coffee with tons of sugar and then let me hang out with him until I got sleepy. Usually it was right after I finished the whole cup. He would never let the cup go undrunk—he always had been told it was bad luck, and he didn't want to start teaching me bad habits. As I grew I learned that coffee has a rich history in magic and enslavement (as I mentioned in the "Foods, Beverages, and Liquors" section). But in conjure there are many things you can do with coffee that are in direct correlation to coffee folklore. Coffee has been a way to help partners stay together. When my grandma was having issues with my grandpa (they would argue or not speak to each other), she would write messages under the sugar bowl to encourage sweet words to be said. Whether my grandpa had his first or twenty-third cup of coffee, the sugar bowl would have the magic of soothing the spoken word. Also my family believes coffee is the binding fluid of a strong relationship. My great-aunt told me that the key to her keeping my uncle faithful was putting some of her first morning urine into his coffee.

I can't tell you which of these I have tried and held true, but I do know that today, putting blood or urine in any substance that someone drinks is illegal, unethical, and unsanitary. In updated hoodoo we know that we can still do spells that keep our lovers happy, sexy, and committed without using personal concerns, but it is good to know our history.

There are other benefits to coffee that make it something else to have on hand all the time in your conjure toolbox. I use coffee in my spiritual bath for cleansing and banishing negativity. I add coffee grounds to sock bags, amulets, and bracelets to keep me energized and joyful when I'm procrastinating. I smell coffee beans when I want to increase my psychic energies, because it invigorates me. Coffee in Western medicine tradition is known to have health benefits that reduce the effects of coronary heart disease, stroke, diabetes, and kidney disease. In some studies coffee is also shown to help reduce glucose levels (of course, it's coffee on its own without added sugar).

If you want a Bible verse to add to your coffee in spells, you can use Isaiah 51:17: "Awake! Awake! Put on strength! You who have drunk at the hand of the one deity in the cup and drained it out." So drink up and don't waste a drop!

Want more folklore on coffee? Here are some of my other favorites:

Coffee gives you a bad or muddled complexion. Coffee will prevent you from growing taller. To get rid of anxieties and/or a case of hiccups, eat potatoes three nights in a row, followed by coffee with castor oil in it on the fourth night. Whenever you spill coffee, your partner or lover is talking about you. Bury your coffee grounds or burn them, but never throw them away; it gives you bad luck. Don't throw away any coffee or coffee grounds on New Year's Day so that you have a good year. You will get a sum of money if you see a small bubble on your coffee and drink the bubble. If you pour a cup of coffee and you see a large bubble, then hurry up and drink it so that you will get a large sum of money. Always finish the cup of coffee poured for you. If you do not, you'll cry later. Never stir a cup of coffee with a fork; it is bad luck. If you want to be in a committed relationship, then place some menstrual blood or your blood into their coffee. If you want to have great sex or encourage sexual relations, then make a powder of sugar, peppermint, and grated orange or lemon peel and spoon it into their coffee or wine.

Moderation is good for most things we do, even with coffee. If you need coffee just to wake up or even to go to sleep and want to be relieved of this influence, then recite 1 Corinthians 6:12: "All things are lawful for me," but not all things are helpful. "All things are lawful for me," but I will not be enslaved by anything.

Apples

Apples in the Bible got a bad rap. They are a gift. They have a gorgeous star when you slice them in half at their fullest part. That star reminds me of the North Star, but it is surrounded by all of this sweet, nutritional value, the core being only a small part of the fruit. The flesh is covered by a thin skin with very tight pores that resemble my own. The apple was a gift from Eve to Adam and was one of many fruits available to them several thousand years ago, so I know that it's resilient. It certainly is inspiration in several poems, books, art, and folklore.

In apple divination you would count the number of seeds in the apple to tell if something will be true or not. If there is an odd number, then the answer is yes or the result is true. If even, then it is a no answer or the result is not true.

Here are a few folklore remedies and some information for you: To cure puffy and swollen eyes, lay a piece of rotten apple on them and go to sleep. If you harvest an apple in the moonlight, it will rot less quickly. You'll have bad luck if you accept an apple that's already been bitten into. If you rub a rotten apple on a pimple or wart, it will go away. Take seeds from an apple and place them on your face or forehead. The number of seeds that stay on your head will foretell the number of days it will be until you meet a new lover.

In Grecian tradition an apple represents love, and to make sure that the one you love loves you, you would take an apple seed and toss it into a fire. If it spoke to you (pops or crackles), then your love is true. If you do not hear anything, then this is a sign that the love is not going to work out. In Scandinavian tradition you need to sleep with half an apple under your pillow so you will dream of your next lover.

In science, Isaac Newton was sitting in a garden and saw an apple fall from the tree, and he wondered why the apple didn't fall sideways and upward. That made him begin the discovery of gravity—that something that was drawing the apple to the center of the earth. Did you also know that scientists that study apples are called pomologists? I'm not a pomologist, but I do know that apples are great options when you want to conjure up a love spell. This spell gives you your first step into making hoodoo dolls, so hold on to your gris-gris bags!

Hoodoo dolls are easy and hard. They are the manifestations of energies into a physical space. They are physically possessed objects. They represent the person that you want them to represent and require a birth and a death to give them a complete circle of life. Making a doll is creative and worthwhile and long lasting. I use apples to create mine because apples are inexpensive and malleable. I can make the head look like pretty much anyone, and they hold paint well. I then attach sticks for bodies and I give them clothing that is basically fabric, either from the person that they represent or fabric choices that are similar to their objects.

This spell is to make a relationship apple pairing that can withstand the test of time. I only do this pairing for committed relationships. It is inspired from my very own love binding from Song of Solomon 6:3 "I belong to my beloved and my beloved is mine."

2 apples (or more to represent each person in the relationship)

1 cup of lemon juice

1 tablespoon of salt

Objects or representatives of the person (hair, urine, mucus, snot, nails, blood, lashes, clothing)

Tongue depressor (craft sticks)

Glue or hot glue

Fabric

Paints to paint the face of the apple after it has dried (or even before it is water soluble and can handle the drying process)

Song of Solomon 6:3 Bible verse to give the apple its energy and protection and also to bind it to the other apple "lover(s)"

I start with two or more fresh red or pink apples (you can use green, but I would only do so in a souring spell). I skin the apples first and keep the apple peel just in case I need it for anything in the future—I always find something I can use it for.

I use a skewer to push holes into the apple to hold the personal concerns (or objects) I use a cotton swab to push the hair, nails, body fluids, or other personal concerns into those holes. I scrape out some flesh from the apple and seal the personal concern hole with it so that the effects do not slip out. Carve Song of Solomon 6:3 (either the verse itself or a phrase or the word "mine") on each apple. I add the craft stick to the bottom of the apple because this is where my fabric will be attached.

Then I carve faces into the apple. This is my favorite part because I can use a paring knife or any kind of carving element (even a spoon and fork). On each apple I write the names of those in the love relationship, so if I have two individuals, say Gery and Jerry, I will write on one apple "Gery" and on the other apple "Jerry." It also helps me with remembering which apple belongs to which person.

The apples will need to be dried. To do this, you soak them in a mixture of lemon juice and salt for thirty minutes. Take care to make sure the hole you made to hold the effects is sealed nicely before this step. Scrape and push more of the fruit into the hole you made earlier if necessary.

Take the lemon-soaked apples, place them onto a baking sheet, and put them in the oven, on its lowest setting, for up to two hours. You may think you could just leave the apples out for a natural dehydration. This will take quite a bit longer and can result in a rotten apple, not a nicely dried one, and will certainly be a less broken down and moldy apple.

Let the apples dry until cooled and then paint them to make them represent the energy and creativity and likeness of the lovers. Once this is finished, I attach the fabric choice to the craft stick with hot glue. Sometimes I add craft sticks to represent the body, arms, and legs and drape the fabric over them.

After the dolls are all completed, I whisper my intention, faith, and direction into each one. In my example I may say, "Gery, I breathe into you extreme kindness and forgiveness. I will that you love in honesty and that we keep each other satisfied in all areas. You will love and hold onto Jerry until we decide to part." And then to the other apple, I may say, "Jerry, I breathe into you sensual pleasure and the desire to give and receive. The fairness and listening skills. All my love to you I give to Gery until we decide to part."

Using hot glue I physically connect them (either by fabric or by craft sticks) and place them in a safe place where they won't get damaged or wet.

Using apples gives me so much joy. Apples represent beauty, sensuality, love, choice, and options. Use them in this way to enhance your updated hoodoo. Ask your ancestors how to add more apples to your daily spell and ritual work. Use dried apples in amulets and bags that you carry to add more love to your life. Simmer apple and cinnamon on a stove before selling or leasing a home to bring in the right tenants. Slice up apples and write in your messages of peace (using a paring knife or stick) and leave them on a trail as you walk in nature. Pray and bless apples and give them to those that you are forming new relationships with to keep the friendship sweet. If you do not have a fresh apple to share, then send over a photo of an apple to a new friend or to someone that is ailing. An apple a day keeps the health practitioner away, they say.

Lemon

Lemons are high in vitamin C, folate, potassium, flavonoids, and compounds called limonin. In human beings vitamin C deficiency leads to symptoms of weakness, anemia, gum disease, and skin problems. African healers (ethnomedicine practitioners) use plants, fruits, faith, intention, and direction to heal. In the book *African American Slave Medicine*, Herbert Covey helps us to understand that, traditionally, those who were enslaved had to go to their own people for healing.

These tart lovelies are part of my souring spell. What is a souring spell? It is a spell that is concocted when you want something to go intentionally wrong or you want to deflect or distract an energy from moving toward you. This could be for any purpose. I've used lemon sour spells on relationships, jobs I do not want any longer, and odd rashes that have appeared on my body. Energies that are just not comfortable get a sour spell too. My updated sour spell uses lemon, a piece of paper, and a freezer or refrigerator. Some call these ice box or freezer spells; they're the same thing. I carve the name of the person that I want to "sour" into the skin of a whole lemon with a knife or needle. Next I cut a slit into the lemon. I then write my wishes onto a piece of paper, sign the paper with my name, the date, and what Bible verse it is covered under, and then fold it so that it is the size needed to slide into the slit I made. I then insert it into the lemon, put the lemon in a rag, and toss it into the back of the freezer. Why the back? Because I do not want to accidently see or think about it. I want it to be just as abandoned as my thoughts about the person.

Lemons aren't always sour. The lemon actually goes through a process when it changes from green to yellow—when the green (the chlorophyl) is taken over by carotenoids. This can sound a bit overwhelming, but understand this: the chemical makeup of the lemon gives it its color. It's the same for other fruits like plums, tomatoes, and grapes. The vitamin found in lemons is called ascorbic acid (what we call vitamin C). Many of us may remember that this helped prevent sailors from becoming sick from scurvy on excursions in the 1700s.[3]

Lemon juice mixed with water is used to wash amulets, jewelry, and other magical items. The washing ensures that any negative vibrations are swept away from the object in question.

The juice is purifying, and it helps to heal wounds between former friends (and it can banish friends to being enemies—use intention, faith, and direction to match). The dried flowers and peel can be added to sachets and amorous mixtures, and the leaves can be used in teas. Adding sweet to your lemon changes the energy, and adding salt draws out anything that needs to be addressed. Write with lemon juice around your home to purify and protect, but follow up with sweetgrass afterward (or something sweet) so that your home receives sweet. Never use sour or fire without following up with something sweet if you are dealing with a home you are living in. Test for allergies and staining issues with objects if you use lemon juice to bless, due to the acidity.

Last-minute lemon mentions:

◆ Spiritual baths, washes, and sprays

◆ Souring jars, dolls, request or petition papers

◆ In candles to sour a situation (dried only)

◆ Sour text messages—when I want to add a sour-like feel to a text message, I will use sour words and the lemon as an emoji

Teas

There are so many good homeopathic uses of teas. They have healed, and there have been revolutions (like the Boston Tea Party in America) because of this mixture of herbs and water brewed or steeped to perfection. During slavery and in many folklore traditions, teas were used as medicine. For example, you can use a tea made of lemon, honey, and onion to help with colds. Tree bark and onions can be boiled down to make a sipping tea for a cough. Mullein tea is used for soothing respiratory issues. Mint teas are used to calm upset stomachs. Sassafras tea was once used as a way to remove cataracts and prevent blindness. Sassafras roots and bark were used to purify and to reduce fevers, chills, and general sickness. If there is an herb out there, someone in our ancestry has probably made a tea with it. Of course tea is a product that is used in trade and revenue, so that means that for BIPOC communities, tea was inherent to slavery and enslavement for those that were responsible for harvesting and processing those teas.

Why is this important in hoodoo? More specifically, why is this important in updated hoodoo? As a practitioner it is important to know where your tea comes from. Try to use sources that are local first (I try to grow my tea leaves right in my own garden. That way I know exactly what is in them and I can make sure that the energy and the intention is added every time I hang out with the plant). When you are first starting out with your hoodoo teas, start with a plant that you can grow on your own. Many grocery stores now carry basil and mint plants. Take one of these home and look at the plant. See the leaves and stems. See how it grows, and water it for a couple of days. Try to keep it alive for as long as you can, and then pray over it. Ask it to give you energy and to heal your body. Next, ask it if you can have a few of its leaves, and then, using herb shears or some other cutting tool, cut the delicate leaves (you'll need a few). Using your fingers, rub the leaves to release the plant medicine. Place the leaves into a cup and add hot or boiling water. Let it steep. While it is doing its work, hold the cup in your hands and ask the tea to give you guidance and to energize all of your cells. Now sip the tea with gratitude and kindness. Enjoy this plant for as long as it will stay with you in this way, and when it is completely gone, find a nice place to bury it. Who knows, it might take root for someone else in the future. If it's mint, then please know that it will take over any space, so only replant it into another container or give it away—try not to toss it, please!

Onion

A few years ago, I was hired to do a spiritual cleansing on a home. The house had a negative energy that encouraged self-harm. When you walked into the suburban split home and looked upstairs you didn't feel it, but once you went into the tiny basement, opened the door that separated it from the rest of the house, went down the stairs painted white, and into the concrete area, you could feel it everywhere. This haunting, creepy need, and voices. Several voices, but not of the same spirit. They would circle you with one solid chant: "Leave this place and come with us." They were almost soothing with their ability to entice you into thinking that you really weren't wanted or even needed. It was powerfully large, even though the space was small. I protected myself thoroughly before entering and was reciting my Bible verse excerpted from Psalm 23:6: "Surely goodness and mercy will follow me all of the days of my life, and I will dwell in the house of the Highest Spirit forever." I cleaned the home with Tall Man, meaning I invited Tall Man to possess me and help me with the words and wisdom to move this spirit out of the home. Before he would let me go into the basement, we first took three onions, which I sliced widthwise and stuck onto the fence posts of all four corners of the property. In hoodoo the onion is used to keep things away. Onions are one of the several types of flowering plants in the genus *Allium*. This also includes leeks, garlic, spring onions, shallots, and chives. All of these can be used in the same way as onions.

They are all glorious protectors. Onion is my favorite because it is so smelly and it is so accessible. Nearly all of us have one or two around the kitchen. The scent of onions can be so pungent and sour that it can cause you to walk away. Tall Man never told me why I was to use the onions on the fence posts, but I can imagine he wanted me to begin with a boundary of energy, and the onions held that line for me while I worked. When I was finished with the cleaning of the home, I removed the onions (that were dark hours later and had attracted just about every ant in the yard) and removed them from the property. I placed them in a bag, thanked them for protecting me while I did my work, and threw them in the trash receptacle of the nearest church. In my tradition, the church grounds are especially high in protective properties due to the nature of the work done there (similar to taking objects and placing them on grounds where a jail holds an energy captive).

Whenever I got sick as a child (cold, flu, asthma), my great-grandmother didn't give me an inhaler or pill. No, she would make me a poultice (like a magical bandage of medicines) and lay it on my chest with onions and lemon peels. Smelled just horrible, but as the odor of this concoction wafted up my nostrils, I would breathe better by the next day.

Another thing that we would do for colds and flu was to slice red onions and add honey and lemon and boil them down until it was almost a syrup. I would take that by the spoonful, or she would even add it to a hot tea that I could sip (I still use this remedy today). There is science behind this as well (other than because my gran gran said to use it). An onion has antimicrobial effects, is anti-inflammatory, helps reduce cardiovascular issues, and can battle some bacteria, according to the PDR for Herbal Medicines. One cup of onions gives a person about 20 percent of their daily dose of vitamin C. This makes it a perfect root vegetable for rootwork. When I need healing or to de-escalate a situation or want to allow the client to speak their own truth, then I'll use onion.

Onions also hold the secrets of your clients really well. Take an onion and slice it in half, have the client write down their secrets, things they would never tell anyone but are holding on to. Let their words flow until they are completely free of them and then place the words into the onion (on folded paper sandwiched between the two halves of the onion). Wrap the onion in twine or red yarn, and let it stay on your altar until it has dried out. If you have a home that is prone to having insects, then you can keep the onion in the refrigerator (if you can handle the smell) for fifteen days, and then toss it. If you cannot handle the smell, then take the onion, boil it in one cup of water, and add the words. Place this onion "tea" on your altar in a safe bowl until it has dried out.

Cromniomancy is usually done by interpreting the onions' sprouting behavior, after performing a ritual to state the topic of the divination. This often involves inscribing the onions and dedicating them on an altar or something similar.

Candles

When I make my own candles I use beeswax, lard, soy, and even vegetable shortening. Candle making is a skill that you can acquire by experience. Start small by using a candle that is premade and melting it down and adding your own intentions and energies into it. I use a double boiler to do this. I add a label to replace the label that the manufacturer added so that I can take advantage of my own hoodoo, and I add my own herbs and Bible verses. I place my hands around the candle and pray my intention into it. Then I let it cool down (I let it cool on its own, never in a refrigerator or anything). When I do make my own candles, it is quite a process. I recommend finding some great books on candle-making basics. I started with some that I found at my local craft store, and they gave me all the information I needed. You may also want to work with a local beekeeper to see if they can assist with beeswax. The important thing I think of when making candles is burn time and quality. I use candles for different purposes. If I am doing a quick spell (around thirty minutes to an hour), then I only need a tealight candle or a votive candle. I also use these candles during my prayer time. When I am working with a client during a session, I need a candle that has at least an hour of burn time. I use rolled candles or my hand-dipped candles for those. Finally, I use pillar candles for hoodoo spiritual bathing or home cleansings because I need the candle to be sturdy on its stand and be able to burn for hours and hours.

There are superstitions about how to allow the candle to burn out (naturally or to blow them out). I personally let the candle get blown out if I'm in a hurry, with no judgment. My guides know my heart and are not worried about the small things. Stay true to what you and your ancestors need, and you will be fine.

Why do I use candles? In folklore magic work is typically done around a fire. Many of our shared ancestors have spent countless hours around a fire. Sharing myths and stories. Helping deliver magic to those that needed it. Cooking spells over a cauldron. Using the candles as a light source for safety or another purpose. Something in me goes back to the old days of using animal fats and a handmade wick to light the way to freedom or to keep safe from whatever dangers were outside. There's an entire difference between how our ancestors used candles and how we use them. Think of your ancestors and spirit guides as you use candles that are blessed with intentions. How did they use the candle?

How are they asking you to use the candle? Is the color for a specific reason? If so, what? Do you have to add to the candle by placing it near a certain charged crystal? Then do so. If you need to scry by looking just above or around the flame to receive a message from Spirit, then do that. Think of any sounds, scents, or memories that this candle is bringing back; you may even want to journal or record your findings.

Perfect match to me.

When I create a candle—whether it's wickless (to be used in a candle warmer), a mini candle (with a wick but not contained in a container), or a fully contained candle in glass or other suitable holding space—it was made with an intention in mind (which is the selection you chose: money, joy and bliss, self-love, etc.). I've already added the herbs and oils. Now all the candle needs is an intention and energy and direction to meet any deliverance need.

All of the herbs that I use are in the hoodoo tradition, which means there might be hyssop, pepper, five-finger grass, salt, chamomile, burdock, and other herbs that I found that most enslaved Africans or those who practice folklore magic use.

I use essential oils to add fragrance to my candles. Right now I'm really into lemongrass and sage. The new batch of money/increase candles are now cedar and camphor. The joy candle is infused with orange peels and lemon verbena, giving a fresh citrus aroma.

For the candles and candle melts, I've used soy and paraffin/soy blends. The blend throws a scent better from the warmer, so you may see more of those in my later batches.

CANDLE SAFETY TIPS

- Be sure to take all of the precautions necessary as a responsible candle owner. Light them in a safe environment where the flame or wax will not harm anyone or anything around it. Wax spreads.

- Only use a candle warmer for the candle wax melts. Don't leave the candle warmer on while it is unattended. Follow all manufacturer's directions and warnings.

- Do not light a candle without it being inside of a solid fireproof container. If you do not feel comfortable handling or using a candle, then do not do so. You can enjoy and meditate on the candle without it being lit. Never consume the candle or store it in a warm environment. With the purchase of the candle, you are accepting all liability of any injury with its use.

- Do not consume the candles—even though they smell tasty!

- Keep the candles away from children.

Hoodoo Dolls and Fetish Dolls

Even as a practicing hoodoo worker I have maybe only made a couple dozen dolls for hoodoo. I use candles, petition papers, card divination, bibliomancy, herbs, roots, cowrie shells, and prayer work first before ever touching a doll. Dolls are powerful and can become possessed or possess the hoodoo worker if you are not careful.

I was personally ridding a doll of an energy years ago and had some works on the altar to help me with my deliverance request. The doll, mind you, wasn't even in my home but at the home of the client. I recited my prayers, started my spell work, and lit my incense, and the incense holder shattered into several pieces.

This didn't prevent me from continuing but inspired me to keep going, as I knew I was getting close to getting deliverance. But this is an advanced practice. Dolls are energized with Spirit and spirits. They take on the life force of the energy you breathe into them, so they become like babies in every sense of the word. They need care, nourishment, and shelter. If they don't get this, then they can die, act out, or look for ways to get into mischief.

Fetish dolls are used in honor of someone who has passed away. It is similar to having a memorial altar for a loved one. You make the doll in the image of the person that is no longer in this physical space, recreate their energy and spirit using objects and personal concerns, and breathe in their life as a proxy.

In the Yoruba pantheon, Elegba is a deity, the divine messenger of Olodumare. Elegba is a guardian, protector, and communicator. Through divination, he guides the fate of man. He is revered in West Africa and all through the diaspora. The Fon call him Legba. He is called Èsú (Eshu) Èlegbara among the Yoruba. For the practitioners of Candomblé in Brazil, he is Exu. The Lucumi of the New World know him as Eshu Eleggua. These references are sacred praise names or *oriki* for Eshu-Elegbara. Oriki is used to describe the attributes or to recount the adjectives that describe an orisha. You make an Elegba doll in honor of this messenger.

DOLLS IN THE REAL WORLD

We have more opportunities to use premade dolls in updated hoodoo. As hoodoo is for everyone, I encourage us to make our dolls out of materials that are near us, but you can also purchase them as well. Be inspired to source dolls that are made by artisans from all walks of life. For Purpose Kids has a line of dolls that encourage cultural awareness and sharing of cultural history.[4] The brand Teni and Tayo teaches African culture, folktales, and geography (www.teniandtayo.com). ISH dolls teach and inspire those that are of Hindu faith. Doll-making brand Maisonette has a line of diverse dolls that inspire leadership, self-esteem, and inclusion (www.maisonette.com). Finally, *Reader's Digest* wrote an article on the multitude of changes to Barbie dolls that reflect "more than 170+ new looks, including body diversity, abilities, skin tones, and hair colors and textures."[5] Shopping for and buying from inclusive brand makers is something I encourage any hoodoo worker to do. Where we spend our dollars, to me, will be visible in how our world looks around us. If we shop for and buy only one brand or skin tone of doll, that is all we will have. The moment we demand more choices we get them (intention and direction at work).

The energy of the doll is important, but so is the material. Just like beings are made of flesh and blood, dolls are made of representations of flesh. Fabrics should be carefully chosen. If it is an effigy doll, I don't want to use a very cheap material. If I want to have a doll that will do a bunch of work, then I use a durable fabric. If you have a precious or fragile doll, then use a delicate material like silk or satin. You can also use objects like fruits, vegetables, and eggs as proxies for dolls. Eggs represent the soul in many cultures. If this is your cultural education and understanding, then go ahead and use an egg if you want to have a doll that has a true soul and spirit.

Egg dolls are good because eggs have the following attributes:

* They are signs of life.
* They are signs of the soul.
* They are a source of fat, nutrients, and energy.
* They are a way that chickens are born.
* They have an inner and outer world that is difficult to penetrate.
* They have to hide life until it's ready to be born into the world.

You can also make dolls from root vegetables, tomatoes, pomegranates, squash, peas (snap peas), peaches, nectarines, plums, zucchini, and pumpkins. Fruits with seeds are perfect substitutes for eggs—you need representatives of the sign of life, which include ovaries and eggs. Life inside of life. Flowers and gemstones can also be representatives of life, fats, nutrients, and birth.

When do you dispose of a doll? When your doll's purpose is met. Burn your doll if its energy is beginning to take over or is causing you personal harm. Work with a solid and well-researched conjure if you start to see your doll in your dreams doing harm to you or others.

You can and should remove the doll from your property when it no longer serves you and if it's serving a vengeful purpose toward someone in your home. You can bury your doll if the energy is something you want kept in your home—like a home-blessing doll or a doll that was created in effigy of someone.

How do you store a doll? Store your doll in a safe and dry space while it is working (after its been energized), and destroy it once you have set the energy free. You can say, "Doll, you have served your purpose and are free." Store your doll without stuffing. I recycle my dolls when I can—no need to add to the landfills with magic work. That just feels right in my spirit. When energy is added, store it on an altar or in a sacred space. Keep it safe from falls as you would a human or animal spirit.

What kinds of dolls can you make? Here are a few different kinds:

- Love doll—Use premade dolls that represent you and the chosen partner. See if you can choose a doll that looks like the couple and add clothing, jewelry, and hair from the couple.

- Keep-the-job doll—Make the doll in your image. Pay attention to the details. For example, if the job I want is to be a judge, I will dress my doll in a robe. If I want to be an activist, I will place a sign in my dolls hands. Add your hair and your expressions. Use colors to represent the money you will make (it would be green in North America but a different color in other parts of the world).

- Fetish honor doll—In remembrance of a loved one, choose a flesh-like material like pantyhose or muslin or even a root vegetable.

- Anger or revenge doll—When obtaining revenge in hoodoo tradition, there is no judgment (there are always consequences so use best judgment and protect yourself before making). Choose Bible verses that speak to the spirit of revenge and anger.

* Get-you-back doll—Use a living fabric, like cotton, and inject your essence into the doll (personal concerns are encouraged).

* Sour doll—Easy doll made from sour objects, muslin dipped in vinegar and dried, dehydrated lemons or grapefruit, a sour playing card (like the joker). Add sour faces and words.

There are many items you can use when stuffing, breathing life, cleansing, and anointing your dolls. Here are my go-to tools for carrying out hoodoo work. (You don't need any special dirt from the graveyard for any doll. This is a myth, just like red brick dust and hot foot powder, in my opinion.) A true conjurer can get the job done with water just as well as someone who needs a special oil.

* Coffee
* Oil (liquid)
* Salt
* Sugar
* Pepper
* Dirt or dust
* Insects
* Water (blessed)
* Aluminum
* Mainstay items (cinnamon, ginger, galangal, dandelion, grass, poke salad, sunflowers, sweet potatoes, peanuts, animal fat, bones, pine needles and cones, jasmine, angelica root, devil's shoestrings)
* Ammonia/Pine-Sol
* Pins, needles, thread
* Gemstones

- Dehydrated foods
- Words
- Candle wax
- Personal concerns
- Elements
- Bible verses
- Breath

◇◇◇◇◇◇ CHAPTER 5 EXERCISES ◇◇◇◇◇◇

Candle Ideas

Using candles for hoodoo is a gentle way to become introduced but still powerful. Pick a candle that you like. Hold the candle in your hand. Smell it. Touch the waxy surface. Look into the candle and view the dried herbs that were hand-selected for its purpose. If using in a graveyard, I recommend keeping it in a place where it can't be blown over by wind. Now sit in a space that is yours and light the candle.

USING A WAX MELT (WICKLESS CANDLE)

Using the wax melt is very similar to using a candle. I prefer to use my wax melts in a burner once a week for a few weeks until I get the deliverance I'm looking for. Each time I turn on the candle burner, I recite the appropriate Psalm (see the next section for ideas).

DELIVERANCE IN THE LIGHT

In a safe place search for a perfect Psalm to meditate or call the candle to do your work. Anoint yourself with your favorite oil or blessed water, then tell the candle to do your work. Thank your ancestors for giving you deliverance, then direct the smoke or fire in the direction of your plea by carefully waving your hand over the flame; do not get too close to it. Allow the candle to burn out naturally or quench the flame if it is not safe to leave it burning.

A mini candle will burn for around ten to thirty minutes; a medium-sized (heart shaped or clover) candle will burn for up to two hours. Anything larger will burn for several hours and is sufficient for a five- to thirteen-day hoodoo or conjure work ritual.

Ideas for Psalms:

+ Protection—34, 54, 59

+ Money/Increase/Job—23, 90:17, 94:18–19, 81

+ Love/Healing—20:4, 29:11, 37:4, 119:28

+ Joy/Happiness—47:1, 95, 30, 112

If you don't use the Bible, then use any other text that you like, or even song lyrics. For example, I like Metallica's song "One" if I'm doing any work with the graveyard candle where I'm asking a soldier to help me with deliverance for a battle that I'm facing. I like Bill Withers's song "Lovely Day" with the joy and bliss candle.

Blessings on your hoodoo work and praying for your deliverance!

Banishment Protection Text Spell(s)

Hoodoo banishment and protection texts are updated hoodoo using your phone. Typing conjures desires and needs into text that are sent to a recipient. When I wanted to banish someone from harming me, I would type to the person,

First message:

Ancestor of Gery, I banish the energy that causes you to harm.

Second message:

For it is written in 1 Chronicles 16:22, "Touch not mine anointed, and do my prophets no harm."

Third message:

It is as written, and it will be done by the power Tall Man. In faith and love.

Text messaging can be used for protection texts in this manner (again using intention, faith, and direction):

First message:

Jen, I am so glad for your new home. Recite this in every corner of your home and sprinkle with salt water.

Second message:

Isaiah 32:18—My people will live in peaceful dwelling places, in secure homes, in undisturbed places of rest.

If you don't want to text your messages, you can also take a photo of the spell and send that in its place. Using photos of your intentions is so powerful. Be warned that any text you send needs to be with your intention, faith, and direction and with the understanding that these texts cannot be taken back and can be forwarded to others. The energy will continue to bear fruit as it stays on the person's phone and when it is viewed or shared.

Take my Instagram posts. I combine a spell and add my Bible verse for my followers to do on their own. They then do the spell and share it to their pages. Then it gets picked up and added to Facebook or TikTok. It gets sent as a text or email to others. And every time this happens my intention, faith, and direction multiply.

This happens with any energy and intention. Even if you want revenge or fear perpetuated. Therefore we as practitioners need to be cautious. I consider all the ramifications before posting. I know that whenever my energy is multiplied then the results are too. Also, I consider if there are legal or ethical considerations. My intention, faith, and direction are powerful, but not omnipotent. There are consequences in this world of social media. Once something is posted it is never truly forgotten or deleted.

My eyes see the downfall of my enemies; when evildoers attack me, my ears are open. (Psalm 92:11)

Here is what you can do to cause the downfall or stumbling of an enemy:

You need a newspaper clipping of a person, place, or object that represents the enemy or a photo of the person. You will also need a very smelly herb called asafetida (I'll say more about this herb later).

After cleansing and connecting to your spirit guide and the enemies, say an incantation. Though you should use your own, you can use mine as an example. But please make it your own:

To _____ name(s),

You are a liar and deliverer of half-truths.

I call you mother of lies because you both lie and then nurture and allow your minions to suckle on your putrid teats so that they proliferate the same vile milk that fills your soul.

You and your energy of nasty, dirty trash are getting the hell out of my head and my space.

You are yesterday's news.

I wrote your name nine times and sealed the deal on you.

(Write hexed name nine times on paper.)

You are history. Your words have no energy. Your rank is under my feet.

Burn the newspaper and asafetida and spit or add phlegm to the burning pile. Relight as necessary until it becomes ash. Take the Sash and offering to the crossroads. Don't walk over what you laid down. Leave in the opposite direction. Don't mention the person's name again in fear, judgment, or retaliation. Go on with yo' life, gurl.

Repeat if you are hardheaded.

Asafetida, as I mentioned, has a unique smell. Its vibrant yellow color is second only to sulfur, in my opinion. I first started using this when instructed by Spirit to help me with menstrual issues. I had powerful cramping brought on from uterine fibroids. I used it in my spiritual baths (just a teaspoon or two because of its smell and potency) to rid my body of what it was holding on to. I would sit in this tub of hot water, asafetida, and chamomile and let the energy do its work.

Afterward I would take a shot glass of the bathwater and flush it down the toilet to encourage the pain and the symptoms to go away.

I've read that other hoodoo practitioners use it for similar purposes. The asafetida plant originated in India, and I have read it is used in cooking as a substitute for onion in recipes. It is also an ingredient you can find in fish sauce and other saucy combinations.

I can't imagine my own ancestors using it, but I can tell you it works wonders for removing negative energies, banishing spirits that hang out too long on objects, and increasing your psychic powers when doing shadow work. If I had to guess, I would say this is because of the smell. Just like peppers are known to add fiery energy and action to a spell, smelly herbs work to banish (like sulfur and asafetida). If you can't find it in your magical bookstore (or are in a pinch and need a temporary alternative) try these things: powdered onion and garlic; powdered mustard; salt and lemon pepper; and mustard, vinegar, and Worcestershire sauce (all liquid form).

The Olive Spell

After learning about how foods, beverages, and liquors have enslaved us, it may be a good opportunity to discover how they can help us. There are a few hoodoo items that I keep on hand that I recommend you do as well. These are things that are many times very inexpensive, are available in most locales, and allow you to do your magic work in plain sight of others without suspicion. That is my favorite hoodoo—the hoodoo I can do while someone else is right in front of me, without them knowing a thing.

My favorite way to do this is a quick color banishment spell. Never done this? It's quite easy. Say someone that rubs you the wrong way comes near you. Without saying anything to them or while they are speaking to you, think of a color that doesn't suit you. For me it's the color olive. Then use that color in this chant: "(Insert color here, color) go away, (Insert color here, color), you shall not stay!" Say this nine times and notice that the person magically walks away. Works on text messages and social media as well. If I have someone that is bothering me on Instagram, while looking at the person's profile I'll say, "Olive, olive, go away! Olive, olive, you shall not stay!"

NOTES

1   Joe Avella, "How the Bible Has Changed over the Past 2,000 Years," Business insider.com, November 15, 2015, www.businessinsider.com/bible-changes -altered-jesus-testament-dead-sea-scrolls-gospel-2015-11.

2   William White, "Alcohol and Slavery," 1996, http://williamwhitepapers.com /pr/dlm_uploads/2014-Alcohol-and-Slavery.pdf.

3   Manon Wilcox, "Why Was Scurvy a Problem for Sailors?" Colors-newyork .com, February 15, 2021, https://colors-newyork.com/why-was-scurvy-a -problem-for-sailors/.

4   "For Purpose Kids' Global Dolls are Designed to Inspire Empathy through Play," www.prnewswire.com/news-releases/for-purpose-kids-global-dolls-are -designed-to-inspire-empathy-through-play-301403013.html.

5   Stacey Marcus, "Meet the Most Diverse Barbie Dolls Ever Made," *Reader's Digest*, March 30, 2021, www.rd.com/list/most-diverse-barbie-dolls/.

CLEANSING

In the first chapter I stressed the importance of cleansing as folklore practitioners. If you've watched a medical drama, one of the first things the teams do before they operate is clean, but you also can assume that the tools they use are also cleaned. We clean all of our tools cyclically. This means clean altars, clean tools, clean spoons, clean jars, clean cauldrons, clean books, clean, clean, clean. What do you use to clean? You can make a simple blessing cleansing water using water and vinegar, water and salt, or water and alcohol.

VINEGAR

Douche. I said it. Douche. A douche is a jet or spray of water or a cleaning substance that is poured directly into a cavity. I don't ask you to buy many things for your hoodoo work, but it is imperative that you keep on hand these staples: water, salt, sugar, and vinegar. These things are super easy to have in your hoodoo tool belt and have hundreds of applications. If you need to clean something, you can use any one or a combination of these objects. If I want to wash out a substance that no longer belongs, then I can use vinegar and water. I can add more vinegar to add more acid or remove vinegar to only add the element and limit the amount of acid.

My first introduction to douche was as a teenager. Was this the same vinegar that I used on fish and chips, an occasional salad, and to clean windows? Of course it was. As long ago as 3000 BC, vinegar was made by mixing dates, figs, and beer. Its medicinal benefits are known to several cultures, including Chinese, Grecian, Roman, and European. Vinegar is a special type of wine, if you will. It is made when bacteria is added to an alcoholic beverage (like beer or hard cider) or sugar and then is allowed to ferment until it becomes acetic acid. There are several types of vinegars, including apple cider vinegar, white wine vinegar, and balsamic vinegar. In hoodoo I've used mostly distilled white vinegar and white wine vinegar. I use the other special and infused vinegars for culinary purposes. Vinegar's properties are acidic and sour. I know what the attributes of vinegar are from what happens when I taste it. When I have a sip of vinegar, I pucker. When I pucker, it isn't a good thing. This helps me think of ways to use it in updated hoodoo. When I want to sour things, I use vinegar. When I want to clean things (my body, my magic tools, my mate), I use just a splash of vinegar and water. If it is good enough for the womb of creation, then it's good enough for my hoodoo work.

SALT

Ye are the salt of the earth: but if the salt has lost his savor, where-with shall it be salted? it is thenceforth good for nothing, but to be cast out, and to be trodden under foot of humans. (Matthew 5:13)

My doctor keeps reminding me to cut back on salt, and I imagine myself pouring salt from the shaker in one hand, with scissors in the other—snip, snip. Salt is extracted from sea water, minerals, lakes, and springs. It is as old as our earth's beginnings and is tied to our census, taxes, revenue, and conflict. It is used in religious and cultural traditions. As healers, medicinal uses for salt are for purification, preservation, relief of diarrhea, and to reduce swelling. Salt is used in culinary arts, literature, superstitions, exorcism, fertility, relationships, curses, and other things. I can find salt in restaurants, gas stations, and hotels. Salt is needed for us to live. We can't reproduce it in our bodies; it has to be added to us in what we consume. Salt cures and it preserves.

Because of these traits, we also use it for these purposes in hoodoo. As hoodoo workers, we use salt in blessing and cursing rituals. We use it to cleanse in baths and showers and washes. You can put it on the tip of your tongue to ground you and to bring you back from a possessed state. It helps our food stay fresh for longer periods of time, and our spells too.

In our shared ancestors' time, salt was collected from lakes and oceans in dry seasons when water had evaporated. During the Civil War salt was used to tan leather and to dye clothes, as well as preserve the foods of the soldiers. The words *salary* and *salad* both come from salt (*salary* because Roman soldiers were given salt as currency for pay; *salad* because the Romans used salt to season their leafy greens and vegetables). Around 2700 BC a Chinese pharmacology text was published and showed around thirty to forty variations of salt. Enslaved people were bought and sold for salt in ancient Greece. Salt is believed in some religions to keep negative energies away to prevent takers of salt from committing "bad" acts. When mixed with water, salt can assist us in clearing and cleansing objects and homes because of this protective power. I put salt on my tongue when I want to ground myself before entering a space that I am concerned or suspicious of. I wash my hoodoo altar and techniques with salt and water that I have blessed.

There are many salt spells that other workers have written about, but let me show you what I appreciate about salt: it's the healing and drawing power. When I use salt and an herb in a shower or bath, I know that it will draw out any of the negativity that I need it to. It will also draw out any other energy as well. If I want more sweetness, I will combine salt and that sweetness. Holy basil is my jam. What I mean by that is that holy basil is my go-to herb when I have a choice. Its scientific name is *Ocimum tenuiflorum*, also known as tulsi. Salt, when I combine it with basil that I've rubbed between my fingers, draws out the power of the basil to reduce stress, alleviate respiratory issues, heal insect bites, and help with eye diseases and ulcers. In a tea (even without salt) basil gives those same benefits, but think of salt as a multiplier for metaphysical work. In my spiritual baths I use basil and salt in a pair of pantyhose or knee-high stockings. I use about a tablespoon of salt and a tablespoon of basil so that the herb doesn't interfere with my plumbing but still releases the magic. It's easy to grow and have in the home; most stores (even dollar stores) carry some type of basil and salt because of its uses in cooking.

Salt in grounding is important. Before I head into a cemetery for graveyard respect, I place a grain or two of salt in my mouth to push away any negative ideas or emotions or fears and to protect me from allowing any energies that want to interfere with my work from doing so. When I am nervous about a prayer or spell or want to draw myself out to have the best possible outcome, I will eat or press salt between my fingers. Another way I use salt is when I want to add more psychic power before going to bed. I recommend putting orange peel and salt in hosiery, tying it off, and then putting it in your pillow before going to bed. The psychic abilities and magical powers will be drawn out and released. If you cannot find orange peel, then use orange extract or essential oil.

ALCOHOL AND ALCOHOL

A jar full of sour wine stood there, so they put a sponge full of the sour wine on a hyssop branch and held it to his mouth. (John 19:29)

Give strong drink to the one who is perishing, and wine to those in bitter distress. (Proverbs 31:6)

I gave this section its title because of the duality of alcohol. It is used for two specific purposes in hoodoo. When I use alcohol (like colorless isopropyl alcohol) it is for cleansing and clearing work. The smell and purity of alcohol instantly makes me just happy because of how clean I am about to make something.

When I'm making a spiritual hoodoo spray and mix alcohol with water and other hoodoo objects, it is a perfect choice. If you have two ingredients to work with that are going to give you a clean removal of negative energies, then go with alcohol and water all the time. When I do home clearings, I use this combination. I pray over it and then wash the steps, sidewalks, patios, door handles, doorknobs—anything and everything that I see and feel that my ancestors are asking me to clean.

The other alcohol is the distilled spirit. I would be remiss without mentioning how addiction and trauma has ruined our community. The systemic alcohol consumption that was given and forced upon my people, my race, my family. When people that want to free themselves from abuse or tragedy, they sometimes turn to psychedelic products—both chemical and natural agents. During slavery, alcohol was restricted by enslavers but then given in abundance to enslaved Africans to alleviate pain during harvest to ensure more cotton, more sugar cane, and more work could be done. Today we do the same. Instead of receiving help from our past, we reach out to marijuana, cocaine, alcohol, methamphetamine, molly, and the list goes on. Our neighborhoods are drenched with liquor stores and dispensaries but not recreation centers, skating rinks, or art and science and technology centers.

If you or your client struggle with alcohol or substance addictions, then it is not necessary for to add or take those things when doing hoodoo. I personally don't feel as balanced or secure in my conjure if I am not present in my body. This means being 100 percent available and in charge of what and who is in my body. When I take substances, I can't guarantee that I will be. If you can be available and in charge, then feel free to partake. Know yourself on and off the substances. I encourage my clients and students to not use substances to mask or dull their senses. Part of knowing your ancestors is also knowing their addictions while they were here in the physical world. If they had addiction issues, for example, I would not use alcohol or marijuana when working with them (and when honoring them with offering). If they enjoyed a particular alcoholic beverage or enjoyed marijuana, then I would do that while they are working through me.

Then there is the other chemical—alcohol. Isopropyl alcohol. When the COVID-19 pandemic began, finding this alcohol was like trying to find toilet paper—you couldn't. This is because it is a cleansing agent and has so many uses—cleaning, disinfecting, as an antibacterial, and in magical work, makeup, spiritual washes, soap, and antifreeze.[1]

For hoodoo, I use isopropyl alcohol when I cleanse my altar, my body, and my rootwork objects. I take the alcohol and mix it with distilled water and local flowers. I first simmer the water and the flower petals and leaves for half an hour. I find a Bible verse that I want to protect myself with or use for my intention, and I rip it out of my Bible, or I copy it and add the page to my water solution. When it is all cool (and not near an open flame!), then I add the alcohol (one part alcohol to the same amount of water). I then bottle that and use it as a spray.

I use rubbing alcohol to prepare my body for blessing work (away from open flames). I anoint myself with it (when I am not using oil). A quick recipe when you are studying is to add two parts rubbing alcohol, seven parts distilled water, and one part oregano or peppermint essential oil. Do not cook or heat this up, please! Mix these three ingredients, and put it in a bottle. Label the bottle for safety. When it is time to concentrate, part your hair and spray it liberally on your scalp.

HOODOO BATHING: FROM TUB TO SPRAY

Taking a bath or shower is so important in hoodoo foundations. Before I do any hoodoo work, I want to make sure that I have a clean body and clean state of mind (even if I have alcohol or a stimulant in my system). This is another part of updated hoodoo. Cleaning yourself before doing any spell or conjure work gets you in the right state of mind—fresh and ready to move ahead with a new attitude and body. Using spiritual baths is familiar in so many traditions and rituals. How many of us would have our wedding, go for an interview, or perform for a special event without cleansing ourselves? Very few times, right? I have a tub in my home that probably gets used once a year. I shower very frequently; I bathe in a tub ... not so much. I bathe when I want to de-stress and add Epsom salts and herbs in a bag so that they don't ruin my plumbing.

Bags could not be easier to use in baths. You don't have to go around looking for expensive bags either. Use or recycle existing socks, stockings (we used to call them pantyhose or knee highs), or baby socks—the thinner the better. Baby socks are easy because they are small, and they only need a rubber band or ribbon or twine to close them after you fill them with fresh or dried herbs. I like using stockings or knee highs because I can use them several times and I can see all of that medicine goodness, so it satisfies me on several points. If you do not have access to any of these items, then reuse or recycle rag remnants, old shirts, linen pants, or leggings.

When I want to be possessed or I want to conjure an ancestor or guide to help me with a deliverance request, I use the hoodoo bath to clean, but also to allow them to use that emotional element of the water mixed in with the herbal elements representing the earth. The herbal elements can also represent the cardinal directions and the five elements of life (earth, water, fire, air, and spirit). All of these combined into one bath! But sometimes we don't have time to take a full-on bath. In updated hoodoo we don't need to. If we are on the go, we have several options: bath, shower, and spray.

Hoodoo Bath

This is full immersion. It's drawing a bath (after having a physically cleansing one) whose purpose is to spiritually clean and get yourself ready for the conjure work you will do. It needs to include the Bible verses you want, the intention, faith, and direction of the conjure you will be doing, and all five elements. When I take a full-immersion hoodoo bath, I will set aside uninterrupted time and prepare everything beforehand. I will carefully pack my herbal bath to represent the work at hand (if I am doing active energy work, I'll add cinnamon, and if I want to relax, I will add vervain). I also add or remove items that I've mentioned in chapter 5. If it is a love spell, I will add sugar. If I want to banish or reject something, I will use lemon. If I want to protect myself,

I will use salt, onion, chives, or garlic. Afterward I will stay in my meditative state and anoint myself with my oils. The sensibility of hoodoo is to continue using the same standard hoodoo plants and objects in several different ways. This way you are extending the usefulness of the precious plant. Wasting our resources is against the definition of what we do as hoodoo workers. We want to squeeze out as much of the magical power from anything we use for as long as we can.

Hoodoo Shower

Sometimes you may not be near or able to have a bath, but you need the connection with Spirit to continue your work. Also, some of us just really do not enjoy baths—I get that. When I bought my home, I loved the bathtub, but I've used it maybe two times in the fourteen months I have lived here. I use baths only when I am cleansing for ritual time or for mental health purposes when I need to relieve stress and anxiety. The warm or hot water seems to permeate my soul. If you do not have time for or want a full immersion, you can achieve the same results in a pinch during a shower.

When showering for a ritual, do so after you have cleaned your body. Chant your invocation and drop the hoodoo bag into shower with your works. I use several things in my bags for showers. Salt is primary, then sugar if I want sweet intentions in the cleansing, lemon if I want to deep clean, tea if the tea herbs contain the magical properties of my intention, and any scents (essential oils, citrus fruit peels, dried flowers), all packed into a sock or pantyhose that has been cut into the shape of a pouch.

I place the pouch on the tub floor, and as the water drains, I squish the contents of the pouch with my toes and concentrate on my faith and the direction of the cleansing. When I have finished my cleansing and have the messages I desire, I hang the pouch to dry and begin my ritual work.

For those who are without houses, it shouldn't prevent good hoodoo work from being done—especially as times of need are the best times for hoodoo. In these times, you can do your spiritual hoodoo shower by using a small bottle of water and blessing in each cupped hand, then sprinkling the water as you ask for your deliverance work.

In January 2020 there were 580,466 people experiencing houseless-ness in the United States.[2] This number includes people that may want to do hoodoo work but are restricted due to their home status. This does not have to be the case. A simple blessing and protection bag can be easily made with a clean, new or gently used infant or child's sock and packed with the hoodoo ingredients. I recommend sugar or salt with a cleansing herb that is locally sourced like a mint plant or dande-lion. Crush these items together and place them into the sock. Capture this bag in your hands and pray onto it, adding your energy to protect and bless the person showering. If you want, add an essential oil that gives you the intention, faith, and direction desired. Tie the sock with a rubber band or hair tie (it will look like a little ball)—no need to fill the entire sock. Consider giving out these cleansing bags to those that are in need as a community service. They can take their bag/pouch, run it briefly under any water source they have, and place the bag in their hands or use it to wash their feet and hands.

Side note: Being physically and spiritually clean should be a human right. Cleanliness helps to protect us from infectious diseases that remain on our skin and sink into our skin cells. When we travel from place to place, we emit odors from physical activity. The more physical we are, the more sweat, grime, and dust we have attached to our hair and body. Showers can be of any length. Being odorous leaves negative connotations for those that interact with us. Spiritually in many tra-ditions the first part of any ritual is to be clean and prepared to wash away the old and get ready for the new.

Social justice can be accomplished in the form of a shower. In justice work and community building, it is important that our houseless com-munity has these options as well to support their own deliverance work. There are organizations like The Right to Shower (therighttoshower.com) that help those that are experiencing houselessness and have limited or no access to showers. They offer volunteer and mobile shower services across North America. In the Pacific Northwest we have organizations like Hygiene 4 All (www.h4apdx.org), which provides access to public health and sanitation opportunities in the form of sanitized portable toilets and shower trailers.

Hoodoo Spray

Have you heard of Florida Water and hoodoo? I think that's one of the first things I hear people ask me about when we talk about hoodoo. They bring up Florida Water and guess that I will think they are a practitioner. Well, I say this: if you created your own Florida Water using flowers from your garden or your local florist and added your own Bible verses and kept the Florida Water on your altar for several days before using it—then yes, I would say you have some hoodoo Florida Water. If, however, you purchased Florida Water because you saw a post online, then I would say no, you probably aren't a hoodoo worker—yet.

Hoodoo sprays are colognes. That's it. What is a cologne or perfume? It is scented water. A hoodoo spray is scented water with intention, faith, and direction that is used for a ritual or magical purpose, many times to take the place of a spiritual bath when a bath or shower cannot happen.

Hoodoo sprays do not take the place of cleaning your body and are not used to mask odor. They are a conjure tool. As the scent goes into your nostrils, it is a reminder of the intention, faith, and direction. The ingredients should mirror these tenets.

There are manufactured go-to sprays that hoodoo workers and other faith-based practitioners use. The Florida Water brand that most use is bottled by Murray and Lanman. It has been used since the early 1900s, and it stuck around because of its citrusy scent. Citrus is used by many faith-based traditions to cleanse objects. I personally enjoy the scent of Kananga water more (bottled by Crusellas & Co.; Murray and Lanman make their own version too). Kananga water is an all-in-one cologne. It can be laid down and given to an ancestor, it cleanses, it increases psychic energy.

Don't just stop at Florida Water. Here are some other spiritual sprays that you can make into hoodoo sprays (if you want bottled, manufactured versions).

When I am getting ready to go into a meeting that I know will be tension filled, I spray Kolonia 1800 Vertiver (the black label) on my back and feet. It calms and relaxes me and keeps my feet moving in the right direction (soft steps). If I am doing some work where I want to encourage myself to focus and take charge, then I use Siete Machos cologne (there is also a soap and other forms, but I prefer the act of spraying, rubbing my hands with it, and deeply smelling it). Siete is believed to have a "take charge" scent that is muskier.

Kolonia 1800 Lavanda (purple label) is popular for prayer work and dream work and smells like lavender. It can be sprayed when you want to de-escalate a situation. I tend to find it too sweet smelling for me to wear, as it overpowers my senses, but try it!

Hoyt's Cologne is what you would use if you were playing games of chance. In some spells, you use upward of half to a whole bottle of this before you go buy lottery tickets, go to the bingo hall, play at the casino, or before any betting activities.

Now that you know what a hoodoo spray is, I encourage (and challenge you) to create your own custom sprays. Start using other perfumes and sprays to do your work. You don't have to do the old-ways methods in updated hoodoo. If you want to use your favorite cologne from a fashion house or even a drugstore, do that!

A word about spraying on others. Okay, I get it. Sometimes you want to spray that coworker in the cube next to you so that they stop gossiping about you or throwing negative energy your way. Spraying anyone without their consent can be illegal and may be considered assault. Also remember most of these colognes contain large amounts of alcohol and are flammable, so never use this near flames! Finally, if making your own sprays, limit the amount of inflammatory herbs (like cinnamon and pepper) that can irritate the skin, eyes, and mouth.

Hoodoo Baths and Spell

I like to have full-body immersion in a bathtub. You can use a mixture of ingredients that includes the tenets of hoodoo, which is intention, faith, and direction. What I mean by this is when you are preparing to bathe, you start with your intention. Why are you cleansing your body? What do you want to achieve? How many baths does your ancestor want you to take? What deity is requesting you to bathe, and what ingredients should you add?

Bathing is the washing of the body with a liquid, usually water or an aqueous solution, or the immersion of the body in water. It may be practiced for personal hygiene, religious ritual, or therapeutic purposes. By analogy, especially as a recreational activity, the term is also applied to sunbathing and sea bathing.

Bathing can take place in any situation where there is water, ranging from warm to cold. It can take place in a bathtub or shower, or it can be in a river, lake, water hole, pool, the sea, or any other water receptacle. The term for the act can vary. For example, a ritual religious bath is sometimes referred to as an immersion, the use of water for therapeutic purposes can be called a water treatment or hydrotherapy, and swimming and paddling are two recreational water activities.

Bathing ritual is an umbrella term that can refer to a wide variety of concepts within the bathing world, including:

+ flotation tanks,

+ hot springs,

+ whirlpools,

+ traditional and infrared saunas,

+ cryotherapy,

+ water-based massage.

Bathing around the World

I explained hoodoo baths previously, but it is important for us to go into history to understand where bathing came from. Bathing to many of us is luxuriating in a warm or hot body of water where we can soak away our worries and stress. The bathing experience wasn't always like that, of course. Poverty and access are two reasons. Bathing in some traditions includes bathing in a public area. Homes that had indoor plumbing were just being built and were for the very wealthy (1800s–1900s in North America). These tubs were made of metal, like copper. Physicians instructed people to take colder baths to cure themselves of disease. Another group of experts would tell the masses to go to a public bath and bathe in the same area where others were washing clothes with bleach and lye. There was nothing peaceful and relaxing about those baths.

Bathing is a technique that we use to cleanse away negative energies, feel good about ourselves, and even to cleanse the body as part of a ritual. Other traditions share this philosophy. You may have seen videos or images of people being submerged in the water, baptizing themselves as a show of faith to a deity. Folks dressed in water being plunged backward into chilly water and coming up saved and sanctified.

Even before that time people used a public bath where everyone bathed together in an area with no privacy. For example, in Rome and Greece, you would be washed down with water or oils (sometimes after exercising) and then scraped with a tool.[3] Of course, that is the experience for the wealthy. Enslaved people would accompany the whites and do the washing and scraping.

In other parts of the world there were similar traditions where baths were for invigorating the body and to prevent disease. The temperature of the baths wasn't like what we use today. They were ice cold, as brisk baths were touted by health professionals to be the most beneficial in helping to reduce inflammation from gout or to combat diseases like diabetes. The baths contained oils or water or milk. Scrubbing and scraping was done with stones, brushes, and other tools.

Religious bathing was a different experience as these baths had everything to do with tradition and faith and, many times, heat. Significant, intense heat was used to sweat out negative energies, to purify the faithful. The faithful would worship in these huts with hot stones in the center of the building. A firekeeper would add to these stones, herbs, and grasses.

Other cultures believed in modesty. Having separate rooms with a place to bathe away from others entirely. For example, in Japan they had a nice-sized bathtub in a room that allowed the bather to look outside at nature. Bathing happened only after the person was already cleansed. They then could take a long soak.[4]

In hoodoo, I try to honor all these traditions. Especially realizing that my ancestors would rarely have had the access to any of them. You see, my ancestors would have been the ones scrubbing and scraping.

Carrying buckets of hot water up and down the stairs of Southern mansions. Having to clean the tubs and dealing with the dirt that came from the same people that enslaved them. To think of them lounging in that same tub for magic work is almost laughable at best and unforgivable at worst. In this realization, I respect the old traditions by having a clean body first, using nature as my guide, and using oils and heat to open my thoughts and mind to the joy that is ritual with an eye toward respecting my roots.

Creating Your Own Wash

In respecting our roots, it is important to honor the lack that came with our ancestry. There weren't shops at our disposal, resources were limited (soap, candles, oils, cleaning agents). My great-grandmother would only use a small number of things when she did any prayer work. She didn't use a gallon of olive oil; she only used a dab on our foreheads when she blessed us. With that in mind, how much of the blessing agents do you use in your baths?

- For purification ingredients like Pine-Sol or ammonia, a thimbleful is fine; you want to add the ingredient but not bathe in it.

- For water, coffee, or oil, you can use a lot or a little. If you are making a batch to use now and later, then usually the liquid base is the largest part of your work.

- For dry ingredients like sugar, salt, or pepper, it depends on how much you can take. For example, if you want to make a pepper bath to remove negativity, that's fine, but don't try to light yourself up with fire. You only will need a tablespoon or two.

- For essential oils or scents, use your sense when adding these, and allow them to dry completely before bottling. I can use about ten drops in a container of salt or sugar bath that will make about ten batches to sell. A little goes a very long way.

STORING THE WASH

If I am storing the wash to use later, I like to use glass, plastic, bags, and the like to keep the wash fresh. If I'm using a dry base, I keep it in a bag that breathes or in a nice glass jar. If I'm using a jar or container (like Tupperware) I write the ingredients of the mixture on it in marker so that I remember, and it also helps for allergies. I always allergy test things and let my clients know the ingredients so they can test for themselves.

WASHES AND HOW YOU CAN USE THEM

- Brewed as a tea—Use a tea bag or strainer. Don't let herbs go down the drain—save your plumbing. Steep the herbs for as long as you like—use your life path number. Use blessed water, coffee, or oil, and mix in your other corresponding herbs for the bath you desire. A quick bath of salt, pepper, and water can be done most anywhere and is easy to do.

- Simple purification wash—Choose your favorite salt, pepper, and base (liquid or dry). Add ingredients together into your chosen base. Bottle it up and pour it over your body if you are getting rid of something or take the wash and work the liquid up your body if you want to attract (it's better as a full immersion or sprinkling of the liquid).

- Double-dip—Using a tea-brewing method, brew the tea once in an herb bag. Let it steep until it's cold. Using a second tea bag, adding newer ingredients, brew again in a different substance. Combine both brews into one wash, and that will become the principal wash.

- Love wash—Pick out ingredients to represent each person in the relationship (two or more). Use orange, water, and cinnamon as a love tea to represent one part of a couple. Use grass, water, and tree bark to represent the second person. Use other ingredients of your choosing for other partners. When you are ready to bathe, combine the ingredients to bring in the intention of commitment, joining of two spirits as one.

- Cold dip—This is the same method as brew, except leave the herbs and basic ingredients in oil, water, coffee, or the like in a container out during a moon phase to attract or reject thoughts or patterns.

- Total immersion—Use the bath in your soaking tub.

- Money-drawing wash—Use sassafras (to heal your money issues), greens (represent money), oil, and your favorite money-drawing gemstone. Use the number of ingredients that match your life path or birth path number or use the lucky number seven. Add a tarot or playing card that corresponds with money to you, like the playing card seven of diamonds. Place all into a jar (write the ingredients on the jar). Write the intention of the money drawing onto the jar and turn the jar clockwise using your numerology. I like to use magnets and dill or parsley in money-drawing wash. I also use a dollar bill in my oil with the words "give me money now" written clockwise on it. Fold the dollar bill toward you because you want the money coming to you. The number of days you let the money wash sit corresponds to your life or birth path number (I explain how to do this in the numerology section). Add any other ingredient that makes you feel like money (song lyrics, an old paycheck, etc.). Oil and water don't mix, so use any oil wash as a moisturizer for your skin after you have cleansed. Do this work during a waxing moon. Starting with your feet, oil yourself upward. You can let the oil sink in or if it is too oily for you, you can wash afterward (I like to leave the oil on my skin).

- Protection wash—Start with salt, pepper (or spicy protection like ginger, sriracha), hyssop, High John the Conqueror root, tree roots, dirt or rocks from a place that protects, dandelion roots, a bag of hair or feathers from the animal that is your spirit animal, a copy or picture of someone in your ancestry that protects you, coffee (to pick you up), gemstones for protection (pyrite is a good idea), object of faith (cross, ankh, prayer beads), paper with "protect me" lyrics, Bible verse, or inspirational quote, and protection essential oil (camphor, garlic, ginger, nutmeg, mint). Mix all ingredients by leaving them out in the light. Shake it daily, and add another ingredient until all ingredients are added (this is a tip for making your wash more potent than others). Start this work on a full moon or your corresponding astrological date.

- Foot cleansing—Pour your concoction over your body after a bath or shower.

- Pour your wash into a container, and sprinkle it in water for a quick bath.

- Leave the wash ingredients in the oil or coffee in a bottle as a quick "cologne."

What to do after the bath:

- Meditate

- Pray

- Rest

- Journal

- Go out into the day with your intention in mind

- Have sex

- Create more magic

- Dispose of ingredients (fire, water, air, earth)

Basic ingredients:

- Purification—angelica, basil, chamomile, cinnamon, ginger, grass, pepper

- Cleansing—water, salt, Pine-Sol, ammonia, natural soap, or cleansers

- Calming—flowers, herbs, gemstone, candles, aromas, ginseng, blue cohosh

- Coffee
- Oil (liquid)
- Salt
- Sugar
- Pepper
- Soap
- Water (blessed)
- Herbs
- Ammonia
- Pine-Sol
- Gemstones
- Music
- Words
- Candles
- Numerology
- Astrology

Method to prepare your washes:

- Select literature, music, quotes, colors, scents.
- Cleanse the area and objects for preparing your work.
- Combine a liquid or dry base with each ingredient: purification, cleansing, or calming (or a combination).
- Add your intent, needs, love, inspirations, feelings into the work while making it.

Herbs to add:

- Chicory or coffee weed—It helps to "unstick" situations where you no longer are getting results! Gets you or the person you use it on excited about your ideas, love, and passion.

- Orange—Oranges lend their energy well to love magic and floor washes (orange peels smell so good in floor washes and spiritual washes). I use orange essential oil (just a drop) on my money and increase bags because citrus is protective and energizing.

- Licorice root—I couldn't stand the smell or taste of licorice as a kid. It wasn't until I worked in a metaphysical shop in Denver that I understood that real licorice root (when chewed) was very sweet and tasty. I read up on this and found that the candy has additives in it because it is cheaper and easier to produce that way. (https://foodiosity.com/what-does-licorice-taste-like)

- St. John's wort—I use this to help with concentration and to give me more focus, and others use it to feel more upbeat. I can tell you I use St. John's wort, valerian, and some dried rose tied up in a bag and stored under my mattress to give me better psychic dreams, and it works every time.

- Jasmine flowers—Jasmine flowers are the main ingredient in my own Florida Water. I use dried jasmine flowers, dried local flowers and some cinnamon. I let all that simmer down with a pint of water. You can also use some jasmine in sex magic with hibiscus or pomegranate seeds (fresh flowers) as kind of a potpourri. Let it simmer in a pot when you are calling spirits to help you gain and enjoy a fruitful sex life.

- Rosemary—It increases female power, especially in connection to relationships and the household. It is often seen planted right outside the home or as hedges in the yard of a house to keep the home safe and the women in the house safe from sexual predators.

- Blue cohosh—It helps with sleep and with eloquence in speaking. Gets your best voice out there.

- Ginseng—Ginseng looks like a human being to me, a lustful, gorgeous being. And this is why I use it in lustful magic work.

NUMEROLOGY

Numerology isn't really hoodoo, and it may be a bit random, but adding a knowledge of numbers is important when you are making washes (like using tarot or adding crystals into your wash), and it's helpful to have range in your practice. Numerology is the divination or reading of numbers to foretell the future or to help those in the past. In hoodoo there are true numbers that we watch and use in practice. It is my experience that even numbers are weaker because they can be separated, halved, and made into other numbers evenly. Odd numbers stand on their own. They create change, they stand alone, they join, they separate, they cause change and confusion, they are what we hope and dream of. One singular sensation, three wishes, seven wonders of the world, you can be on cloud nine or dressed to the nines, eleven is an angel number, and so on. Here's a brief explanation of three of my favorite numbers.

The number 1 is a number that cannot be divided. I think of being on "one accord" meaning we are all of one mind. I think of a 1 as something that solidifies that work. It can stand on its own without needing any help. Doing a spell for one day because it is strong enough to handle it. Adding the number 1 to a spell (a single-ingredient spell is prayer). The number 1 is called a unifier in sacred texts outside of the Bible. In math (a very sacred text of its own) the number 1 cannot be lessened or subtracted from. There is power in that statement. When I do work using the number 1, I am using intention, faith, and direction that cannot be divided or lessened by anything else. Number 1 work is very powerful. It is made by me, with my own energy, for my own purpose. I use an Ace of Spades to do death, change, or final separation work. A quick one-ingredient spell to protect is using spit or urine. You spit or use your urine on things you want to claim as yours (while obeying the law). I chew and spit ginger, tobacco, galangal root, licorice root, lemon, grapefruit, or orange peel, pomegranate seeds, and other things, and then spit them onto the ground, on the four corners of my property, onto the wheels of my bicycle or tires of my car. The number 1 is a powerful number.

The number 3 is a sacred number because it is a combination of others—the unifier with two other objects, spirits, ancestors, deities, energies, sacred texts, and so on. According to Biblestudy.org the number 3 is used in the Bible 467 times. When using hoodoo spells, pick out Bible verses with the number 3 to give a balance using this number. Three is a trinity, it is a group of persons, a period to worship, three gifts given (law, inheritance, and calling). In Buddhism there are three higher trainings (morality, concentration, and wisdom). I use three-ingredient (called trinity) blessing work, so my trinity is usually salt, water, and sugar that I use as a base for any work, which keeps it stable and balanced because it has those three legs. In card divination I use threes when I am bringing together hearts and souls and for separating those hearts. This is because of the tarot card Three of Swords, with the heart with three swords running through it, and the Three of Cups that shows a trio celebrating with cups full of deliciousness.

The number 5 is a number that has done me well. Back in my tarot days I used and identified the number 5 as the "trouble" number. The Five of Cups, Wands, Coins, and Swords usually depicted tragedy, war, or strife. So now, when I think of confusion and anger, it usually comes in the number 5. Five is something that you also see when you cut an apple in half (number of seeds, mostly). Tree branches grow in branches of five. We generally have five senses. The pentagram is a five-sided star. When you're playing poker, each player gets five cards. This means the game is on. It also means the same for hoodoo when I use five ingredients, I'm willing to change or take a chance. I am okay with risking the outcome of the spell to whatever Spirit wants (which I think is the smartest way to work with Spirit). Here's my petition paper spell using five ingredients:

1 candle (any color)

1 piece of paper

1 writing utensil

1 wish (to write onto the piece of paper)

1 match or way to light the candle

Wash your hands and call for your help from the deity, ancestor, and guide that will help you. Write your wish onto the piece of paper. Fold the paper into an envelope (you can find instructions online) while saying your wish over and over, like this: "Ancestor ____, you see what I can't see. Grant me this _____ (include your wish) if it is your will." Set the envelope to the side. Light the candle. Using your fingers, carefully seal your envelope by folding the envelope shut and using the wax as the glue to hold the paper shut. Leave it on your altar for at least five days but never an even number of days, like ten.

Finding Your Life Path Number

Finding your life path number is an exciting way to find out more about yourself as a practitioner that isn't true hoodoo but highlighted by numerology. My way below is what I have learned from several numerologists, but it isn't the only way. You can search online for others and find one that works best for you.

Once you calculate your number, add that meaning into your wash.

Don't know your life path number in numerology? Here's an easy how-to guide for calculating your life path (or birth path) number:

1. Begin with your full birth date. Example: December 19, 2009.

2. Reduce the month, day, and year down to a single digit by adding them.

MONTH:
December is the twelfth month.
$1 + 2 = 3$
DAY:
The day of birth is 19
$1 + 9 = 10$
Add again to get down to a one-digit number:
$1 + 0 = 1$
YEAR:
The year of birth is 2009
$2 + 0 + 0 + 9 = 11$

Continue adding until you get a one-digit number:

1 + 1 = 2

Now add the resulting single digits together to get the life path number.

Month = 3 + Day = 1 + Year = 2

3 + 1 + 2 = 6

The life path number is 6.

Quick guide to numerology number associations:

If your number is 1, then you are certain of a good outcome.

If your number is 2, then you are going to have an easy time getting what you want.

If your number is 3, then you are going to add life to your wash.

If your number is 4, then add more luck to your wash (visualize a lucky totem being added).

If your number is 5, then add nothing else, as your internal luck will give you the best insight.

If your number is 6, then the wash is going very well indeed, but add a smooth rock, coin, or smooth object to make it even more perfect.

If your number is 7, then you need to balance the wash with banishment energy.

If your number is 8, then add prosperity to your wash.

If your number is 9, then add the hair of an animal, or visualize adding some.

MOON PHASES

When you take a bath, you can do so to match your understanding of moon phases and cycles. For me, my ancestors tell me when to take baths, which is outside of a moon cycle. But I know of other practitioners that swear by it. I have provided brief ideas on when to take your baths to align them with intention, faith, and direction. There are apps and sites you can use to find out the moon phase. The beauty and flexibility around hoodoo are you can add other divination tools into your hoodoo. Doing work by the moon phase is one of those ways. You take a bath with the intention, faith, and direction that is inspired by the magical properties that are associated with those moon phases. That also can mean getting your bath water by bathing it in the light of the moon during its phase to match your intention.

- Moon water—Moon water is exactly that: water that is blessed by the moon. You take a bucket or vessel, fill it with water, let it stay under the moonlight night after night until your ancestor or deity says it is ready. In hoodoo I keep spells on my altar for only an odd number of days. My gran gran believed in the luck of an odd number. In the Bible the numbers 1, 3, 7, and 9 are special because they are mentioned many times (I spoke on this a bit before).

- Waxing moon—What the heck is a waxing moon? If you are asking this, there is no shame. I'm going to explain it to you how I understand it. It's the moon you can see right before the full moon, so it is the moon that goes from a half moon to right before the full moon. I have read that *waxing* means to get bigger or get larger. Gibbous is added in the description of the moon and its shape and how round it is with that oval side too. If you take a bath during this moon phase, you are doing so to make things bigger. Love life, sexuality, increase, health, wishes, and dreams. When you want to bring things full circle, you can take a bath during the waxing moon phase.

- Full moon—It is typically seen as a time of great power. That's when many practitioners currently do their most important rituals. Some say the full moon is the best time for works of black magic. It is worth noting that police and other emergency services regularly report more extreme behavior around the full moon. This has long been recognized, hence the term "lunacy."

- Waning moon—This time is best for works of lessening, such as reducing poverty, losing unwanted and annoying people. It's also good for works of destruction, hexing, and cursing.

Here are ingredients I recommend in hoodoo baths and spells:

- Blue cohosh
- Ginseng
- Angelic root
- Galangal
- Orange peel

Here's my very own version of a general feel-good wash, which provides sleep, protection, love, and harmony: brew in the tea-bag method and use with the immersion method, or put the brew into a bottle or another vessel and allow it to drip over your body. Air dry if you can, or pat yourself dry, and then go out for the day.

FLOOR WASHES

Floor washes are hoodoo equivalents of spiritual bathing (which I will detail later). They are made of water, some type of soap (I use Murphy's Oil Soap, organic soap, like Dr. Bronner's, Pine-Sol, ammonia, and Fabuloso), and a mixture of strained blessed plants or essential oils. Some of the items in a wash can stain (like when I use hibiscus for washes that are to assist with bringing in love). I recommend testing for staining prior to doing any ritual of washes. Think about what you will be washing. If you are doing a whole house, then use something that will have long-term cleaning power and will last through a large amount of foot traffic. If I want to do a front step, I use something that I may not mind causing staining issues because my stairs may be made of concrete or wood that won't be stained. The recipe that I use for floor washes consists of five parts:

One part water

Half part organic soap

Half part salt

Quarter part Bible verse that states your cleansing need. You get this by tearing the verse from the Bible, or by writing the verse and putting the paper in the finished water mixture or by burning the verse and allowing the ash to be added to the water mixture.

Quarter part herb or plant material that is strained in water.

Mix these ingredients together and either spray the mixture onto your floors or use as the water to mop your floors.

There are a few considerations:

- Do not use the washes near an open flame.
- Do not consume or drink the washes or soaps.
- Test the soap for any allergies and be sure to use it in a protective pouch.
- Keep the washes in their original container or transfer them to a glass container, as they contain alcohol (do not store for long periods of time in a plastic container).

Feel free to dilute the wash, as the magic will withstand dilution. Two-to-one dilution is just fine, if not more! For bath washes you may only want to use a tablespoon or two.

Why Use Washes/Floor Treatments?

Hoodoo, the oral, enslaved African American conjure work, has already shown itself to me to be a powerful ally in my magical practice. Use conjure/hoodoo when you are begging and pleading for deliverance from an external force, internal struggle, or just situation. You use a treatment of floor or body washing when you want to ask for deliverance and you prefer to use a liquid form of calling your ancestors to help.

Think of your ancestors and spirit guides as you use my floor washes and blessed washes in your ritual bath or for cleaning of floors and other items you want blessed. It is very simple to use the washes. You wash, spray, or clean an object with the liquid while reciting your chosen Psalm that will call the energy of what you want cleaned.

Add your herbs, but you do not need to add any oils (only essential oils and your intention and energy and direction to meet your deliverance need). I really recommend that you make your washes yourself or bless your bottles of Pine-Sol or Fabuloso and mark them with the Bible verse to give them the intention.

I make several batches of floor wash in my home in my very own kitchen. I do this using an Instant Pot or a slow cooker. This way I can put all of my ingredients into one pot, turn it on simmer and low, and walk away. Many take almost fourteen hours to get to a point that I think they are good. Once they have simmered down, I take it out of the Instant Pot or slow cooker and let it cool. After it is cool, I pour it into a vessel and leave it on my altar for up to twenty-nine days (never thirty, as that's an even number). Don't feel nervous if you need to leave yours awhile before using. All of the herbs that I use are in the hoodoo tradition, which means there might be hyssop, pepper, five-finger grass, salt, chamomile, burdock, and other herbs that I found most enslaved African or folklore magic uses.

I use essential oils for fragrance in my washes. Right now I'm really into camphor, lemon verbena, and clove.

Using the Wash

When you clean your home or body with washes you use intention, faith, and direction. You intend to get deliverance, right? But remember *why* you want deliverance. Keep that in your mind as you prepare, pour, and use the wash. Next, faith. Have faith that the magic and deliverance will be achieved. Even if you do not see immediate results, any work of faith is acknowledged by your ancestors, even if you do not see it. Then, direction. There are ways to bless an object. For example, when blessing your home, you will use the floor/blessed wash in a Swiffer or from a spray bottle or even poured on a rag.

Open the windows and doors if you can and move the mop, Swiffer, or rag in the direction you want the energy to move. For example, if you want to move the energy out, then wash from the furthest part of your home to the door that is open out. I prefer starting from the top floor, then the bottom floor, and then middle floors as you have them, moving the energy toward the exit. If the exit is a back door, then I prefer you move the energy out the nearest exit that is open (not where there is a brick wall or building preventing energy from going out into the clouds).

When you are done, scoop a small amount of the water and take it outside and toss it on pavement, or if it is not full of harmful chemicals, you can pour it down the toilet.

If you don't use the Bible, then use any other text that you like or even song lyrics. For example, I like Metallica's song "One" if I'm doing any graveyard work where I'm asking a soldier to help me with deliverance for a battle that I'm facing. I like Bill Withers's song "Lovely Day" when cleaning, or "Respect" by Aretha Franklin for getting respect from an employer or when in a relationship.

Here we are at the end of your hoodoo foundations journey! I am so excited to have shared my hoodoo foundations with you. I hope you have found this information useful and that you can come back again and again to this reference, this sacred text, for many years to come. What are some things you can do afterward? I encourage you to keep learning and growing by connecting and communicating every day with your hoodoo ancestors, guides, and deities. Keep their wisdom close like a jewel upon your chest. Consult with them, honor them, and bring offering to them for guiding you and helping you with the task that you have now taken on. Here is the briefest of recaps:

- Clean body, clean self.
- Intention, faith, and direction are all you need to be a hoodoo worker.
- Love and respect yourself in this process—there is no judgment of your goal as long as you remember this.
- Bring in shared ancestors, guides, and deities as they match your intention, faith, and direction.
- The method you work is not as important as your intention, faith, and direction.
- Use nontraditional methods of conjure because we are in a nontraditional experience that is open and affirming for all.

Now with all of the intention, faith, and direction that I have, and in conjunction with my own ancestors that have spoken in this text, I give you these final words:

Sacred Deity,

We ask that you consecrate this reader as a hoodoo worker blessed with all of the gifts that are given from our shared ancestors, guides, and deities. May we open up our way of thinking and give ourselves life that is always inclusive, fair, and equitable.

Give us this day, in prosperity and protection, a better understanding of all of the hoodoo traditions of the past so that we may upgrade them to better build our future.

Help us to protect our earth, our society, and ourselves in love— even if this means banishing or protecting ourselves from those that may attempt to harm us.

We know that in faith and science we have prevailed. Just as our shared ancestors have battled and won, then so too will we.

Show us in chants, prayers, cleanliness, and offerings that conjure is a perfect match for when we need deliverance.

Help us to see more clearly the way to hoodoo with respect, in respect of those that have paved the way for us.

It is written in Jude 24–25.

Now unto the science of gravity and life force that is our universe, incapable of allowing us to fall, presenting us faultless before the presence of all glory with exceeding joy, to the only wise shared life force, be glory and majesty, dominion, and power, now and forever—go forth hoodoo worker—love you! Ase!

That Hoodoo Lady

◇◇◇◇◇◇ CHAPTER 6 EXERCISES ◇◇◇◇◇◇

Opening and Closing for Baths

When starting your spiritual bath, do this with intention, faith, and direction of bath as a spiritual practice and not your ordinary bath. To do this I like to have a beginning set of words and an ending.

Before each bath you may say

Our ancestors,

Open us up to what we need to hear.

Close our ears to what we don't need.

Open our mouths to ask questions and speak when necessary.

Help us to trust our instincts, guides, and resources as we learn together the ancient tradition of herbal washes and baths.

After your bath is complete, then close with

We have honored our ancestors by cleansing our bodies.

We thank you for giving us the intention of cleansing, the faith that this is done, and we are now clean and ready to do our conjure work and direction that anything that does not belong in or on our bodies is now going down, down, down with the water and down the drain.

Our clean bodies are lifted up and up.

Energies that do not agree with your ritual are now told, "Go away. Away and far until we request of you again."

Then take a small amount (around an ounce or so) of the water and toss it at the crossroads after you have completed your spell work.

Vinegar Doorway Wash

This is a simple vinegar wash for your doorway. I use this during Samhain when I am bringing in the last of my garden harvest and saying hello to fall (my favorite time of year).

2 cups of water

1–2 tablespoons of vinegar

3 handfuls of juniper or pine needles or dried pine cones

2 tablespoons of regular salt

Mix the items together and let them sit under the moonlight for a few days (odd number of days, please). Let your ancestors tell you how many days.

Once it has set up, then breathe into the mixture your favorite cleaning Bible verse, poem, or chant. If you can't think of anything, pray over it, saying, "This is my home. All that enter here are cleansed of anything that may harm me and mine. I ask this and know that it is so."

Pour the mixture over your front doorway (and back door if you have one), and use a broom to sweep the water over the entry so that it soaks all the way in.

Let it hang out there overnight, and then sweep it again, saying the same chant. Follow it up with some sweet water (orange peels and water or dried apple and water will do nicely) that has been set out in the sun for a few days.

For your ancestor or deity that gives you comfort and peace, be sure to leave an offering, like a slice of the apple or orange or a shot glass of wine or whiskey.

NOTES

1   "Isopropyl Alcohol," PubChem, https://pubchem.ncbi.nlm.nih.gov/compound/Isopropyl-alcohol.

2   "State of Homelessness: 2021 Edition," National Alliance to End Homelessness, https://endhomelessness.org/homelessness-in-america/homelessness-statistics/state-of-homelessness-2021/.

3   Anna Hoffman, "Quick History: Public Baths & Bathing," Apartment Therapy, May 6, 2019, www.apartmenttherapy.com/quick-history-baths-bathing-146544.

4   "The Standard Guide to Global Bathing Cultures," February 20, 2018, www.standardhotels.com/culture/bathing-cultures-hydrotherapy-rituals-Finnish-Japanese-Russian-Korean-Turkish.

APPENDIX

The appendix contains my personal suggestions on how to use the places, people, and events that have made the book what it is. You can use this as a field guide or resource, or imagine that I'm right by your shoulder giving you just a bit more help to give your hoodoo life.

THAT HOODOO LADY ANSWERS YOUR QUESTIONS

1. What's one thing you want me to do to get started in hoodoo?

   Release any notions that you can't do this because of X or X. Also washing your body and home is critical to hoodoo. Your situation and housing state does not make a difference. Cleanse yourself with alcohol wipes, water, and soap, put salt under your tongue, sweep the floors of wherever you are staying. Not allowing yourself to live in dirt gives you a perspective that is a direct connection to our shared spirits.

2. What do you do if you are afraid before you do a conjure or work?

   Listen. If something is telling you to back away, then do so. Don't test fate. Of course, if you are one that enjoys risk, then you will

have to deal with the consequences. These may include possession, harm, illness, and even worse. Do I mean to scare you? In
the kindest of words, *yes*. Because work as a practitioner has
consequences for you, your psychological, physical, financial,
relationship, and mental health, and the same for your client.

3. I have a guide that I would like to use in spell work, but there
isn't a lot of information about them. What can I do?

If there isn't good quality information about them, you may
want to guard yourself in a protective Bible verse first. See my
section on prayer and start with making your own prayer, and
do that before the next step. Then and only then do you have
a quick conversation with them. Ask them who they really are,
how they will help you, and what Bible verses, herbs, and methods of laying down the work is appropriate for them. Remember,
there is more risk in doing work with an unknown. Protect yourself, or leave it alone and go to an ancestor that is known. Your
choice and your consequences.

4. Is hoodoo the same as voodoo, Lucumi, or Santeria?

No, hoodoo is a practice of using folklore magic that developed
in the Southern tradition. You do not need to believe in any religion to practice hoodoo.

5. I'm Christian, Buddhist, atheist, Satanist, Jewish, Muslim, or
other faith or no faith, and I want to practice hoodoo. Can I?

Yes, any religious belief (including anyone that does not have a
religious belief) can practice hoodoo. Hoodoo is for those that
want deliverance using faith, intention, and direction that was
orally taught to hoodoo practitioners and rootworkers of old
using folklore and Southern African American magic.

6. I am not Black. Can I still practice hoodoo?

Yes, but learn Black history and understand the causes and suffering of enslaved people. Next, figure out how to practice hoodoo
in your way. That means adding your own influences in protection
and blessing by adding herbs, roots, and incantations from your

own identity. Respect the heroes and legends that you have chosen by embracing who you are and reaching out for what you want to become. Doing hoodoo without this respect of our ancestors is disrespectful to me and makes hoodoo watered down. Just like doing hoodoo without the Bible or without knowing the oral traditions passed down through hoodoo practitioners or by blending it with other tools that the enslaved Africans did not have access to waters it down and changes its face.

7. I want to put a hex or jinx on someone. Is this possible with hoodoo?

Hoodoo is not like other folklore magic where there are rules about who or what you can use hoodoo for. However, you must know that any work that you do with the Bible should be for deliverance from something. I think of it like this: if you are doing this for deliverance *and* you are right in asking for it, then go for it. If you can do it in good conscience and your ancestors agree with you, then do it.

8. I'm adopted or don't know my ancestors. What do I do to connect to an ancestor?

You are not alone. We all share several common ancestors. Think of Mitochondrial Eve or Kwan Yin or Shirley Chisolm or Malcolm X. So many ancestors are there with great stories to help you in your work. Research historical figures that speak to you, and ask them to be your ancestors and guides. Hoodoo heroes and legends are universal. They are to be accessed by anyone that wants the connection and wisdom. It's okay to reach out and ask for deliverance.

9. I want to begin learning more about herbs that I use with #hoodoo. What do you recommend?

There are great online resources out there, but when I ask my deity and guides first, then I get the best answers. When you ask your heroes and legends for help they will be there for you. Start with finding just one that speaks to you and spend time learning about that one. For example, if I choose to work with suffragist Sophia Singh, I will do research on her and understand why she is calling you and what herbs were available to her at the time. I will research her location, her likes and dislikes, and find herbs that bring in that energy. Having your own personal relationship to herbs is key as well. You don't want to rely only on what I write in this book. I am your tour guide, but after I'm gone, you have to go home and unpack what you learned on the tour and let it integrate into your daily conjure life.

10. When is the best time to practice conjure?

The best time to practice conjure is when you are led to begin and when you have a need for deliverance. You may not want to start with a huge deliverance need first (like protecting your property from an entity or negative spirit) for your first try. Start with blessing your own anointing oil or blessing your own lotions or toothpaste or even front steps. See how it makes a difference.

11. What's it like to be possessed during a reading?

This is different for every reader, in my opinion. When I am possessed, I am (with consciousness and in full control and acceptance) allowing that spirit to speak through me to my client or in my conjure. I set up boundaries for when this can happen and set up a ritual for when it needs to stop. Once the possession is complete, I physically and spiritually cleanse myself to make sure nothing has attached itself. Coming from an African-based lineage, possession is only natural. Coming from a Church of God in Christ background, it's practically required. See the section on possession in chapter 3.

12. Is possession necessary?

It is *not* necessary to become so possessed or in tune with your guides that your eyes roll in the back of your head and you speak in tongues. I have had a couple of disappointed clients that didn't get to witness this for a reason #sorrynotsorry. It is important to have a connection with whatever feels comfortable to you, and it's important you feel comfortable enough to obtain the information on how you will seek deliverance using your Bible magic and determine how to shape the verses to match your need perfectly (or to your level of comfort).

13. Is it legal to conduct rootwork/conjure or hoodoo?

I'm not an attorney or lawyer—always seek advice from a legal professional if you have questions—however, here are my personal thoughts:

Yes, the First Amendment states,

United States Constitution prevents the government from making laws which respect an establishment of religion, prohibit the free exercise of religion, or abridge the freedom of speech, the freedom of the press, the right to peaceably assemble, or the right to petition the government for redress of grievances. It was adopted on December 15, 1791, as one of the ten amendments that constitute the Bill of Rights. (Congress, Librarian of, 2021)

But performing any nontraditional spell work should only be done with the guidance and knowledge of your state, county, city, and federal laws. For example, if you make a hoodoo spray and remotely bless or vex your neighbor and harm comes to them and law enforcement can prove (and substantiate) it, you may or may not be held liable. Always check the laws first. If in doubt, then don't try it. Another example, throwing dirt, works, blood, personal concerns, and even Bible verses (the paper itself) can be a criminal activity if it is shown to violate laws (harassment, stalking, hostile workplace, assault, etc.).

Here's an excerpt from an online article of one person that was imprisoned for practicing conjure:[1]

U.S. District Judge Paula Xinis sentenced Bennett on July 31. Jurors who convicted Bennett last October heard testimony that she used investors' money to pay more than $800,000 for prayers by Hindu priests in India to ward off federal investigators while her business collapsed.

An FBI agent said investigators found evidence in Bennett's home that she tried to silence U.S. Securities and Exchange Commission investigators by casting "hoodoo" spells.

CHAPTER 1 NOTES

WHAT IS A CONJURE WORKER? NOTES

As a reminder, the notes for the third glass of water exercise can be triggering or harmful. You are advised to use your own discretion before reciting or even reading them. If you wish to proceed, please do so knowing that the harmful verses may trigger additional pain.

CHAPTER 2 NOTES

HOODOO, FOLKLORE, AND DEATH

Death has many forms, but in hoodoo it is all about protecting yourself from jinxes—being "hoodooed," where sickness or death will overtake you—or causing someone's death with a hoodoo trick. Some hoodoo practitioners use a powder called goopher dust (made with cemetery dirt and other items). But in my gran gran's day there were other ways to bring about illness and pain that didn't require all of that. Using hair, blood, urine, animal bones, feathers, sausages, and beans could cause some havoc. My favorite folklore tales can be found in Harry Middleton Hyatt's *Folk-Lore from Adams County, Illinois*.

My gran gran would always tell me that I had to be careful when I heard my name being called. I was never to answer unless I saw the person call me or if I heard them call twice, because the person could be death calling to take me. There is a folklore that putting a blade, scissors, or an opened Bible under your bed will ward off death.

During Christmas time, people would wish for a white Christmas (a Christmas with snow on the ground) because there were several sayings such as "A white Christmas, a lean graveyard. A green Christmas, a fat graveyard" and similar versions that carried the same message.

If you hear a church bell and a dog howling at the same time it, signifies death.

If you hear a ticking of a watch behind the walls, then it is a death clock ticking.

It is considered bad luck for a pregnant person to see a coffin or to be near a coffin—it would cause a miscarriage or stillbirth.

If you see a light over your bed, that is an omen that a death angel is coming.

A pigeon is known in some traditions as an agent of death, and if it lands on your house or you hear it cooing in front of your house, it was a bad omen.

If a mouse or rodent chews on your clothing, it is an omen of an impending death visit.

It is bad luck to search for and dig up hidden treasure, as folklore says you will die within the following year.

Dreaming of being caught in the rain is a bad omen.

HOODOO, FOLKLORE, AND FIGHTING

In hoodoo, you can use several different objects to cause arguments and fights. This folklore typically starts with an argument, causing a bad omen of arguments, and ends with a way to conjure or hoodoo someone into being jinxed and not having peace. For example, if you are pregnant and get into an argument with another person, then the baby will resemble the person you argued with, and so on. It is important to understand the superstition behind fighting so that you understand what roots, herbs, and objects you will need to reverse the condition.

As a hoodoo practitioner, you are expected to know these types of folklore sayings and stories so that you can be fully ready for anything you may encounter. As a community activist, fighter, suffragist, or other fighter for a cause, you will want to help bless and protect your community by applying the knowledge of the folklore with your understanding of how to heal and protect them when they are going out. By calling their ancestor guide as mentioned in chapter 2 and reading up on folklore, you should be fine.

THE BLUE LADY SPELL

The Blue Lady is one of those heroes and legends that many of us have. Maybe she isn't a Blue Lady to you, but if you've lived long enough, you've seen a version of her. She is beautifully tempting and peacefully serene and beguiling. She encourages you to come with her, be with her, learn from her. She is a siren and a shadow. Many say she is a mermaid that causes ships to sink or captains to go too deeply into treacherous waters. Whatever she is, she is a force that is worthy of offering and acceptance. We have opportunities to call to the Blue Lady when we need something that is just too scary to even face, whether it's an opportunity that we think is too large for us to grasp or a relationship that is good, but we are worried it is too good to be true. Maybe you need her when your parent or loved one is in hospice and you want someone to escort them home. The Blue Lady, in her gentle and loving outreach, welcomes us home to another place and time. She is never forceful, but she can slightly guilt you into doing just a bit more than what you would have before. Be careful when calling her or using her in spells because she can lure you and hypnotize you. If you need that in a spell, then call out to her.

To work with the Blue Lady, you will need some things that she loves, like things from the sea (seashells, seaweed, fishes, and water). Do this spell early in the morning and never near sunset because she may take it literally that you indeed want the sun to set on the person the spell is intended for.

You will chant "Blue Lady, sing. Blue Lady, work with me. Blue Lady, I'm here, Blue Lady, for you" three times and wait for her. You will smell the ocean and sea breezes, and you will see her transparent, cobalt blue frame as you do any attraction, luring, or beguiling spells.

Once you have completed your spell work, take the items you used with her (after thanking her for giving you your desire) and dispose of them in fire—do not give them to her as an offering. Believe me, she has plenty. Do not go to open water, rivers, or streams while you are working with her. Use protective Bible verses before going to sleep after you have worked with yourself, and put a small amount of sea salt on your tongue after you have finished your burnt offering and for seven days after you have finished your spell.

The Blue Lady encourages us to not be afraid of change and death. She appreciates receiving gifts and offerings of things that she enjoys that make her feel at home—water, things of the ocean and sea, salt, seaweed or kelp, mermaids, things found in the ocean. She would not appreciate things that she could not use in the sea or things she could not bring back and forth between worlds. She gets hungry too, but for things that are refreshing and have a high moisture content (watermelon or squash instead of savory herbs). When you connect with her, feel free to see if she asks for something, and she will reply to you.

FATHER'S LOVE SPELL

Intention—Norvette (or Burney, his nickname), let me see clearly. Let me feel unbiased love. Let me see which way I need to go.

Faith—Faith in the type of protection and love that comes from parents that are nurturing and caring protectors.

Direction—South/Down. The ground. The earth. Warmth, getting to the core of a situation. Starting with the basics. Simply and without any need for extras.

My dad is a kind soul. He teaches that the best way to move toward revolution and psychic connection is by being quiet and listening first. I receive some of my best advice from my dad. As imperfect as he was and is, he is perfection to me.

My dad trained us by being an example. Whether you may judge this as a positive or negative, he was our example. All his children, in some way, are the culmination of that example. Now that we are older, we truly don't depart from it. I am bound to my own psychic talents. My brother is a wonderful husband and father and spends his time raising his children, not worrying about being a breadwinner. My sister is a powerful healer in her own right and has used her abilities to solve problems for governments in her own million-dollar business. Me, of course, I'm an author but also have a totally unrelated focus in the nonspiritualist community where I use my resources, time, and effort to bring about powerful change to my communities and justice groups that I support.

Use my dad when you want to see and need his encouragement, as a parent that you may need, as a sounding board from a father figure (whatever that looks like for you) when you want to understand your vision. Call him either Norvette or Burney. He likes tobacco and sweets. You know you have connected when you smell internally the cigar smoke or hear R&B music. He doesn't try to impress you with big words. He speaks quietly and clearly. He doesn't like being called a lot.

Once per year is about all he may give you, but that time is precious, so please give him adequate time (at least sixty minutes of meditative contemplation with him).

Use this when you want to increase your psychic ability and see the problem for what it is. Other times you need to look through the smoke. You may be surprised what you can see when your vision isn't exactly clear. We, even as practitioners, put too much faith in what we can see and not enough in what Spirit is telling us.

INGREDIENTS:

Eyeglasses that blur your vision (from a dollar store)

Quiet place to dream or meditate

Tobacco or similar herb to produce smoke

Timer

When you have found your quiet place, set a timer for sixty minutes minimum and chant this verse: "Norvette (or Burney or Dad), give me sight; let me see!" Think of your needs and light the tobacco. As it burns repeat as a chant, over and over: "Norvette (or Burney or Dad), give me sight; let me see!"

Now put the glasses on. Repeat the verse again. "Norvette (or Burney or Dad), give me sight; let me see!" while you very carefully look through the glasses for just a moment. Now, take the glasses off and see with new sight.

Try this again and again as you think about your situation and what you want to see.

Once my dad, the imperfect hero, gives you clarity and you have your true vision, then you can stop the meditation. Thank Dad and extinguish the tobacco.

My dad loved sweet desserts, especially things with raisins. You may want to remember that when thinking of offerings. Rice pudding with raisins, bread pudding with raisins. Chocolate-covered raisins. Raisin bran muffins. He also enjoyed cigars and smoking his pipe.

CHAPTER 3 NOTES

CHAPTER 4 NOTES

CHAPTER 5 NOTES

CHAPTER 6 NOTES

BIBLE VERSE ON BURNT OFFERING

The Lord said to Moses, "Tell the Israelites that they must give their gifts to God at the proper time. The smell of the gifts when they burn will make him happy. You must say to them, 'This is the offering by fire that you must offer to the Lord: It must be two male lambs that are one year old. They must not have anything wrong with them. That is the burnt offering for every day. You must give one lamb in the morning and one lamb in the evening. With the lambs, you must also offer to God one kilo (2.2 pounds) of flour that you have mixed with one liter (2 pints) of good olive oil. It is a regular burnt offering that God told you about. He told you about it on Sinai mountain. It is an offering by fire to the Lord. The smell as it burns makes the Lord happy. Then the drink offering with it will be one liter (2 pints) of wine for each lamb. In God's Holy Tent, you must pour out a drink offering of the best wine to the Lord. You must offer the other lamb when it begins to get dark. Offer it with a grain offering and a drink offering like the offerings in the morning. You must give it as an offering by fire. The smell of the smoke from these sacrifices will make the Lord happy.'" (Numbers 28:1–8)

COFFEE PROTECTION AND MEMORY BATH

Use this blend when you want to encourage feelings of comfort and protection. Coffee keeps us awake. It gives us the ability to act. It sharpens our memories and reflexes. Before doing any work where these things are desired, take one bath in these waters. Always check and respect your own issues with allergies or sensitivities and adjust the ritual as necessary.

½ cup of dark, brewed room temperature coffee

Bible verses to add to the coffee.

Use this blend when you need to awaken your spiritual abilities as well, like before a bath or in a bath.

A NEW DAY RITUAL TEA CAKES

These cakes are to be blessed and shared with others. I no longer have the exact recipe, but I found this one and modified it a bit to match what I do. They are perfect for spring celebrations, when you want new things, new days ahead, for new life, for new love, new jobs, and other similar things. You can get creative with any flour, sugar, or other sensitivities, and mix and match ingredients to your liking. For variety you may want to use edible flowers, like lavender, or infuse your favorite tea flavors into them.

Add nuts if you'd like, as this brings increase and prosperity. I like them plain, just like my great-grandma made them, so I don't add a thing. I like to pray over them three times: once in the beginning as I'm preparing the ingredients, the second time as I'm mixing and putting them in the refrigerator, and the third time when they are finished baking and cooling.

1 cup butter or shortening, or a mixture of ½ cup butter and ½ cup of shortening

1 ¾ cups white sugar (substitute with acceptable sweetener to your liking)

2 eggs (substitute with acceptable egg substitute for baking—I use eggs and don't substitute)

1 teaspoon vanilla extract

3 cups all-purpose flour (substitute with plantain, almond, or coconut flour)

½ teaspoon baking soda

½ teaspoon salt

¼ teaspoon ground nutmeg

In a medium bowl, cream together the butter and sugar until smooth. Beat in the eggs one at a time, then stir in the vanilla. Combine the flour, baking soda, salt and nutmeg; stir into the creamed mixture.

Knead dough for a few turns on a floured board until smooth. Cover and refrigerate until firm.

Preheat the oven to 325 degrees F (165 degrees C). On a lightly floured surface, roll the dough out to ¼ inch in thickness. Cut into desired shapes with cookie cutters. Place cookies 1½ inches apart onto cookie sheets.

Bake for 8 to 10 minutes in the preheated oven. Allow cookies to cool on baking sheet for 5 minutes before removing to a wire rack to cool completely.

BIBLE VERSES BY TOPIC

These verses are taken from my first book, *The Hoodoo Guide to the Bible*. I brought them over so that you can have them available to you without having to flip between books.

Bible Verses for General Topics

Your ears will hear a word behind you, "This is the way, walk in it," whenever you turn to the right or to the left. (Isaiah 30:21)

If He should determine to do so, If He should gather to Himself His spirit and His breath, All flesh would perish together, And man would return to dust. (Job 34:14–15)

Psalms:

- Protection—34, 54, 59
- Money/Increase/Job—23, 90:17, 94:18–19, 81
- Love/Healing—20:4, 29:11, 37:4, 119:28
- Joy/Happiness—47:1, 95, 30, 112

Bible Verses to Banish or Bind

Thy words were found, and I did eat them; and thy word was unto me the joy and rejoicing of mine heart: for I am called by thy name. (Jeremiah 15:16)

As they moved, they would go in any one of the four directions the cherubim faced; the wheels did not turn about as the cherubim went. The cherubim went in whatever direction the head faced, without turning as they went. (Ezekiel 10:11)

Do not be afraid of them; your guides will fight for you. (Deuteronomy 3:22)

I will pursue them with sword, famine, and plague. I will make them a horror to all the kingdoms of the earth—a curse and a desolation, an object of scorn and a disgrace among all the nations where I have banished them. (Jeremiah 29:18)

I will bring the four winds against (insert person) the four corners of the heavens, and I will scatter them to all these winds. (Jeremiah 49:36)

Let all bitterness and wrath and anger and clamor [perpetual animosity, resentment, strife, fault finding] and slander be put away from you, along with every kind of malice [all spitefulness, verbal abuse, malevolence]. (Ephesians 4:31)

They will pay the penalty of eternal destruction, being banished from the presence of the guides of old and from their glorious majesty. (2 Thessalonians 1:9)

Get rid of all bitterness, rage and anger, brawling and slander, along with every form of malice. (Ephesians 4:31)

Bible Verses about Faith and Overcoming Obstacles

Because you know that the testing of your faith produces perseverance. (James 1:3)

If you believe, you will receive whatever you ask for in prayer. (Matthew 21:22)

Now faith is confidence in what we hope for and assurance about what we do not see. (Hebrews 11:1)

I have fought the good fight, I have finished the race, I have kept the faith. (2 Timothy 4:7)

But you, are never far from me. You are my strength; come quickly to help me. (Psalm 22:19)

When you pass through the waters, I will be with you; and through the rivers, they shall not overwhelm you; when you walk through fire you shall not be burned, and the flame shall not consume you. (Isaiah 43:2)

Even though I walk through the valley of the shadow of death, I will fear no evil, for you are with me; your rod and your staff, they comfort me. (Psalm 23:4)

Bible Verses for Love

There is no fear in love. But perfect love drives out fear, because fear has to do with punishment. The one who fears is not made perfect in love. (1 John 4:18)

For the Spirit that were are given does not make us timid, but gives us power, love and self-discipline. (2 Timothy 1:7)

I have said these things to you, that in me you may have peace. In the world you will have tribulation. But take heart; I have overcome the world. (John 16:33)

Love never fails. But where there are prophecies, they will cease; where there are tongues, they will be stilled; where there is knowledge, it will pass away. (1 Corinthians 13:8)

And above all these put on love, which binds everything together in perfect harmony. (Colossians 3:14)

Hatred stirs up strife, but love covers all offenses. (Proverbs 10:12)

So now faith, hope, and love abide, these three; but the greatest of these is love. (1 Corinthians 13:13)

A friend loves at all times. (Proverbs 17:17)

Hatred stirs up conflict, but love covers over all wrongs. (Proverbs 10:12)

Anxiety weighs down the heart, but a kind word cheers it up. (Proverbs 12:25)

Bible Verses for Change

He reveals the deep things of darkness and brings utter darkness into the light. (Job 12:22)

Be not ashamed, but receive strength in thy mind, through the commands which I am about to deliver unto thee. For, said he, I am sent to shew unto thee all those things again, which thou hast seen before, but especially such of them as may be of most use unto thee. (II Hermas 1:5)

I do not consider myself yet to have taken hold of it. But one thing I do: Forgetting what is behind and straining toward what is ahead. (Philippians 3:13)

He sent his word, and healed them, and delivered them from their destructions. (Psalm 107:20)

Vengeance is mine, and recompense, for the time when their foot shall slip; for the day of their calamity is at hand, and their doom comes swiftly. (Deuteronomy 32:35)

But if your enemy is hungry, feed him. If he is thirsty, give him something to drink. For in so doing you will be heaping fiery coals on his head. (Romans 12:20)

The Lord will send on you cursing, confusion, and rebuke in all that you set your hand to do, until you are destroyed and until you perish quickly, because of the wickedness of your doings in which you have forsaken Me. (Deuteronomy 28:20)

"To what can I compare this generation? They are like children sitting in the marketplaces and calling out to others 'We played the pipe for you, and you did not dance; we sang a dirge, and you did not mourn.' For John came neither eating nor drinking, and they say, 'He has a demon.' The Son of Man came eating and drinking, and they say, 'Here is a glutton and a drunkard, a friend of tax collectors and sinners.' But wisdom is proved right by her deeds." (Matthew 11:16–19)

NEW BEGINNING

Behold, I will create new heavens and a new earth. The former things will not be remembered, nor will they come to mind. (Isaiah 65:17)

LOVE

Dear children, let's not merely say that we love each other; let us show the truth by our actions. (1 John 3:18)

Bible Verses for Strength

It is the part of a brave combatant to be wounded, and yet overcome. But especially we ought to endure all things for spirit's sake, that they may bear with us. (Polycarp 1:14)

ENCOURAGEMENT

No weapon that is formed against thee shall prosper; and every tongue that shall rise against thee in judgment thou shalt condemn. This is the heritage of the servants of the Lord, and their righteousness is of me, saith the Lord. (Isaiah 54:17)

And He said to His disciples, "For this reason I say to you, do not worry about your life, as to what you will eat; nor for your body, as to what you will put on." (Luke 12:22)

PREVENT NIGHTMARES

If you lie down, you will not be afraid; when you lie down, your sleep will be sweet. (Proverbs 3:24)

CROSSING; GOING AGAINST YOUR GUIDES OR GOD

Whatever you devise against the Lord, He will make a complete end of it. Distress will not rise twice. (Nahum 1:9)

They will soar on wings like eagles; they will run and not grow weary, they will walk and not be faint. (Isaiah 40:31)

Be on your guard; stand firm in the faith; be courageous; be strong. (1 Corinthians 16:13)

For anger lasts only a moment, but favor lasts a lifetime; weeping may stay for the night, but joy comes in the morning. (Psalm 30:5)

Blessed [is] the man that endured temptation: for when he is tried, he shall receive the crown of life, which the Lord hath promised to them that love him. (James 1:12)

Love the Lord, all you faithful followers of his! The Lord protects those who have integrity, but he pays back in full the one who acts arrogantly. (Psalm 31:23–24)

Even though the fig trees have no blossoms, and there are no grapes on the vines; even though the olive crop fails, and the fields lie empty and barren; even though the flocks die in the fields, and the cattle barns are empty, yet I will rejoice in the Lord! I will be joyful in the God of my salvation! (Habakkuk 3:17–18)

But he that shall endure unto the end, the same shall be saved. (Matthew 24:13)

Remember his marvelous works that he hath done; his wonders, and the judgement of his mouth. (Psalm 105:5)

Rescue me, Lord, from evildoers; protect me from the violent, who devise evil plans in their hearts and stir up war every day. They make their tongues as sharp as a serpent's; the poison of vipers is on their lips. Keep me safe, Lord, from the hands of the wicked; protect me from the violent, who devise ways to trip my feet? (Psalm 140:1–4)

A patient man needs to stand firm but for a time, and then contentment comes back to him. For a while he holds back his words, then the lips of many herald his wisdom. Among wisdom's treasures is the paragon of prudence, but fear of the Lord is an abomination to the sinner. (Ben Sira 1:23–25)

Overhearing what they said, Jesus told him, "Don't be afraid; just believe." (Mark 5:36)

Bible Verses for Health

As a practitioner, I am asked all the time for health hoodoo spells—when someone is hurting or traumatized or needs healing from an illness or from the common cold. These verses are ones that you can use in these types of deliverance requests. Just these alone are powerful and do not require more than intention, faith, and direction to make them work.

For He wounds, but He binds up; He shatters, but his hands heal. (Job 5:18)

Heal the sick in it and say to them, "The kingdom of God has come near to you." (Luke 10:9)

When Jesus saw her, he called her over and said to her, "Woman, you are freed from your disability." (Luke 13:12)

And he said to her, "Daughter, your faith has made you well; go in peace." (Luke 8:48)

For I will restore health to you, and I will heal you of your wounds, says Yahweh; because they have called you an outcast, [saying], It is Zion, whom no man seeks after. (Jeremiah 30:17)

Behold, I will bring it health and cure, and I will cure them; and I will reveal to them abundance of peace and truth. (Jeremiah 33:6)

Heal the sick, raise the dead, cleanse those who have leprosy, drive out demons. Freely you have received; freely give. (Matthew 10:8)

Pleasant words are a honeycomb, Sweet to the soul, and health to the bones. (Proverbs 16:24)

Bible Verses for Job, Increase, or Career Change

Ask and it will be given to you; seek and you will find; knock and the door will be opened to you. For everyone who asks receives; the one who seeks finds; and to the one who knocks, the door will be opened. (Matthew 7:7)

Give, and it will be given to you. A good measure, pressed down, shaken together and running over, will be poured into your lap. For with the measure you use, it will be measured to you. (Luke 6:38)

Call unto me, and I will answer thee, and shew thee great and mighty things, which thou knows not. (Jeremiah 33:3)

Whatever you do, work at it with all your heart, as working for the Lord, not for human masters. (Colossians 3:23)

Every man received full rations and a generous sum of gold and silver from the king's purse. (Judith 2:18)

On the first day of every week, each one of you should set aside a sum of money in keeping with your income, saving it up, so that when I come no collections will have to be made. (1 Corinthians 16:2)

The Lord was with Joseph so that he prospered, and he lived in the house of his Egyptian master. When his master saw that the Lord was with him and that the Lord gave him success in everything he did, Joseph found favor in his eyes and became his attendant. Potiphar put him in charge of his household, and he entrusted to his care everything he owned. From the time he put him in charge of his household and of all that he owned, the Lord blessed the household of the Egyptian because of Joseph. The blessing of the Lord was on everything Potiphar had, both in the house and in the field. So Potiphar left everything he had in Joseph's care; with Joseph in charge, he did not concern himself with anything except the food he ate. Now Joseph was well-built and handsome ... (Genesis 39:2–6)

Bible Verses to Offer Gratitude

We all can be more grateful. When I had an asthma attack recently, after letting myself go through the fear, anxiety, and stress, I allowed myself to thank my ancestors for this gift of asthma. It slows me down when I need rest. It reminds me to breathe. It reminds me to take care of my body and soul. It's a constant reminder of my roots and that I come from strong and weak ones.

And the Lord said unto Moses, Take unto thee sweet spices, stacte, and onycha, and galbanum; these sweet spices with pure frankincense: of each shall there be a like weight. (Exodus 30:34)

Take thou also unto thee principal spices, of pure myrrh five hundred shekels, and of sweet cinnamon half so much, even two hundred and fifty shekels, and of sweet calamus two hundred and fifty shekels. (Exodus 30:23)

How abundant are the good things that you have stored up for those who fear you, that you bestow in the sight of all, on those who take refuge in you. (Psalm 31:19)

Let every skillful man among you come, and make all that the Lord has commanded: the tabernacle, its tent and its covering, its hooks and its boards, its bars, its pillars, and its sockets; the ark and its poles, the mercy seat, and the curtain of the screen; the table and its poles, and all its utensils, and the bread of the Presence; the lampstand also for the light and its utensils and its lamps and the oil for the light; and the altar of incense and its poles, and the anointing oil and the fragrant incense, and the screen for the doorway at the entrance of the tabernacle; the altar of burnt offering with its bronze grating, its poles, and all its utensils, the basin and its stand. (Exodus 35:10–16)

In everything I did, I showed you that by this kind of hard work we must help the weak, remembering the words the Lord Jesus himself said: "It is more blessed to give than to receive." (Acts 20:35)

SAYING THANK YOU WITH SOMETHING THEY CAN MULTIPLY

Give, and it will be given to you. Good measure, pressed down, shaken together, running over, will be put into your lap. For with the measure you use it will be measured back to you. (Luke 6:38)

SAYING THANK YOU WITH LIVING THINGS, WATER, AND OIL

You shall command the people of Israel that they bring to you pure beaten olive oil for the light, that a lamp may regularly be set up to burn. (Exodus 27:20)

But he would feed you with the finest of the wheat, and with honey from the rock I would satisfy you. (Psalm 81:16)

And shall take the cedarwood and the hyssop and scarlet yarn, along with the live bird, and dip them in the blood of the bird that was killed and in the fresh water and sprinkle the house seven times. Thus he shall cleanse the house with the blood of the bird and with the fresh water and with the live bird and with the cedarwood and hyssop and scarlet yarn. And he shall let the live bird go out of the city into the open country. So, he shall make atonement for the house, and it shall be clean. (Leviticus 14:51–53)

And he shall kill the lamb in the place where they kill the sin offering and the burnt offering, in the place of the sanctuary. For the guilt offering, like the sin offering, belongs to the priest; it is most holy. (Leviticus 14:13)

Bible Verses for Wisdom

FIRST of all believe that there is one God who created and framed all things of nothing into a being. He comprehends all things, and is only immense, not to be comprehended by any. Who can neither be defined by any words, nor conceived by the mind. (II Hermas 1:1–3)

WISDOM

If any of you lack wisdom, let him ask God, who gives generously to all without reproach, and it will be given him. (James 1:5)

WISDOM/ENCOURAGEMENT

The Child continued to grow and become strong, increasing in wisdom; and the grace of God was upon Him. (Luke 2:40)

WORTH, DIRECTION, VENGEANCE

Then I saw when the Lamb broke one of the seven seals, and I heard one of the four living creatures saying as with a voice of thunder, "Come." (Revelations 6:1)

TEACHING, PERSEVERANCE

Pay close attention to yourself and to your teaching; persevere in these things, for as you do this you will ensure salvation both for yourself and for those who hear you. (1 Timothy 4:16)

For wisdom is better than rubies, and all the things one may desire cannot be compared with her. (Proverbs 8:11)

Bible Verses for Sexual Pleasure, Dating, Marriage, or Love

When I mentioned that the Bible was the largest collection of spells, I hope you are now seeing proof of this. Whether you come from a background in monotheistic religions or polytheistic religions or none at all, the very act of love and sex and desire has caused many to want to put spells or "roots" on people to obtain what they want. If only it were that easy. Do I do spells for love? Yes. Do I do spells for love against someone's will? For me, not usually, but if you need to do that for your deliverance and recognize your need for it *and* have considered any consequences or your own moral and legal boundaries, then please feel free to conjure away. My favorite tenant of #hoodoo is that there is no rule or law or entity that manages or certifies or restricts us other than ourselves and the ancestors that work through us.

Taking this into consideration, read through this beautiful language and allow yourself to think of how it speaks to you, excites you, or even pisses you off.

> *Then I passed by you and saw you, and behold, you were at the time for love; so I spread My skirt over you and covered your nakedness I also swore to you and entered into a covenant with you so that you became Mine, declares the Lord God. (Ezekiel 16:8)*

> *For this reason, a man shall leave his father and his mother, and be joined to his wife; and they shall become one flesh. And the man and his wife were both naked and were not ashamed. (Genesis 2:24–25)*

SPICES, HERBS, ROOTS, AND OBJECTS

Once you have read about using salt, sugar, lemon, coffee, onion, and other objects, you will want to add herbs and roots to them. There are some great books out there that I recommend for learning more about herbalism. I ask you to work with someone and research from those that have an ethnobotanist background, and here is the reason why. I can tell you quite a few mixtures that I've thrown together intuitively. That doesn't mean that they are safe or even should or can be called medicine. The use of the word *medicine* is for actual physicians, doctors, and experts—those that received years of practice and study on the topic (and not a few courses in common culinary herbs like chives, peppermint, basil, thyme, and others). Also, when choosing an online store the same suggestions apply. Here are some places I recommend for finding real roots, herbs, and wisdom.

Goddess Isis Books and Gifts
2775 South Broadway
Englewood, Colorado, 80113
www.isisbooks.com/Herbs-Magical-Herbs-Medicinal-Mortar
-Pestle-s/164.htm

Haus of Hoodoo
1716 Saint Charles Ave
New Orleans, LA 70130
https://hausofhoodoo.com

Original Products Botanica
2486 Webster Ave
Bronx, NY 10458
www.originalbotanica.com/about-our-store

Here are my favorite herbs to use from my own research of the most flexible and accessible:

NAME	USES/ATTRIBUTES
Water	Cleansing, purifying, making new, refreshing, protecting (with prayer/versus), unifier, base for other hoodoo work
Basil	Protection, clearing, cleaning, sweet
Cinnamon	Spicy, heat, anger, revenge, sweet, love, passion, sensual
Valerian	Calm, sleep, relaxation, love, contentment, ease
Ginger	Fiery, hot, healing, burning, lungs, heart
Pepper	Banish, rejection, hot feet, causes people to move and situations to go your way
Cayenne	Spiciness, revenge, exorcism, sensual, respect, justice, courage, strength, force, masculine
Rose	Sweet, peace, mourning, parental love, commitment, honor

continues

NAME	USES/ATTRIBUTES
Wine	Offering, sweet, love, dignity, relaxation
Peanut	Business, increase, nutrition, energy, slowness, satisfaction
Coins	Promotions, new job, justice, offering, requests, demands, change of path, good luck, asexual, choices, yes/no answers, justice, court cases, bags, amulets
Cilantro/mint/chives/parsley	Money, increase, agility, rewards, luck, money bags, amulets
Echinacea	Health, communication, relief, reduce anger, heal relationships, resolve conflict
Hibiscus	Sexual pleasure, passion, love, feminine
Gargoyle	Asexual, challenge, protection, evil, conqueror, strength
Potatoes/sweet potatoes	Masculine, penetration, grounding, steadfast, respect, slow growth but steady growth
Sugar, syrup, sweetener, stevia	Bribery, inducements, sweetness, love, positive relationships, encouragement, addiction, offering
Maze	Confusion, destruction, creating distraction
Hair, footprints, fingernails, urine, blood	Personal concerns, used for personal attacks and blessings, used for possession, dolls, amulets, charms, bracelets, mourning fetish dolls/effigy dolls
Lemon	Souring spells, freezer spells, cleaning, clearing, withdrawal, banishment, clear nonsense, force truth from lies
Onion	Choices and decisions, petitions, demands, requests, grounding, earth based, growth, opportunities
Oil	Fluid, asexual, loosen up tongues, encourage truth to be told, justice, court, law, base for other hoodoo work
Apple	Dolls, bags, spiritual washes, feminine, fertility, relationships, commitments, yes/no answers
Sulfur	Clear homes, rejection, banishing, connecting with ancestors that will eliminate evil
Lysol, Pine-Sol, dishwashing soap, Murphy's Oil Soap	External object cleansing, clearing and making fresh and new, spiritual baths and washes, floor washes
Charcoal	Rituals, hiding or smoking out your enemy, demanding respect, psychic ability, amulets, bags, foot washes, foot work

HERB SUGGESTED READING

Scott Cunningham's *Encyclopedia of Magical Herbs*: In this book, fellow pagan and practitioner Cunningham gives a complete listing of herbs and their magical powers, spells, procedures, intentions (which follow along with hoodoo and the importance of intention), categorization, genders, planetary rules, colors, and so on. It is very thorough and a must-have on any conjure worker's bookshelf.

Herbert C. Covey's *African American Slave Medicine of Herbal and Non-Herbal Treatments*: In this book, from an academic standpoint, you will receive wisdom from Covey's experience interviewing subjects that speak on medical care, medicine, and the enslaved worker's experience when needing and receiving medical care, diseases and their cures, herbal and plant treatments, nonherbal treatments (using dung, meat, animal fats, hair which are the roots of traditional conjure). This book is thoughtfully written from an anthropological standpoint but also tells important stories about the African American experience in healthcare and the integration of Black healthcare with white healthcare—as told by enslaved Africans themselves.

Judith A. Carney and Richard Nicholas Rosomoff's *In the Shadow of Slavery Africa's Botanical Legacy in the Atlantic World*: This book is more about the understanding of African foods, clothing, gardens, and grasses. It is an important piece of work for any practicing hoodoo worker because we need to understand the history of our ancestors and what they did before so that we can replicate them in a respectful manner. Doing hoodoo just by what you see on YouTube (in my opinion) is never a great idea. Study, study, study.

Michele E. Lee's *Working the Roots: Over 400 Years of Traditional African American Healing*: This book has a special place in my heart, as it was gifted to me once and I purchased it once. This was my ancestors' way of making sure I read this text through and through. Lee's excellent and thorough explanations of many of the hoodoo herbal and nonherbal remedies in this book are worth investing in. Lee provides so many nuggets of wisdom that I have marked up this book so much—it's like one of my gran gran's old cookbooks. I don't see every herb I use in here, but there are so many of substitutes and real working examples of conjure that it isn't necessary. Invest in this as your next book purchase.

NOTE

1   "Woman Appeals 20-Year Prison Sentence For $800K Ponzi Scheme To Pay For 'Hoodoo' Rituals," Associated Press, August 21, 2019.

BIBLIOGRAPHY

Admin. (2021, 02 20). *Origami Instructions—How to Fold a Paper into an Envelope*. Retrieved from Origami.photobrunobernard.com: https://origami.photobrunobernard.com/origami-instruction/how-to-fold-a-paper-into-an-envelope/.

"American Battlefield Trust." (2020, 10 11). Retrieved from The Civil War: www.battlefields.org/learn/civil-war.

Associated Press. (2019, 08 21). *Woman Appeals 20-Year Prison Sentence for $800k Ponzi Scheme*. Retrieved from CBS Local: https://baltimore.cbslocal.com/2019/08/21/woman-appeals-20-year-prison-sentence-for-800k-ponzi-scheme-to-pay-for-hoodoo-rituals/.

Biblestudy.org. (2021, 12 11). *Meaning of Numbers in the Bible*. Retrieved from Bible Study.org: www.biblestudy.org/bibleref/meaning-of-numbers-in-bible/3.html.

Bordewich, F. (2021, 04 12). *John Brown's Day of Reckoning*. Retrieved from Macs History: http://macshistory.weebly.com/uploads/2/7/2/9/27291669/john_brown_-smithsonian_article.pdf.

"Botanica y Yerberia" (2020, 11 19). Retrieved from Botanica y Yerberia's Facebook page: www.facebook.com/Botanica-y-Yerberia-7-Potencias-Gomez-222164411151094/.

Bulk Apothecary. (2021, 02 09). *Bulkapothecary.com*. Retrieved from Bulk Apothecary Herbs and Spices: www.bulkapothecary.com/herbs-spices.

Byrne, R. (2006). *The Secret*. Atria Books/Beyond Words.

Congress, Library of. (2021, 01 14). *The First Amendment*. Retrieved from Constitution Annotated: https://constitution.congress.gov/constitution/amendment-1/.

Covey, H. C. (2007). *African American Slave Medicine of Herbal and Non-Herbal Treatments*. Lexington Books.

Cunningham, S. (1985). *Cunningham's Encyclopedia of Magical Herbs* (Llewellyn's Sourcebook Series) (Cunningham's Encyclopedia Series, 1). Llewellyn Publications.

Darkwah, N. B. (2000). *The Africans Who Wrote the Bible*. HBC.

Debby Herbenick PhD, M. (2013, 07 10). "Erect Penile Length and Circumference." Retrieved from *The Journal of Sexual Medicine*: Debby Herbenick PhD, MPH.

Editors, H. C. (2020, 07 18). *The History Channel - Abolistionist Movement*. Retrieved from History.com: www.history.com/topics/abolitionist-movement/john-brown.

Gladstar, R. (2012). *Rosemary Gladstar's Medicinal Herbs: A Beginner's Guide*. Storey Publishing, LLC. Retrieved from Rosemary Gladstar's Medicinal Herbs: A Beginner's Guide.

Goddess Isis Bookstore. (2020, 06 17). *Goddess Isis Books and Gifts*. Retrieved from Goddess Isis Books and Gifts: www.isisbooks.com/Herbs-Magical-Herbs-Medicinal-Mortar-Pestle-s/164.htm.

Harris, D. (2021, 03 14). "How Did European Colonialism Affect Africa's Culture?" Retrieved from ASEP Association Gathering European Companies: https://asep-european-companies.com/good-to-know/how-did-european-colonialism-affect-africas-culture.html.

Harrison, K. (2020). *The Herbal Alchemist's Handbook: A Complete Guide to Magickal Herbs and How to Use Them* (Weiser Classics Series). Weiser Books.

Heline, C. (1941). *Mythology and the Bible*. La Canada: New Age Press, Inc.

Heline, C. (2006). *Mythology and the Bible*. Kessinger Publishing, LLC.

Herbs and Arts. (2021, 02 13). *Herbs and Arts Online*. Retrieved from Herbs and Arts website: www.herbsandarts.com/online-store/Dried-Bulk-Herbs-c45840169.

Hicks, E. A. (2004). *Ask and It Is Given: Learning to Manifest Your Desires*. Hay House.

Hyatt, H. M. (2015). *Folk-Lore from Adams County, Illinois*. London: Forgotten Books.

Women in the Bible—What Can We Learn From Them?. (2020, 06 20). Retrieved from JW.Org: www.jw.org/en/bible-teachings/questions/women-in-the-bible.

Kyd, K. (2021, 11 13). *Sense*. Retrieved from "The Peanut Industry—Africa": https://timeforsense.com/peanut-industry-africa/.

Lee, M. E. (2017). *Working the Roots: Over 400 Years of Traditional African American Healing*. Wadastick.

Little, Karen Raye HHP & Professor RayeQueen (2015). *The Secret for Sistahs: The Black Woman's Spiritual Guide to Releasing Negativity*. CreateSpace Independent Publishing Platform.

Merriam-Webster. (2021, 12 7). *Merriam-Webster*. Retrieved from www.merriam-webster.com/.

"Miriam Makeba." (2021, 01 03). Retrieved from Miriam Makeba Official Website: www.miriammakeba.co.za/.

"Miriam Makeba." (2021, 02 05). Retrieved from South African History Online: www.sahistory.org.za/people/miriam-makeba.

Mystica, T. (2021, 01 05). *African Mythology Gods and Goddesses list—Creation Myths, Examples, Stories and Creatures*. Retrieved from The Mystica: www.themystica.com/african-mythology.

Ortiz, P. (2018). *An African American and Latinx History of the United States*. Beacon Press.

Pleyades2011. (2021, 01 05). *Creation Myths in Africa*. Retrieved from The information's Depo for the Searcher: www.bibliotecapleyades.net/mitos_creacion/esp_mitoscreacion_0.htm.

Staff. (2020, 12 05). "Miriam Makeba Dies in Italy." Retrieved from Mail and Guardian: https://mg.co.za/article/2008-11-10-miriam-makeba-dies-in-italy/.

RGA. (2021, 01 07). "Grandma's Old Fashioned Tea Cakes." Retrieved from All Recipes: www.allrecipes.com/recipe/25766/grandmas-old-fashioned-tea-cakes/.

Rosomoff, J. A. (2011). *In the Shadow of Slavery: Africa's Botanical Legacy in the Atlantic World*. University of California Press.

Sanborn, F. B. (2021, 03 01). *John Brown Exhibit*. Retrieved from West Virginia Culture Archives: http://archive.wvculture.org/history//jbexhibit/Sanborn188.html.

Shone, S. (2019). *The Hoodoo Guide to the Bible: Advice from a Real Rootworker*. Denver: That Hoodoo Lady Publishing.

Singh, E. (2020, 12 27). *Africa News Analysis*. Retrieved from Two South African, www.africanewsanalysis.com/two-south-african-heroines-miriam-makeba-dr-frene-ginwala-by-eric-singh-ana-snr-editor/.

Sisterlocks. (2021, 12 15). *Sisterlocks*. Retrieved from Sisterlocks Official Website: www.sisterlocks.com/.

Stroyer, J. (2021, 01 05). *Slave Housing*. Retrieved from Spartacus Educational: https://spartacus-educational.com/USAShousing.htm.

Swayne, M. (2021, 01 13). *Lynching Map US History*. Retrieved from Futurity: www.futurity.org/lynching-map-united-states-history-2064252.

"Talking History: Aural History Productions—Slavery and the Making of America." (2021, 03 01). Retrieved from Talking History: www.albany.edu/talkinghistory/arch2005jan-june.html.

Wills, A. (2021, 03 23). *Savvy Homemade*. Retrieved from Candle Making—A Guide for Beginners: www.savvyhomemade.com/candle-making-beginners.

National Organization for Women (2021, 01 12). *Black Women and Sexual Violence*. Retrieved from NOW website: https://now.org/wp-content/uploads/2018/02/Black-Women-and-Sexual-Violence-6.pdf.

SUGGESTED READING

You may ask what titles are on my bookshelf now or even where I drew inspiration from when writing this book (and my first book, *The Hoodoo Guide to the Bible*). If this subject interests you, then perhaps these other books are worth a read or just googling them.

- *African American Slave Medicine: Herbal and Non-Herbal Treatments*—Hardcover, March 1, 2007, by Herbert C. Covey

- *All That's Wrong with the Bible: Contradictions, Absurdities, and More*: 2nd expanded edition—Paperback, September 16, 2017, by Jonah David Conner

- An Indigenous Peoples' History of the United States (REVISIONING HISTORY)—Paperback, August 11, 2015, by Roxanne Dunbar-Ortiz

- *Ashkenazi Herbalism: Rediscovering the Herbal Traditions of Eastern European Jews*—April 6, 2021, by Deatra Cohen and Adam Siegel

- *Backwoods Witchcraft: Conjure & Folk Magic from Appalachia*—June 1, 2019, by Jake Richards and Starr Casas

- *Conjuring Harriet "Mama Moses" Tubman and the Spirits of the Underground Railroad*—Paperback, February 1, 2019, by Witchdoctor Utu

- *Cunningham's Encyclopedia of Magical Herbs* (Llewellyn's Sourcebook Series) (Cunningham's Encyclopedia Series, 1)— Book 1 of 3, October 1, 1985, by Scott Cunningham

- *Missing Witches: Recovering True Histories of Feminist Magic*—Paperback, March 23, 2021, by Risa Dickens and Amy Torok

- *Mojo Workin': The Old African American Hoodoo System* by Katrina Hazzard-Donald

- *Pussy Prayers: Sacred and Sensual Rituals for Wild Women of Color*—October 24, 2018, by Black Girl Bliss

- *The Queer Evangelist: A Socialist Clergy's Radically Honest Tale*—March 16, 2021, by Cheri DiNovo and Kathleen Wynne

- *They/Them/Their*—September 19, 2019, by Eris Young

- *Transforming: The Bible and the Lives of Transgender Christians*—April 7, 2018, by Austen Hartke

- *We Are Everywhere: Protest, Power, and Pride in the History of Queer Liberation*—Hardcover, May 7, 2019, by Matthew Riemer

- *Wisdom of the Natural World: Spiritual and Practical Teachings from Plants, Animals & Mother Earth*—Paperback, March 8, 2021, by Granddaughter Crow

- Women Who Run with the Wolves: Myths and Stories of the Wild Woman Archetype—Mass Market Paperback, November 27, 1996, by Clarissa Pinkola Estés

- *Working The Roots: Over 400 Years of Traditional African American Healing*—Paperback, December 15, 2017, by Michele Elizabeth Lee

- *Atheism: The Case Against God* (The Skeptic's Bookshelf)—Paperback, July 12, 2016, by George H. Smith

BIOGRAPHY

As a professional hoodoo practitioner, That Hoodoo Lady (Sherry Shone) witnesses the power of Spirit in her business with office and home clearings (she has a terrifying accounting of a famous mouse), officiating weddings and going home (funeral) services, and public speaking. She has given classes in hoodoo, conjure, and rootwork traditions for several years, and the culmination of this knowledge is gratefully shared in this book. This is Sherry's second published book on hoodoo and her first on inclusive hoodoo.

Her favorite courses to teach are in hoodoo doll making, old-ways candle conjure, and ceremonial/ritual rootwork brooms.

Being a hoodoo practitioner is a lifestyle and choice that has blessed her to manifest joy, protection, and happiness into her life. But it started as the brave effort to find herself after being ostracized by a church upbringing that shamed her for her sexuality and punished her by using the very Bible she now studies and uses as her primary tool for conjure.

Through prayer, animism, and understanding of true spirituality, she has been delivered and hopes that this book touches you and gives you the same wisdom and strength to drive deep into your own culture and biblical knowledge.

That Hoodoo Lady resides in Oregon with her wife, daughter, and three dogs that have rescued her. She would love to speak at your next event. Sherry is also ordained in Colorado and Oregon and can officiate weddings and funerals and provide other ministerial services. She can be reached at infoplease@thathoodoolady.com, on Instagram at @ThatHoodooLady, or on her website www.thathoodoolady.com.

About North Atlantic Books

North Atlantic Books (NAB) is a 501(c)(3) nonprofit publisher committed to a bold exploration of the relationships between mind, body, spirit, culture, and nature. Founded in 1974, NAB aims to nurture a holistic view of the arts, sciences, humanities, and healing. To make a donation or to learn more about our books, authors, events, and newsletter, please visit www.northatlanticbooks.com.